Some of the critical acclaim for THIS MAN JESUS:

"A distinguished scholar and highly competent popularizer, having thoroughly distilled what Scripture scholars—both Catholic and Protestant—have written in recent years, offers average readers a book that will enable them to develop an authentic appreciation of who Jesus really was. This popular presentation of the latest theological understanding of Jesus deserves wide reading in lay as well as clerical circles."
America

"To say that Vawter's book is worth reading is a great understatement; it is a book that any thinking Christian owes it to himself to read." *Commonweal*

"*This Man Jesus* is an example of scholarship that is both precise and comprehensive. Bruce Vawter is aware of current developments in biblical scholarship and in theological interpretation. At the same time his knowledge of the dogma and the exegesis of prior ages is profound." *The Living Church*

". . . a good book—sound scholarship, sound theology, a sound and exciting approach to Scripture." *Christian Century*

"A serious reading of this book and a reflection on its ideas will be rewarding. The major aspects of the life of Jesus are discussed in a manner that will give the reader a clearer appreciation of the Man Jesus . . . an excellent historical, critical, theological approach to the Gospels as they proclaim the Man Jesus." *The Cord*

"Vawter is that *rara avis,* a creative biblical scholar who theologizes without boring the layman into catalepsy. *This Man Jesus* will be received enthusiastically not only by the professional theologian but the literate Christian with a hunger for information in an area where free inquiry was so long inhibited by ecclesiastical discipline." *Virginia Kirkus Service*

*Jesus of Nazareth, a man attested to you by
God with mighty works and wonders and signs. . . .
God has made him both Lord and Christ, this
Jesus whom you crucified. Acts 2:22.36*

THIS MAN JESUS

An Essay Toward a New Testament Christology

BRUCE VAWTER

IMAGE BOOKS

A DIVISION OF DOUBLEDAY & COMPANY, INC.

GARDEN CITY, NEW YORK

1975

Image Books edition by special arrangement
with Doubleday & Company, Inc.
Image Books edition published September 1975

ISBN: 0-385-02797-4

To his colleagues in
the Theology Department of
De Paul University
d. d. d.
the author

ACKNOWLEDGMENTS

The biblical citations in this book, except when a more literal (and less literary) translation has been called for, appear in the version of *The New American Bible*.

Numerous friends whose judgment I value and whose competence in certain areas is clearly superior to my own have been kind enough to review the book in manuscript form. Their better thoughts, often substantial, have been incorporated into its text. Their names go unmentioned from no sense of ingratitude, for my gratitude is profound, but lest they be thought to have lent their hand to the expression of ideas for which I alone must stand as the responsible author.

In the pages that follow it will become abundantly evident how much I have depended on my colleagues in theology and exegesis who have taken the trouble to put their views on record, for approval or dissent, and to whom, therefore, I am completely indebted. For the most part I have cited them explicitly, though without references to chapter and verse, which I presume most of my readers would find superfluous. There are also, however, many implicit citations, probably far many more than I would willingly recognize, to which I am equally indebted. I trust only, in the one case as in the other, that I have falsified no man's thought in the process of measuring it against my own.

B.V.

CONTENTS

INTRODUCTION | 13
The Priority of Christ | 13
The Priority of History | 16
Beyond Subjectivity | 21
History and Method | 25
Biblicism and Biblical Relevance | 30

1. HE HAS BEEN RAISED | 35
The Transforming Event | 35
The Earliest Witness | 37
The Third Day | 42
Interpreting the Resurrection | 46
Raisedness and Risenness | 48
What Is Bodily Resurrection? | 51

2. HE DIED FOR OUR SINS | 57
Christ Without the Cross | 57
Jesus and the Romans | 61
Jesus and the Jews | 65
The Trial of Jesus | 70
Why Did Jesus Die? | 75
Redemptive Suffering | 77
The Metaphors of Salvation | 81
The Metaphors of Sacrifice | 84

3. LORD AND CHRIST | 91
The Enigma of the New Testament Christ | 91
The Jewish Messiah | 94
Jesus' Attitude Toward Messiahship | 97
The Christian Messiah | 100
A Prophetic or Priestly Messiah? | 103

Lord and Master   109
The Exalted One   113

4. SON OF MAN AND SON OF GOD   117
The Son of Man: Another Enigma   117
The Apocalyptic Son of Man   120
The Heavenly Man   123
A Church Designation?   127
Jesus' Own Title?   129
The Enigma Once More   132
Adoptive Sonship   134
Variations on "Son of God"   137
Miracles   139
The Manifested Son of God   144
"Real" Sonship   147
Jesus' Awareness: Father   150
Jesus' Awareness: Amen   155
Resurrectional Retroactivity   157
The Chalcedonian Formulations   161
What Is Divine "Nature"?   164

5. THE POWER AND THE WISDOM   169
The Wisdom Tradition   169
The Implications of Redaction   173
The Johannine Hymn   177
Why the Cross?   181
The Chalcedonian Formulations Again   183
Beyond Chalcedon   186
The Final Ecumenicism   190
The Unknown Christ   195

6. THE CARPENTER OF NAZARETH   199
The Stuff of Legend   199
The Source of the Legend   202
The Virgin Birth   205
The Brothers and Sisters of Jesus   209

Why Born of a Virgin? 211
And Why Not? 213

A FINAL POSTSCRIPT 217

SCRIPTURAL CITATIONS 221

INDEX 227

INTRODUCTION

The Priority of Christ

To write about christology these days may seem a more than usually laborious way of making an act of faith. At all events, an act of faith it is, and, since all faith involves assumptions, it might be as well that we set forth at the outset the assumptions on which this book is premised.

The first assumption concerns priorities. In 1956 a group of British theologians chose to honor the seventieth birthday of Karl Barth with a collection of *Essays in Christology*, having selected their theme not simply as one possible option from among many but as being itself the very heart of Christian theological concern. In 1966 the same group, now augmented by other English-speaking colleagues from around the world, again responded to Barth's eightieth birthday with a complementary volume on Christian service, the *diakonia* of the church. This order, it seems to the present writer, was the correct one: first Christ, then the church. The two cannot be separated, it is true, as we shall soon be pointing out; nevertheless, that the one ought to precede the other in our thinking should be clear enough.

Apparently it has not been clear, however, not to much of the church of our times, not to many Roman Catholics. In the aftermath of the Second Vatican Council what we seem to have been caught up with, almost to the exclusion of anything else, is church structures and other matters of polity. Church structures are of course important, important most of all, perhaps, to those who would airily dismiss them. But there is no justification either in tradition or in present need for according them paramount importance. Yet even in the Council the preoccupation that crystallized under the rubric *Christus Dominus* surrounded not the author of Christianity but rather the episcopal office in the church. Subsequent crises that have riven us, or which promise to rive us: Have they not for the most part been at the fringes of structure or of what is otherwise ancillary rather than at the heart of what is Christian and substantive to it? Liturgical forms and reform, priestly celibacy and life styles, response to the sexual revolution and the ecological challenge specified in birth control, abortion, and the re-evaluation of basic values human and humane, the recovery of ancient freedoms and responsibilities eroded by a tradition of insulated privilege, all these have been and are existential issues that must be honestly faced. But how often have they been faced, by those who stand above or below the issues, except in ethical or sociological or organizational terms? Terms borrowed from one age and subsequently canonized now seen in conflict with terms borrowed from another. Even when appeal is made, as it is on all sides, to the gospel, it is hard to agree that very much that is specifically Christian is being said about any of these matters. At least, it is not Christian if by Christian we understand what pertains to the person of Christ, a position that has been taken precisely in view of the Christ-event.

It ought to be a truism that concern for the gospel and the Christ-event should carry with it a lively interest in the person of Jesus of Nazareth. Yet neither in professional theology nor in its divulgation within the church has such a lively interest been shown either in our recent past or, for that matter, in the present. The classic "lives" of Christ that nourished the piety of a short generation ago really did not, though they seemed to, betray an interest of this kind. Often they did quite the opposite. Born of the apologetics that rose to the challenge of nineteenth-century historical positivism, the "lives" attempted to render the gospel story plausible by adopting, in all essentials, the same canons of historical reliability by which skeptical critics had determined the gospels to be myth and legend. There is no doubt that they served a useful purpose in making the story come alive: Nazareth, Bethlehem, and Cana (even though rarely the right one) were now places to be photographed and located on a map, the capacity of the six stone water-jars could be calculated precisely in gallons, and the casting nets thrown by the sons of Zebedee were properly illustrated as circular. The story came alive with archaeological authenticity and thus seemed more real, just as *Julius Caesar* seemed more real when done with togas and stolas rather than doublets and farthingales. What the "lives" did not do, however, was look at the gospel story for what it was and identify the Christ of whom it told. For apologists and skeptics alike, in those days, the gospels were efforts at biographical reportage—successful and trustworthy efforts in the view of the apologists, naïve and myth-ridden in the eyes of the skeptics. And because of this, a "Map of Palestine in the Time of Jesus" might be for the gospel story what a map of Middle-earth is for the fairy tales of J. R. R. Tolkien, nothing much more or less. The net effect of the "lives" was to construct the pseudohistory of a Jesus who never was, the Christ of faith mythicized by historicism.

It may be said in extenuation of our so long having failed to face the real issues of New Testament christology that an obscurantist exercise of church discipline fearfully inhibited our scholarship in the pursuit of its proper work. It was precisely in the nineteenth century, as Leonard Swidler has reminded us, in the century of freedom and liberalism, that there occurred in the Catholic church "an extraordinary rolling back of Christian freedom, an extraordinary growth of archconservative authoritarianism, of Catholic ghettoism" in which "all contact with the modern world was condemned as being at best a waste of time and highly dangerous" and in consequence of which "Catholic scholarship was relegated to mouthing outdated, and hence ineffective, formulas." The repression must be admitted, and without too many recriminations, since the guilt is shared by those who submitted to the discipline along with those who imposed it. It formed part of what John Tracy Ellis has called "the exceedingly high price that the church has paid in the past by her members' refusing to make the adaptation and adjustment that the constantly evolving character of the human condition demands." Its effects remain in many a crisis of faith that ought never to have occurred. Because the church so generally tried to pretend that time had stood still, stand still it did for far too much that was churchly. And thus, because it was never permitted to develop naturally in the minds of men as it otherwise would have, the "new" theology of Christ or of any other avowal of faith may seem like some monstrous growth discontinuous with the past, far more radical than it really is. On the other hand, any theology that has been denied a proper history of its own with the right natural to all men to make and learn from their own mistakes will be doomed for a certain time to waste itself on frivolities that a more mature tradition has already tested and discarded.

In any case, however, ecclesiastical obscurantism on the authoritarian level does not alone account for the church's christological apathy. At best, or at worst, it affected only a few peripheral areas of timid exploration and discussion. During its sway there was never any call from the grass roots for a study of christology in depth, the kind of call that stirs the conscience of scholars as well as the deadly inertia of beadledom. Nor do we hear any very clear call today, now that the restriction of authority is no more, or is ignored, and when virtually every other aspect of belief and practice can be subjected to the frankest kind of criticism. We seem, prelate and people alike, to have been possessed of a singular disinterest in the central figure of the historical religion that we know as Christianity. In this respect the Catholic can find himself in the seemingly unusual company of Rudolf Bultmann, for whom there is nothing religiously significant about the person of Jesus beyond the mere fact of his having existed. "What went on within Jesus' own heart," Bultmann has written, "I do not know and I do not want to know."

The Priority of History

We are now brought to a second assumption entertained by this book, namely, the importance of history. We must pause on this word for a moment, for it is today a sign of grievous contradiction.

The Christ of apologetics pictured by the "lives" of the nineteenth and early twentieth centuries was, we have suggested, historicist and not historical. When the picture was first drawn it was an excusable, though nonetheless fatal, caricature of the Christ of faith; however, the last of the "lives" also attempted to survive the evidence that had long invalidated them. Historicocritical study of the gospels had made sufficiently plain that they were the repositories of traditions that had developed through decisive stages and with many variations. They came from their authors' hands not to represent Jesus as he had appeared among his contemporaries in the manner of an historical reconstruction—a quite modern ideal of historiography—but rather to express what the person of Christ meant to the faith of the respective Christian communities of which the gospel story had taken hold and which produced the several written gospels. Redolent though these gospels were of the Palestinian Judaism of Christianity's origins, it was also clear that they contained much that reflected other, alien world scenes and cultures, which would have been altogether out of place in an historical life of Jesus. This discovery was merely corroborated when the gospels were seen in ever better focus against the backdrop of the other sources of New Testament witness. The more sophisticated understanding of the complexities of Christian beginnings that was the by-product of a dozen related sciences had already shown up the folly of an historicist approach to the gospel presentation of Jesus.

The continuing study of the gospels has only reinforced this conclusion many times over. Perhaps the most important role in this study has been played by form criticism. Form criticism—research into the history of the gospel forms—has analyzed the stories told about Jesus and the sayings ascribed to him from the viewpoint of their transmission in the oral tradition that underlies the gospels and in the context of the Christian communities whose needs they served, when these elements circulated as independent bits of instructional, credal, and catechetical material inspired by the memory of Jesus and the significance he had assumed for the church. By reconstructing the ecclesial situation that a given story or saying can be seen to have been shaped to fit, form criticism can often cast doubt on there having been for it a comparable situation in the life of the historical Jesus. At the very least, it has shown the considerable modifications, developments, and adjustments introduced into the material that connects Jesus with the gospels during the process of its transmission. More recently redaction criticism—the study of the further adaptation of the tradition as it was assimilated to the special theological and other interests of the individual or collegial authors of the separate gospels—has confirmed and strengthened the analysis begun by form criticism. Possibly the most important single certainty that has emerged from these studies is that which recognizes the decisive effect of the church's resurrection faith on the formation of the gospels. That is to say, the preresurrection Jesus portrayed by the gospels has nevertheless and inevitably been endowed by their authors with qualities that were ascribed to him only after the resurrection experience: He is not, therefore, first and foremost the Jesus who is of interest to the historian, but the Christ who was preached in the church as its Lord and Savior.

In its dogmatic constitution *Dei Verbum* concerning divine revelation, the Second Vatican Council acknowledged the substance of what we have been saying when it so described the gospels: "What the apostles preached in fulfillment of the commission of Christ, afterwards they and apostolic men under the inspiration of the Holy Spirit handed on to us in writing." The gospels were written, the Council went on to affirm,

> with that clearer understanding which the authors enjoyed after they had been instructed by the events of Christ's risen life and taught by the light of the Spirit of truth. The sacred authors wrote the four gospels, selecting some things from the many which had been handed on by word of mouth or in writing, reducing some of them to a synthesis, explicating some things in view of the situation of their churches, and preserving the form of proclamation.

In these sentences it was repeating words first used by the Pontifical Biblical Commission in an instruction of April 21, 1964, a rather remarkable document which, in language however guarded and hedged, not only admitted but even welcomed the insights into the gospels opened up by form and redaction criticism. It is the task and duty of the exegete, the commission concluded, to recognize in the gospel word three layers, so to speak, each of which he must strive to isolate and explain: (1) the words and deeds of Jesus in their contemporary setting; (2) the dimension in which these were presented by the apostolic tradition (the area investigated by form criticism) in such forms as "catecheses, stories, testimonies, hymns, doxologies, prayers"; and (3) the modifications introduced by the sacred authors (the sphere of redaction criticism).

What is proclaimed by an ecumenical council is, of course, merely the confirmation of the findings of its resource personnel. Not because of Vatican II are no new "lives" of Christ attempted, but because the learned men who once wrote them have now learnt that they can no longer be written. Their cadences endure, alas, in sermons, some devotional literature, and an occasional bishop's pastoral letter; piety of this sort goes on its placid, irrelevant way because it has not bothered to find out that its base of operations has been removed. Equally superficial in its involvement with the central figure of Christianity, however, is the attitude that regards any historical curiosity concerning him as all one with the outdated "lives" and not worth the bother.

Modern criticism has enormously complicated historical enquiry into the gospels, but it has neither made it impossible nor rendered it superfluous. The last point, perhaps, requires some clarification. There are these days many who, whether or not they articulate it quite as well, make much of the position outlined long ago with great eloquence by Martin Kähler in *The So-called Historical Jesus and the Historic, Biblical Christ*. (It was Kähler, it seems, who first used the flexibility of the German language to teach us that "history" has multiple meaning when related to the Christ of faith.) The only Christ who matters, said Kähler, is the Christ of the gospels, the Christ proclaimed in the primitive kerygma of the church. He is the Christ who saves, the Christ in whom we believe. We believe in him because we have seen and accepted him as he appears in the church's preaching, a preaching that has interpreted for us certain historical events—specifically, the meaning of the crucifixion of a certain

Jew by the Romans in or around the thirtieth year of our era,
at least sometime during the governorship of Pontius Pilate as
the Christian creed holds—but a preaching and interpretation
of history that is in any case the only means whereby the
event itself has been made known. Event and interpretation
have come down to us inextricably connected, and there is no
separating them. One either believes the word by which the
saving events are proclaimed, or he does not. But to believer
or nonbeliever, of what use is research into the circumstances
of an historical Jesus apart from those that have obtained a
kerygmatic interpretation? To faith they are irrelevant. They
could have an interest for a neutral historian, but even to him
they must appear so meager and inconsequential as to hardly
merit his attention. Such was the negative verdict pronounced by Kähler over the nineteenth-century "quest for the
historical Jesus" even before Albert Schweitzer read its final
obsequies after the turn of the present century. It has remained for more recent scholars of the same persuasion to
find in these negative results a positive virtue; for, they say,
an attempt to objectify by historical research anything that is
believed is not only futile but also a lapse into the primal
heresy of striving for justification through works rather than
by faith.

This kind of thinking relies on a frame of mind that with
equal impartiality and equal approximation may be styled
Platonic or existentialist or Kantian: Namely, reality for me is
what exists in my mind and has been formulated in my
being; it does not consist in some supposedly objective fact
"out there." A great deal is to be said for this way of thinking
as accurately capturing a psychological truth. In what real
sense can a thing be said to exist for me if it has never
touched my soul, demanded a decision of me, or affected my
actions in any way? However correct and orthodox may be
the affirmations I make about such a thing, as long as I am not
personally involved with it, it is only an abstraction that has
no concrete being. We need more recognition of this truth if
we would avoid repeating some of the mistakes of the past. It
is a truth that the church has often ignored in its approach to
the dogmas of faith. For example, has not the church ap-

peared to deem the formula of transubstantiation the ultimate eucharistic reality, even in preference to the experienced presence of Christ for which the eucharist exists and which is common to Catholics and Protestants alike, whatever their theological understanding or lack of it? Nevertheless, if the existential concept of reality expresses a truth, it does not thereby express the whole truth.

Most men will be hardly persuaded that the sole norm of meaningful existence is what they have discovered in their own experience. If men are to associate, to recognize the areas of agreement and disagreement that guarantee them a society, even to communicate their experiences to one another, there must be some canons of facticity that transcend the personal and subjective. And when, as it does here, the question of facticity concerns supposedly historical events, most men will think it hardly playing the game to avoid the issue by redefining history, by making it no longer refer to what once happened but only to what happens now. For what once happened—the *einmalig* of the German scholars—is that once-for-all fact the knowledge of which and the show of which knowledge first gave the name to history.

Beyond Subjectivity

Historical objectivity, however, may be the wrong term for us to employ, if it gives rise to the thought that historical method can substitute for faith or compel it, or if it insinuates that there is a Jesus recoverable from history who can stand on his own over against the Christ of the church's belief. Therefore transsubjectivity is the term preferred by Helmut Thielicke in his arguments for the necessity of the search in history for this Jesus. First of all, he points out, if faith may not be measured against historical factuality, then man is required to believe at the expense of his reason. We are much reminded these days that faith is not merely a set of mind, an assent to a series of propositions, but rather a commitment of the total man; and nothing could be more profoundly true. Included in the total man, however, certainly must be his reason. If the historical question cannot be or simply is not raised, then reason has not been served, and something less than the total man has been committed.

Second, Thielicke argues, the historical search is necessary in order to show what is and what is not faith, in order to show the meaning that faith bestows on an historical happening. In 1 Corinthians 15:12–19, Paul took up the question with the Christians of Corinth:

> Tell me, if Christ is preached as raised from the dead, how is it that some of you say there is no resurrection of the dead? If there is no resurrection of the dead, Christ himself has not been raised. And if Christ has not been raised, our preaching is void of content and your faith is empty too. Indeed, we should then be exposed as false witnesses of God, for we have borne witness before him that he raised up Christ; but he certainly did not raise him up if the dead are not raised. Why? Because if the dead are not raised, then Christ was not raised; and if Christ was not raised, your faith is worthless. You are still in your sins, and those who have fallen asleep in Christ are the deadest of the dead. If our hopes in Christ are limited to this life only, we are the most pitiable of men.

If this was not an appeal to the facticity of the resurrection of Christ, there never was one: Paul would undoubtedly be bewildered to find his own name and words invoked in proof, as they sometimes are today, that there was nothing special about that resurrection, that nothing occurred at that one time that is any different from what occurs here and now. But let us leave that question for the moment. The point that Paul is making is that unless Christ has been truly raised up, restored to life, the gospel that proclaims him life-giving Savior and embodiment of God's forgiveness to man must be a false message founded in no fact. Yet the fact is that redemption has taken place and sins have been forgiven: the Corinthians had this conviction confirmed through their experience of the life in Christ, and it had never been in question. Insistence on the facticity of the resurrection, therefore, is not to substitute for faith or to motivate it, but to indicate its historical content. Conversely, the unbeliever who is unconscious of the lordship of Christ, who is "still in his old state of sin," can stand mute before the same fact of history. Faith and history need each other, and the one cannot do the work of the other.

Thielicke's final and decisive argument for the need of the historical search, a codicil to his first, he terms "the irrevocability of anticriticism." Put in simpler words, what is meant is that historical criticism has the task of determining whether its results contradict faith or not. It is stipulated that faith may not rightly survive if determinable facts are brought into conflict with what is believed about them. Thielicke quotes Gerhard Ebeling: "Were it to be proved that christology had no basis in the historical Jesus, or even was a misinterpretation of Jesus, then christology would be finished." Paul, despite his notorious lack of involvement with the circumstances of the Jesus *kata sarka*, would surely agree.

Catholic disinterest in the historical Jesus has generally been unmotivated by any fear of alloying the purity of faith in the historic, biblical Christ: It is not the Christ of biblical faith who has preempted the Catholic scene in earlier or in these latter times. Rather, historical inquiry about Jesus is likely nowadays to be regarded as quixotic or at best unnecessary in view of the sufficiency of the Christ who is allegedly experienced in one's fellow men or in the liturgy of the people of God. To these assumptions, too, a word must be addressed.

Christianity, unless it is only a retained habit of mind or is to be newly identified with whatever we happen to be doing at the moment, is inextricably bound up with the biblical word. The only Christ with whom we can have any contact beyond our own imagining, the Christ who is the indispensable referent for any alleged experience of him in life or liturgy, is the Christ of the gospels. We can go further. Since the biblical word about Christ has come to us only in the formulations of the earliest church, part of what it is to accept Christianity—to take seriously a christology—is to accept an ecclesiology as well. Here we say nothing with regard to church structures or polity; we simply insist on the *sine qua non* of continuity of a people and a tradition. A churchless Christianity is historically a contradiction in terms, and by the same token any Jesus who is not at the same time the Christ of the church's biblical faith is merely the mental or emotional construct of those who have parasited on the church's body.

Whoever speaks of a postbiblical Christianity compounds an ambiguity. If he means only that the Bible cannot stand entirely on its own *vis-à-vis* the Christianity that was, is, or will be, he enunciates a commonplace that has never been doubted, not even in the most rigid acceptation of *scriptura sola*. If he means, however, that something else now can or should take the place of the Bible, that the Bible has had its day and that Christianity can do without it, he appears to have fallen into loose and equivocal language. Whatever the faith is that can dispense with the biblical word, it is not Christianity. No one can reasonably object to a personal faith that someone finds rewarding and fulfilling: Any person's own experience is irrefutable by anyone else. But one may quite reasonably object to woolly ways of thinking and speaking that call any and every faith Christian, that rob words and ideas of meaning by making everything equal everything else.

The assumption of this book is, then, that if there is anything of value to be preserved in the way of life and thought that we rightly represent as Christian, there is required of us that lively interest in the circumstances of the historical Jesus of which we have been speaking. It is the means whereby we are prevented from creating a mythical Christ out of pious experience and imagination or, more commonly today, out of our own aspirations and the way we would have things be—the "Jesus as I think of him" once beloved of the Sunday supplements and lately of the recurring Rauschenbusches who fancy themselves radical theologians. Such a lively interest does not ask us to imitate but rather to repudiate the methods of historicism that resulted in the contradictory and equally mythical hero-figures of the "lives" written by both Christian apologists and rationalists looking for a Christ without dogma. Historical research alone—from Reimarus to

Wrede through Schweitzer, and then from Schweitzer down to S. G. F. Brandon and David Flusser—has been able neither to provide an apologetics for the Christ of the gospels nor to construct a convincing substitute. But it can and should offer the believer some help in his desire to be in authentic contact with the revelatory Christ-event as it was first proclaimed and accepted.

History and Method

History is a record of events that have been transmitted with interpretation. This is the definition of all history, not simply that of the gospels. To investigate the interpretation is the only way we have of investigating the event itself. And that is precisely what we set out to do when we undertake an historical examination of the New Testament. It is obviously of some importance that we be able to trace the history of interpretation if we are to come to any understanding of what the event did and does mean. Is the Johannine Christ, like and unlike in so many various ways to the Christ of the synoptic gospels, an interpretation of the meaning of Jesus of Nazareth valid for a Christian church of the time and place of the Fourth Gospel's origins, and for us? Did Paul's reinterpretation of Christian creeds and liturgies that he took from tradition and redacted to suit his own theology retain the sense and spirit of those who first formed them? No one can answer such questions unless he is prepared to submit the New Testament to historical research, to ascertain as best he can what its development has been. Such research can never bring us back to a neutral, uninterpreted Jesus of history, nor should we want it to: Kähler was quite right when he said that this Jesus would be an irrelevancy. If all the words and deeds of the historical Jesus had been recorded on audio and video tape—the desideratum often expressed in utterances of a fundamentalist piety—it would doubtless prove to be a hindrance rather than an aid to Christian faith. The Christ in whom Christians believe is an interpreted Christ, and interpretation, whether it is man's or comes from the

Spirit of God, is never undertaken independently by a machine. What we seek to do, therefore, is to get at the origins of a belief. We can do no more.

But neither should we settle for less. Although it is true that in the main, christology has been an elaboration of the Christian community of faith—for Jesus himself, of course, was not a Christian, let alone a Christian theologian—still, it is not enough just to trace the christological formulations back to their earliest stage within the Christian kerygma about Jesus as though that were the end of the matter. To be content to stop there is to be content with a gnostic Christianity, a docetic narcissism that would permit the church to contemplate itself personalized as Christ. Paul, after all, who made use of some of the earliest Christian formulations in his later letterwriting, had already incorporated them into his thinking and preaching within five years or so of the death of Jesus. The kerygmatic Christ, in other words, as first discerned in the Christian sources that are at our disposal, is not all that removed from the Jesus of Nazareth who inspired the kerygma. A respect for the nature of the kerygma itself, therefore, impels us to approach it as a word concerning a person recent in history and to discover, if we can, which of his words and deeds are historically recoverable through the impact that he made upon it. And in these words and deeds we may find an incipient christology implied in what Jesus knew or sensed himself to be.

Specifically what is recoverable and how it is recoverable is the subject for discussion in the pages that follow. Included in it, it must be stated at the outset, is relatively little of statistical fact to relate Jesus to the larger history of the world of which he was a part. The Christian believer is frequently distressed to learn that the gospels can be depended on for such a small deposit of this kind of thing, which he has been taught to regard as the very stuff of history; but on reflection he should not find it hard to see why this should be so and of what little consequence it is in any case. We can fix only approximately the span of years in which Jesus lived out his ministry in first-century Roman Palestine. His birth: in Bethlehem of Judea? So we have long told the story, familiarized with it by the Christmas legend that we have made of the combined Infancy gospels of Matthew and Luke. And quite possibly it was so: the Matthean and Lucan stories, which are in occasional conflict with each other, may independently testify to an authentic recollection confirmed, perhaps, by the tradition underlying John's gospel. But on the other hand, the whole idea may only reflect an ingenuous interpretation of prophecy as prophecy was then understood, which decreed that one who was not identified as Messiah must have been born in David's native town. With much more confidence we may affirm that Jesus was a Galilean and a villager of Nazareth. There is no reason to question the reliability of such data, which in fact occasioned some embarrassment for those who first told the story of the Christ. Of the same character is the pervasive tradition that links Jesus with John the Baptist, though we cannot determine with certainty what the precise relationship was. We can at least be sure that Jesus received baptism at the Baptist's hands.

Of greater importance, surely, is what we can assert about Jesus' death. The passion narratives of the gospels have quite obviously described it in terms of theological models that belong to a relatively late stage of New Testament development. Nevertheless, certain hard facts can be convincingly retrieved from them, even over and above the hardest ones that were the challenge of the first Christian faith: namely, that Jesus died as a convicted felon under Roman law with his popular movement, of whatever kind it had been, brought down to apparent failure and demoralization. These minimal facts may also be attested to by the rare independent witness of the Roman historian Tacitus—independent, that is, unless he merely echoed the "suffered under Pontius Pilate" article of the Christian creed that he had heard and had no reason to call into question. Possibly we would have other independent access to the historical situation had it not been for some heavy-handed fumbling on the part of the later Christian establishment. The contemporary historian of the Jews, Flavius Josephus, almost certainly wrote something about Jesus; but Christian interpolators have so corrupted his references that it is now impossible to determine exactly what he did write. Jewish tradition preserved in the Talmud was ruthlessly censored in the medieval Christian societies where Jews had to survive, or was suppressed by the Jews themselves to prevent its being censored. As we shall see, however, neutral or hostile testimony would probably add very little to what is recoverable about Jesus from the gospels.

Of the many things told about Jesus throughout the gospels we may sometimes surmise the path by which an event passed from the actuality of his life into the interpretation of the church simply because of the evidence of the effort by which it did so. Where the soul of Jesus is most poignantly revealed—in the agony in the garden, for example, or in the words of desolation uttered from the cross—we often encounter particulars which the earliest kerygma found difficult to interpret, or which it interpreted variously. It would be hard to conceive of the primitive tradition as having first simply contrived such details that it then had to set about trying to blend into its idealized picture of Jesus. They have about them the ring of authenticity. We are not referring here to "eyewitness accounts"; many of these stories describe what could not have been the object of direct witness. Eyewitness accounts, at all events, though endowed by eager apologists with almost mystical qualities, do not hold the same magic for those who have to deal with them as sources of reliable information. We are thinking, rather, simply that a person appears to have inspired the stories and that the stories have not created a person.

Even more rewarding for our purposes, perhaps, is research into the words of Jesus, his teaching. Again, we are not reverting to the old and chimerical quest of the *ipsissima verba*, which sought to isolate the precise pronouncements of Jesus that could be reconstituted with the literalness of auricular recall. In all substance the words that the gospels put on the lips of Jesus are at best a refraction of his teaching and a translation: a translation into the language and the forms required by a Palestinian and later a Hellenist church, quite apart from the more obvious translation into Greek of what was presumably in the beginning a message phrased in

Aramaic. Even in refracted form, nonetheless, words may reveal the personality of their begetter, just as the personality of Socrates comes through to us in the dialogues of Plato. Had we only the words of Thomas More spoken by him on the scaffold, we should already be far towards knowing what sort of man he was. Similarly, in the cadences of the Sermon on the Mount, we hear intimations of a christology, implied in what its preacher evidently thought his own qualifications were. The Sermon on the Mount is a composition of the First Gospel, no mistake about that, compiled from materials that can be found otherwise scattered through the gospel tradition. But it is not an entirely free composition: It has assembled elements of teaching and of personal impact that have their independent claims to an origin in Jesus.

The route of the historical method is admittedly not an easy one, and not everyone will always agree exactly where it leads. There is no infallible criterion of success. Present-day scholars frequently invoke the criterion of dissimilarity, that is, the likelihood that a given teaching points truly to the person of Jesus when it can be shown not to have been extracted from contemporary Judaism nor to correspond with the inventive interests of early Christianity. This is a criterion useful for what was unique about Jesus, and the unique is, of course, a prime affirmation of christology. It is a New Testament affirmation. But it is not the only New Testament affirmation, and furthermore the criterion is not altogether peremptory; for the primitive church with all its inventive interests stood over against contemporary Judaism even more, presumably, than Jesus did. It leaves untouched, in any case, very much that is of extreme importance in assessing the person of Jesus, not the least of which is his identification with the honored tradition of Israel, his character as the one whom Martin Buber could call an elder brother. Who is to say that the one rather than the other is the more distinctive of Jesus? The principle of dissimilarity alone, therefore, is not enough; other probabilities must be weighed along with it. Jesus has meaning not only because of what distinguishes him from the human condition but also because of what unites him with it. Christology must take account of the duality and try to ascertain how it was taken into account by the early kerygma and, possibly, by Jesus himself.

Biblicism and Biblical Relevance

A final word should be said about methodology, since we are on the subject and since it, too, is one of the assumptions of this book. In what follows we shall be concerned mainly with biblical theology, for reasons that hopefully we have already justified. This is out of no intent to limit theology to the Bible, only to insist that a Christian theology must begin with it. We shall have very little to do with what is properly called systematic theology except in an indirect way, namely by presuming to pronounce it either sound or misdirected on the basis of the biblical precedent. The seeming arrogance of this procedure is itself a dictate of biblical theology, which assumes that its controlling word has the last say concerning what is and what is not opportune and relevant.

Biblical theology, however, is not the same as biblicism. Biblicism actually excludes theology by taking for granted that the Bible needs no translation, that the biblical word is immediately clear and relevant. It is an old-fashioned misunderstanding of what the Bible is about, exposed as a misunderstanding in no better way than by examining the process of the biblical authors. For in both the Old Testament and the New we find theologians at work, men who were aware that the word had to be made relevant and who tried to afford faith an understanding by translating it into terms, categories, and frames of reference that their contemporary societies recognized as valid and meaningful, and, while they were at it, discarding some of the terms, categories, and frames of reference that they have inherited. A biblical theology today does neither more nor less than this when it seeks not merely to retrace the steps of the theologians of the Bible but also to judge whether those steps still lead to a desired destination. Part of the task of biblical theology, in other words, is to point out the limitations of the Bible, and to continue its work of translation by acknowledging that its authors have made use of some categories that were either wrong from the beginning or at least are no longer helpful, for which reason it must substitute better categories to take their place. This is a thought abhorrent to biblicism.

Biblicism assumes sophisticated as well as cruder forms, however. It sometimes works in reverse, by ascribing to biblical authors before their time those insights and categories of truth that only a later evolution of human thought has made possible. It is the same kind of game that Catholics have played with ecclesiastical tradition—"as the church has always and consistently taught"—and for the same reason, understandable enough; but it does not much advance the cause of theological clarity. It is more honest and, therefore, in the long run more profitable to biblical understanding when we frankly set forth what there is about the Bible that we cannot and should not accept from it. Cannot and should not, that is, not because it is the biblical word that challenges our faith but because it gets in the way of the biblical word and prevents it from being heard rightly. Paul, for example, believed that the air he breathed was infested by demonic spirits who were at the source of this world's disorders. To admit that Paul has, nevertheless, something to say about this disordered world that we will find useful, it is required of us neither to share his demonology nor to pretend that it was for him a figure of speech for forces and influences that we find it natural to describe in other, impersonal terms. What is required, it seems, to use Ian Henderson's expression, is that we try to see from the outlook of our age what the New Testament saw from the outlook of its age. The implied change of focus is what we call nowadays demythologizing the New Testament.

Demythologizing is an unwieldy word that is not always consistently employed. The scholar with whom it is most characteristically associated, Rudolf Bultmann, has never, as a matter of fact, defined in any comprehensive and exclusive fashion the myth that must be got rid of before the New Testament message can be heard today. By myth he sometimes means only the famous three-layer universe presupposed in most of the biblical period, the heaven that was "up" and the hell that was "down" in relation to the solid (and flat) earth beneath one's feet. (Actually the cosmology was usually more complicated than this, but the simplification will serve.) Theological statements framed in the language of this world-view have been quietly demythologized, even unconsciously, ever since the Bible came to be read by men who had a different knowledge of the cosmos. But of course the mythical constructs with which modern New Testament interpretation seeks to cope are generally of a more sensitive order than this and require a subtler handling.

Remythologizing, some say, may be the better term for what we are trying to do, since some of the categories we use to classify thought may also deserve to be called mythical. Theological statements, and not theological statements alone, must frequently rely on approximations, analogies, metaphors, all of which contain their element of the unreal at the same time that they are making it possible for man to express himself. It is the price that must be paid for intellection, for venturing into areas beyond immediate sensate experience. A scientific hypothesis is nothing more or less than a myth that works. Science itself is a myth for unscientific men, which means most men. And even the older mythological world is closer to us than we like to think, as we prove when we find it natural to kick out at the piece of furniture that has attacked our shins or to beat the machine that refuses to disgorge the product for which we have fairly paid and fed it.

Nevertheless, the basic objectives of demythologizing are clear and definite enough, and they are valid. The New Testament, which has given us the only historical picture of Jesus that we are likely to have, is the product of some half century of disparate Christian thought, all of it formed in an uncritical age. It would be a false issue of faith to require of the believer that he adopt the presuppositions of two millennia ago, and it would do little credit to the object of faith to suggest that it cannot stand the test of the presuppositions of a later age. It is not really a question of weighing one set of presuppositions against the other or of comparing ages; it is simply a matter of acknowledging that one is ours and the other is not.

Miracles may serve as an illustration. We shall have occasion to speak of miracles later on as a question in their own right, but for the moment let us consider them only from the standpoint of presuppositions. The men who wrote the New Testament evidently took miracles for granted, while modern man does not. It can be debated whether a credence in miracles indicates a frame of mind any more receptive to the mythical than one that has on as little evidence put its faith in a causal order that automatically excludes them, but that is not the point. The point is that miracles are not the same thing for the New Testament and for us today; not the same thing, that is, when miracle is defined as we define it in relation to a natural philosophy that the New Testament did not possess. The theoretical possibility of miracles, therefore, as a suspension or contravention of nature's laws, though it is sometimes proposed as a touchstone of orthodox biblical faith, is not really a New Testament affirmation. The New Testament has a doctrine of miracles as great works of God, as signs and portents, but the physics, so to speak, of miracles does not figure as one of the articles of its faith. The present-day believer is free and, it would seem, at times at least he is even obliged, to replace the physics presupposed by the New Testament authors with one in better correspondence with reality as he knows it, though this may require him on occasion to resort to other terms to describe what the Bible knew as miracles. As already indicated, what we say here of miracles is by way of example; the same principles must be free to roam all the highways as well as the byways of the New Testament thought-world. It is all summed up in this: Faith in the gospel does not carry the price tag of any particular science or philosophy of man, ancient or modern.

These, then, are some of the assumptions with which this book has been written. Others will no doubt become evident in the progress of its development, as the reader is made aware of them in what is hopefully the unfolding logic of the pages that follow. The author of these pages asks only that they all be read before any one of them be judged separately and that they all together stand or fall as the sense of this book and its justification.

1. HE HAS BEEN RAISED

The Transforming Event

It began with the resurrection. Perhaps it were better said, it had begun long before, but with the resurrection began understanding.

Sometime in probably the fourth decade of the first century of the era we count as Christian a routine Roman execution had taken place in occupied Palestine, that turbulent outpost of imperialism that a coming emperor was soon to name *Iudaea capta,* marking an earlier attempt at the *Endlösung* of the Jewish Question. The execution, we say, was routine, one of the many carried out under Pontius Pilate, neither the worst nor the best of the governors who enforced the at once capricious and studied rule of Roman order, which even its own historians recognized to be an insufferable tyranny. The mode of execution was routine: crucifixion, a barbarous kind of death by torture, a technique learnt by the Romans from their barbarous enemies, following the most fixed of the laws of war which condemns belligerents to imitate the worst in one another. The cause was routine. Our sources tell us that three men were executed on the occasion, and two of them they call *lestai,* which our Bibles long translated as thieves, but more accurately must be rendered bandits, men who rob with violence. Without question the Roman executioners regarded all three as *lestai:* It was a word they came to use for the Zealots who waged terrorist guerrilla warfare against them. (It was a word sometimes applied by non-Romans as well, since the Zealots were capable of savaging their own people. The Third Gospel, which has pro-Roman tendencies, probably thinks of Zealots as having been the *lestai* into whose hands fell the man journeying from Jerusalem to Jericho in the parable of the Good Samaritan.) These men died because they were judged to be partisans of the Jewish political resistance to the Roman yoke.

"Ironic though it be," S. G. F. Brandon has written, "the most certain thing known about Jesus of Nazareth is that he was crucified by the Romans as a rebel against their government in Judaea." Ironic or not, the conclusion is certain enough. It is confirmed by the title legally affixed to Jesus' cross, explaining the cause for his death. *The King of the Jews* was at one and the same time—within inverted commas, had there been any—a sign of Roman derision and the justification of their cruel deed, not unlike the Star of David which Nazi law decreed to be a yellow badge of shame. Such are the bare facts that underlie the article of the Christian creed: He suffered under Pontius Pilate.

Actually, of course, the creed says much more than this, that it was "for us men and for our salvation" that Jesus suffered under Pontius Pilate. And since it is only under this dimension that the crucifixion of Jesus is of any more interest to anyone than the crucifixion of the two other *lestai,* and the only reason that any of the three has been remembered, it is evident that faith has intervened in these events from the very beginning. Nevertheless, even in the interpreted form in which the events have been transmitted by our sources, it is possible for the historian to see what took place and was capable of other interpretations.

Initially the first Christians, before they became the first Christians, did interpret the facts otherwise. The group of followers who had gathered around Jesus and accompanied him to Jerusalem was at first completely demoralized by the turn events had taken. Their leader dead and his cause apparently dead with him, they scattered and fled. The Galileans among them—and probably most of Jesus' sympathizers in Jerusalem were Galileans—quite likely immediately left the inhospitable city that had shattered their hopes and set out to regain their homeland. Luke tells a story that has every appearance of accurately recalling their mood when he represents two of the disciples walking the road out of Jerusalem and discussing what had happened with a stranger who had overtaken them. Jesus of Nazareth, they said, had been "a prophet mighty in deed and word before God and all the people. . . . We had hoped that he was the one who would

redeem Israel." We had hoped: a hope now seemingly
dashed beyond all repair. The first interpretation of the
crucifixion outside the walls of Jerusalem was doubtless much
the same for Jesus' disciples and for those who had conspired
to bring him to his death. His work, his influence, his power,
all were now ended.

Then came the resurrection. Its first effects were to trans-
form the band of disillusioned disciples, or many of them at
least, into a community of believers, which would later
become a church. In the second chapter of the Book of Acts,
Luke has Peter deliver a proclamation to the Jerusalemites
following the disciples' experience of the Spirit at Pentecost.
The sermon is Luke's composition, and it contains elements of
a fairly advanced theology, certainly later than the setting in
which it has been placed, but it also probably preserves the
outline of a more primitive resurrection faith:

> Jesus of Nazareth, a man attested to you by God with
> mighty works and wonders and signs . . . you killed by
> crucifixion at the hands of godless men. But God raised
> him up: a fact of which we are all witnesses. . . . There-
> fore let the whole house of Israel know beyond any doubt
> that God has made him both Lord and Christ, this Jesus
> whom you crucified.

In this christology there is, as yet, no claim of any redemptive value in the death of Jesus. His death is seen simply as
an evil fact perpetrated by evil men, but now triumphantly
canceled out by the resurrection.

What had taken place to account for this faith? What did
the church mean when it proclaimed the resurrection of
Christ?

The Earliest Witness

To answer this question properly we must first of all try to
get at our earliest sources. This entails getting at sources
behind the accounts in the written gospels. All the gospels
conclude with a resurrection narrative, or, to be more exact,

with a narrative of the Easter event, the finding of an empty tomb where the dead body of Jesus had been laid. None of the gospels (not even Matthew's in the apocalyptic imagery of 28:2–4) has attempted to portray the resurrection itself as an observed happening that had been or could be recorded. Rather, resurrection was the interpretation that faith had imposed on the otherwise ambiguous fact that the tomb was empty. All of the gospels save Mark's add to the story of the tomb various accounts of appearances of Jesus subsequent to the Easter event: The selfsame person who had died and had been entombed revealed himself to those who had known him best as once more unmistakably living, as having somehow transcended the pangs of death. Here, too, resurrection is an interpretation, the only explanation, seemingly, that squared with the experiences of which these first Christians were utterly sure. These gospel narratives have their value, as we shall see, but we cannot begin with them.

We cannot begin with them because they constitute not the beginning but rather the terminal point of a very long generation of early Christian witness, a witness that ended in the combination and partial composition of variant traditions, and, inevitably, in the accretion of details that can only be regarded as legendary. As Thielicke has aptly remarked in this connection, "When men are totally grasped by something, their fantasies also want to testify to it." Thus, while the witness to an empty tomb doubtless points to some authentic fact (that women, barred from bearing testimony considered valid in a Jewish forum, were nevertheless remembered as being the first to witness to the fact is an important factor in considering its historical likelihood), the heavenly *interpretes* of the event—in Mark a young man clothed in white, in Matthew a fearsome angel, in Luke two men in dazzling apparel—are conventional literary figures borrowed from earlier Jewish stories of divine intervention (like Daniel 10:6, for example, or 2 Maccabees 3:26.33). We come up against irreconcilable statements regarding persons, places, and how and when things happened. Apologetical concerns, reflecting later controversies, account for some of the discrepancies and peculiarities, as also do some disparate attempts to objectify experiences whose memory was now remote and secondhand.

There seems to be no doubt at all that the very earliest witness to the resurrection that we possess is the one recorded by Paul in the fifteenth chapter of his first Letter to the Corinthians. Writing sometime in the year 56 or 57 of the Christian era, Paul incorporated into this letter a credal formula that he had previously been taught:

3 I handed on to you as of the greatest importance what I
     myself received:
  that Christ died for our sins
    in accordance with the Scriptures,
4 and that he was buried,
  and that he was raised on the third day
    in accordance with the Scriptures,
5 and that he was seen by Cephas,
  then by the Twelve.
6 After that he was seen by five hundred brothers at once,
    most of whom are still alive, although some have
    fallen asleep.
7 After that he was seen by James,
  then by all the apostles.
8 Last of all he was seen even by me . . .

Paul explicitly states that he is drawing on tradition, and both the stylized structure of the passage and some of its language (for example, "the Twelve" is not an expression Paul otherwise uses) indicate that he had a ready-made text at his disposal. The use of existing formulations of this kind, produced to satisfy the liturgical and other theological needs of contemporary or earlier Christian communities, was, it would appear, normal practice in the writing of the New Testament. Already in the same letter Paul had quoted from a traditional Eucharistic liturgy (1 Corinthians 11:23–26). In this present instance he has revised and adapted somewhat; that, too, was the normal practice. With verse 8 we have to do, obviously, with his own testimony, not that of tradition. But also verse 6, which breaks out of the rhythm of the surrounding verses, looks like a Pauline interpolation, a datum that he had from some other source and that he introduced to strengthen his case. Actually, as we have already suggested in the Introduction, the Corinthians required no real convincing about the reality of the resurrection of Christ: They had accepted it as the foundation of their Christian faith. Their problem seems to have been, rather, a curiously up-to-date one. Theirs was a triumphalistic interpretation of Christianity, which saw the kingdom of God as already having been achieved. In their de-eschatologized theology there was no need for the resurrection hope in which Paul trusted, for all that it promised, they believed, had already taken place. It was to recall them to history, to convince them of the reality of their own coming resurrection, that Paul insisted on the reality of Christ's, since in his mind they were inseparably connected. Christ, for Paul, was but the firstfruits of all who rise from the dead, and the totality of his triumph could be realized only with a full harvest. He reigns as Lord of the church, but only in view of the end, when he turns the kingdom over to God and "the last enemy to be destroyed is death."

Paul did not specify when and where he received the testimony he passed on, and scholarship has not been able thus far to arrive at a compelling consensus regarding the origin of the formulation or just what phase of early Christian theology it represents. It is possible that its original language was Hebrew or Aramaic and that it grew up in the Jerusalem church that Paul visited some half dozen years following the crucifixion, where he met Cephas (Peter) and James (Galatians 1:18f.). Or he may have had it from the Christian community of Damascus, where he first resided after his conversion in the midthirties. Or finally, it could have been a creed of the church at Antioch, also in Syria, of which Paul was a leading member in the forties prior to his embarking on his extraordinary missionary travels. At all events it undoubtedly takes us back to some of the earliest beginnings of the Christian faith, to the Jewish Christian church, whether Semitic- or Greek-speaking, before Christianity's great breakthrough to the Gentile world.

The witness, however ancient, is still indirect as regards an historical occurrence: It testifies to experiences, visions of Christ, which were interpreted as evidence of a resurrection. Doubtless only in a Jewish community would such an interpretation have been made. C. F. Evans has recently called into question the prevalence of the idea of resurrection in the Jewish eschatology of the period, and to this issue we must return in our attempt to understand what the resurrection of Christ ultimately signified for the first Christians. Nevertheless, even though resurrection was not a universal Jewish response to the puzzle of life and farthest destiny, it was a Jewish response, not a pagan one. In the popular dualism of the Hellenistic world, which dichotomized body and spirit and denigrated the former, bodily resurrection would hardly have been thought a necessary complement to survival after death; in fact, the whole idea would have seemed grotesque, and it is represented more than once by the New Testament as grotesque in Gentile eyes. It was an idea that could take shape only in the minds of men schooled in an anthropology that looked on man's being as essentially that of a body: a "primitive" view which corresponds with some present-day human analysis. The school of this anthropology was the Old Testament, though admittedly resurrection was a late-comer in Jewish thought.

Even when Paul joins his own testimony to the tradition that he had received, we still have to do with an inference. We can only surmise the nature of the revelation given to Paul on the road to Damascus. The three separate descriptions of it found in Acts suggest more the hearing of a voice than the seeing of a vision, but in any case these narratives depend on sources that do not necessarily take us back to the historical Paul. Paul himself may allude to the experience in Galatians 1:12.15f., when he speaks of God's having "revealed his Son" to him, but even if so, he had to assume that what had convinced him that Christ was living in his church was the same kind of thing that had first brought men to believe that the Jesus who had died and been buried had been raised to life again on the third day.

The Third Day

"On the third day" in this ancient creed probably has nothing to do with the gospel chronologies that date the finding of the empty tomb and the beginning of the appearances of the first day of the week (viz., Sunday), after a burial that had taken place on the eve of a Sabbath (viz., Friday). If there is any connection, we would expect that a credal formulation of this sort has influenced the gospel traditions, determining their details to correspond with what had become a conventional way of thinking of the resurrection of Christ. An argument could be made to the opposite effect, since there are details in the gospel narratives that do have historical as well as theological significance. The resurrection appearances of which they speak—differing both among themselves and from the traditions invoked by Paul—might well have begun on a third day following the crucifixion, especially if we prefer as the more likely scene of the appearances the Galilee of Matthew (and of the supplement to John in Chapter 21) rather than the Jerusalem of Luke and the major tradition of the Fourth Gospel. (Despite the efforts of the final editors of John's gospel, the two geographies and chronologies appear to be irreconcilable., However, the empty-tomb tradition, which obviously originated in Jerusalem, has been brought into conjunction with a third-day chronology only with some difficulty, a difficulty of which the gospels are sensible and which they resolve in conflicting ways.

Actually, despite our liturgical habituation to Sunday as the day of the Lord *par excellence* because of the resurrection event, it is by no means certain that it was so in the earliest accounting. The first Christians continued to keep the Jewish Sabbath, as Jesus had before them. In Acts 20:7–12 Luke describes a Christian gathering "for the breaking of bread" that took place on a late Saturday night and was protracted into the early morning—presumably a eucharistic celebration appended by the Christians to the normal Sabbath observance. If this picture is a true paradigm of early Christian worship, it is possible that "when the Sabbath was past . . . very early on the first day of the week" (Mark 16:1f.) had earlier become in its own right a significant setting which was only later adapted to the resurrection story. As a matter of fact, it seems that only in the second Christian century was the celebration of Easter firmly fixed on a Sunday, and thus dissociated from the coinciding Jewish Passover which could have caused it to fall on any day of the week.

"On the third day" probably reflects, instead, the same kind of early resurrection theology that we saw in the second chapter of Acts. In the formula cited by Paul we note a series of "ands" connecting together the confession of death, burial, and resurrection. This is an example of parataxis, a characteristic of Semitic speech and of Semitic-flavored speech, which lacks more discriminating ways of relating one clause to another than by simply piling them up one on top of the next. The sense of verse 4b above is "*but* that he was raised on the third day"—as before, the force of the resurrection is felt principally in its having canceled out the apparent disgrace of Jesus' death. True, this death is not here represented as pointless; rather, it was "for our sins"—an interpretation to which we shall return. But neither has there been any attempt to make of the resurrection anything other than a fact that had occurred and was witnessed to. There is no looking forward, as another theology would, as Paul's theology did, to the hope that has been grounded in the resurrection; the formulation looks backward from the resurrection as the means of interpreting a life and death that had been recently experienced and were otherwise ambiguous. "On the third day" was essential to this interpretation.

The third day was traditionally the day of deliverance, of reversal, of victory snatched from the jaws of death and defeat. "Come!" the prophet cried hopefully to his fellows in Israel. "Let us return to Yahweh. He has torn us, but he will heal us; he has struck us, but he will bind up our wounds. After two days he will revive us; on the third day he will raise us up, that we may live in his presence" (Hosea 6:1f.). On the third day Abraham tried to sacrifice his son Isaac, performing an act of obedience that apparently spelled the end of all his hopes but that in actuality made their realization possible (Genesis 22:4). On the third day Joseph freed his brothers from prison (Genesis 42:18). On the third day Yahweh finally appeared to his people in the awesomeness of Mount Sinai (Exodus 19:11.16). On the third day the fugitive David heard news of the event that inevitably made him king in Israel (2 Samuel 1:2). On the third day Hezekiah had been delivered from a sickness unto death (2 Kings 20:5). On the third day Esther began her work for the salvation of Israel when everything appeared to be lost (Esther 5:1). On the third day, or more precisely, after three days and three nights, Jonah's prayer was answered and he was freed from the belly of the fish (Jonah 1:17, 2:10). Three days were the interval in divine vindication: such seems to have been the meaning of the as yet unbelieving disciples whom Luke put on the road to Emmaus, who had hoped in Jesus as the prophet who would redeem Israel but now thought him discredited, since the third day had passed without incident (Luke 24:21).

If this expression was so pregnant with meaning in the days of Jesus, there is no reason to doubt the persistent gospel tradition that associates a third-day or after-three-days pronouncement with the historical Teacher of Nazareth. The saying, to be sure, now appears in a form that makes it unacceptable as strictly historical witness. Its talk of a third day (Matthew 17:23, 20:19, 27:64, Luke 9:22, 18:33, 24:7.46) or of a time after three days (so in the Marcan parallels, but also in Matthew 12:40, 27:40.63) cannot as it stands speak to an authentic situation in the life of Jesus. Apart from other elements in the passages that can hardly be historical, had Jesus really predicted his own passion, death, and resurrection in such meticulous detail, the rest of the gospel story would be rendered incomprehensible. If anything is certain it is that the resurrection was totally unexpected. The suffering and death of Jesus, far from being awaited with complacency as a regrettable *sine qua non,* had quite scandalized the disciples and caused them to remove themselves as far and as quickly as possible from the powers who condemned their Master to death. As they stand, therefore, the sayings about suffering, death, and resurrection betray a theology that is not only later than Paul's sources but also later than Paul himself.

Yet something may be retrieved from them that does put us in contact with the historical Jesus. Somewhere along the course of his preaching and teaching it is most likely that he did speak, and perhaps more than once, of a vindication of what he was doing, a triumph of the kingdom of God that he was proclaiming, in terms of the three-day tradition. Such a statement or statements could later have been interpreted to refer to his resurrection by those who remembered his words and now, in their Easter faith, found them fulfilled. We have in mind such sayings as we mentioned in our Introduction, words that it would be difficult to imagine simply having been invented, both because of their enigmatic character and their having been the source of some embarrassment to the New Testament writers and redactors. There is, for one thing, the persistent association of Jesus with a polemic against the temple: destroy it, he said, and he would rebuild it in three days (Mark 15:29, Matthew 27:40, Acts 6:14). Mark, probably because he did not understand it, branded the tradition a lying witness that had been fabricated against Jesus, and in this instance he seems to have been followed by Matthew (Mark 14:58, Matthew 26:61). But John recognized it as a true saying of Jesus, which he understood as referring to the resurrection (John 2:19.22). We do not have the means to reconstruct perfectly the historical circumstances that originated the saying, but it may well be one that connects Jesus with a strand of thought elsewhere represented in the New Testament (the speech of Stephen in Acts 7, for example, and also Matthew 12:6 and Acts 17:24) and shared by other elements of contemporary Judaism, both normative and sectarian, with deep roots in the Old Testament: an hostility to, or at least a mistrust of, the Jerusalem temple, coexisting with the more usual tendency to glorify the temple as the place of the divine presence. We do not intend at this point to explore further the reasons for this attitude or to connect Jesus with it more intimately; we are interested simply in recognizing as plausible on his part a three-days saying that later, not unreasonably, could have been related to his resurrection.

Another instance of the same kind is the rather obscure interlude described in Luke 13:31–33. The passage has been taken by Luke from special material that was available to him and employed by him—not without some additionally puzzling details in the process—as part of his going-to-Jerusalem theme, the major emphasis that he has imposed on the career of Jesus beginning with 9:51. What was the original episode all about? It is difficult to say, so difficult in fact that it is more reasonable to assume that it was an historical datum imperfectly remembered than that someone made it up for no assignable purpose. If it is an historical datum, Jesus on some occasion spoke of an eventual culmination of his chosen destiny as taking place on a third day. The circumstances we cannot know, and they are not to the point. Why and under what respect had he attracted the hostile attention of Herod Antipas? What role did the Pharisees play in the drama: foes (the customary part they have been rather simplistically assigned by the gospels), friends, or merely disinterested bystanders? We need not ponder the details, but merely recognize that with some probability the three-days tradition later associated with the resurrection did go back to a situation in Jesus' life when he may have spoken of his career in terms of Hosea 6:2.

Interpreting the Resurrection

Resurrection, we have said, was an interpretation given to certain events by the first Christians who experienced them. Since the resurrection itself was not such a witnessed event, it cannot in that sense be described as historical. What was witnessed were the appearances and the empty tomb. The latter may not be dismissed, as it once was, simply as a crude attempt to establish an apologetics for the resurrection by inventing "objective" evidence. The tradition of the empty tomb is not reflected with certainty in the primitive creed of

1 Corinthians 15:3–7 and is undoubtedly later than the tradition of the appearances, but it was not a story invented for apologetical reasons. (There may be a trace of apologetics in the story of John 20:3–9, but if so, it is an isolated emphasis in the gospel tradition.) As Matthew 28:11–15 shows very clearly, an empty tomb of itself was an ambiguous fact that could be interpreted in various ways, as indeed it was interpreted then and since, ways that could be entirely contradictory. On the other hand, a tomb that was not empty would not be ambiguous at all: It would stand in irrefutable witness against those who held the resurrection faith. It would be difficult to imagine how Christianity with its belief in a resurrected Christ could have survived a single day in Jerusalem had there been a tomb there to which men might point as the occupied last resting place of Jesus of Nazareth. There is little doubt, therefore, that the emptiness of the tomb is an historical fact, even though historical method cannot establish how it became empty. As previously noted, that the original witness to the empty tomb depended on the testimony of women—who or how many we cannot fully determine in view of the conflicts in the stories, though the name of Mary Magdalene occurs in all of them—is a further persuasion of authenticity.

In the Introduction we dwelt at some length on the principle inherent in demythologizing, that it is not required of us to accept the biblical authors' presuppositions and thought forms as the price of sharing their faith. That is to say, it is possible to believe in a God in heaven—a transcendent God—without localizing him in some special way in the sky. It is possible to agree with the New Testament that nature is not a totally benign sphere in which man moves by his own efforts to an inevitable higher fulfillment without at the same time ascribing a demonic character to the cosmic forces against which it is his lot to struggle. In the same way, as Willi Marxsen has argued, among others, it is possible to believe in the resurrection without having to carry along with this belief the outdated baggage of Semitic anthropological concepts which underlie its formulation in the Bible. The message of the resurrection, insists Marxsen, is that Christ lives, he is Lord of the church, he has survived death. Therefore Bultmann's understanding of the meaning of the resurrection is substantially correct. "Christ rose into the kerygma": Through the Easter faith what Jesus was he continues to be.

Marxsen maintains that the New Testament itself began the process that demythologizing only concludes. He points out that the typical language used to describe the resurrection appearances, *ophthe* ("appeared," "was seen") is that employed throughout the Greek Bible for theophanies and other divine visitations. From this fact he draws the conclusion that the primary thrust of the biblical message concerns the living presence of Christ, not his "risenness." On this precedent he accepts the resurrection appearances as having mediated a valid word for the present and future of the church, but with no power to bind Christian assent to any literal resurrection of the dead Jesus of history. He does not question the reality of the appearances. Bultmann can be quoted to the same effect:

> What the disciples saw was the product of imagination in the sense that they projected what they saw into the world of space and sense. But that does not make what they saw imaginary. The faith evoked by the preaching of the gospel is no more subjective than a man's love for his friend. It is directed towards an object which is not purely external to him, but which operates as a reality within him.

This is, in other words, no return to the old rationalist accounting for the resurrection as a visionary response to wish-fulfillment. It is simply the attempt of men to come to terms with resurrection faith without at the same time obliging the believer to accept what they see as an absurdity.

Raisedness and Risenness

However, it is by no means clear that such an interpretation really preserves the Easter faith that the New Testament proclaims. That faith is not, in the first place, belief in a Lord of the church who merely survived death. It is, rather, belief in an *act* of God who *raised* Jesus from the dead. Whatever this act may have been, it could not have been simply a conviction that grew in the minds and hearts of the disciples concerning their crucified Master. Whatever the nature of the resurrection appearances, they could hardly have been the product of imaginations that were unconditioned to create them. Something happened, something unexpected, even shocking, to account for the church's Easter message.

Here it may be apposite to recall the point made by C. F. Evans that we mentioned earlier, regarding resurrection as a peripheral idea in the Jewish world that produced Christianity and the New Testament. We have agreed that resurrection was an interpretation given to certain experienced events and an interpretation that would have hardly occurred except to Jews; yet even to the Jews who had experienced the events, resurrection was not the inevitable and only interpretation possible. And in Christianity resurrection has certainly moved from the periphery into an absolutely central position. In this connection Evans finds highly significant the variety and contrariety of the resurrection traditions:

For what have to be combined are not a number of scattered pieces from an originally single matrix, but separate expressions of the Easter faith. Each of these is complete in itself; each has developed along its own line so as to serve in the end as a proper conclusion for an evangelist of his own particular version of the gospel. Behind and within all the traditions, of course, is the conviction that Jesus of Nazareth continues to be and to operate, and that in him past, present, and future are somehow related; but the mode of this continuation is differently conceived in the four gospels, and in each case is closely related to the theology of the particular gospel concerned. . . . In one sense, therefore, the Easter tradition may be said to be strong. It is multiple and varied, and has a wide spread. It is not single, uniform or stereotyped. Whatever the Easter event was, it must be supposed to be of such a kind as to be responsible for the production of these traditions as its deposit at whatever remove. The events themselves, however, both the resurrection appearances and the empty tomb, lie so deeply concealed within the traditions that they can be glimpsed only very indirectly, so that the principal difficulty here is not to believe, but to know what is it which offers itself for belief.

All of which can suggest, among other things, that what has been paramount in the Easter faith is not an interpretation that performed a paradigmatic function but rather a controlling fact, however elusive it may be to the tools of historical investigation, which provoked interpretation with many variations.

Furthermore, those who first came to believe in a resurrection did not profess only that Christ lives; they professed that he lives the life of God, that he has passed from this world into the next. Belief in the resurrected Christ, in other words, was not to affirm that a corpse had come to life again but to affirm that in Christ had been realized the eschatological age of apocalyptic expectation. This is another, far more important factor, which again removes the resurrection from consideration as a strictly historical phenomenon. It does so because in the resurrection Jesus has transcended history and entered into a sphere that is outside the control of man's historical experience. It would appear to be a truism, then, to confess that historical experience cannot confirm or define whatever fact lies behind faith in the resurrection.

Neither, however, can it disqualify it by offering itself as the grounds of another, contrary faith, such as Swinburne's, for example:

> From too much love of living,
>   From hope and fear set free,
> We thank with brief thanksgiving
>   Whatever gods may be
> That no life lives for ever;
> That dead men rise up never;
> That even the weariest river
>   Winds somewhere safe to sea.

For if this other faith can appeal for its plausibility to a certain amount of human experience and to the laws of nature as they are now known—in which sense, of course, these laws are a human construct—it also comes up against other human experience that is equally valid. Wolhart Pannenberg has argued from the phenomenology of hope, including its role in modern psychotherapy, that the desire of life beyond death is one built into the nature of man—man who alone of all creatures knows that death is his destiny. Nor is the consistency of this human testimony negated by the apparent equanimity displayed by modern man in the face of the inevitability of death. Ernst Bloch has warned against accepting this attitude too easily at its face value, since it is often unconsciously sustained by hopes that were once consciously articulated in an earlier age. The desire has found expression historically in many other forms besides resurrection, but in some form or other it has always appealed to the mind of man as it is made, and the mind of man as it is made is the only determinant of truth that we possess.

What Is Bodily Resurrection?

Resurrection is, inevitably, a partly mythological concept, though as we have previously said it may be less mythological than other conceptions of the hope of immortality, such as a disembodied soul, for example. At all events, in removing myth from the gospel we must be wary lest we remove the object of faith along with it. In biblical faith the resurrection of Christ was something; something did occur to account for the appearances. It is not to retreat into obscurity or equivocation to confess that we have no better way of defining that something than to call it resurrection. We cannot define what is undefinable in terms of human experience; we can only describe it in some fashion by the use of the pictures we call analogies. The picture we use following the New Testament precedent to describe both what God effected in Christ and, with it as the proleptic example, what its faith promises to all who share in God's kingdom, is mythical to the extent that, taken in all literalness, it might equally well serve to describe the resuscitation of a corpse, which we have said the New Testament does not intend to do. Some of the later developments of the tradition represented in the gospel stories—Luke's particularly, perhaps—may at times give a contrary impression, dwelling as they do on matters like the marks of the crucifixion visible on the body of the resurrected Christ. So-called objectifying details of this kind, however, like those that have him eating, drinking, and living familiarly with the disciples after the resurrection (Luke's forty-day interval leading up to a visible ascension partly fits in here), usually have antidocetism as their justification. Docetism, the heretical tendency to portray Jesus as a divine being who had only appeared to be a man who could suffer and die, made itself felt early in christological thinking, and it is one of the tensions against which gospel materials like these have been formed. The stories wanted to make the point, even by means that now seem rather crude and clinical, that both before and after the resurrection Jesus was very man, and that the risen Lord was the very Jesus of Nazareth and no apparition. They really did not purpose to caricature the Easter mystery as the awakening of dead flesh to life, after the naïve fashion of a medieval painting of the general resurrection. In fact, the same stories indicate more than once quite the opposite when they represent the resurrected Christ as at first unrecognized by those to whom he appeared, as now clothed in a new state of being that had to be disclosed before it could be believed.

Paul, too, for all his insistence on the resurrection as a reality, did not think of it as a resurrection of dead flesh:

Perhaps someone will say, "How are the dead to be raised up? What kind of body will they have?" A nonsensical question! The seed you sow does not germinate unless it dies. When you sow, you do not sow the fullblown plant but a kernel of wheat or some other grain. God gives body to it as he pleases—to each seed its own fruition. . . . So is it with the resurrection of the dead. What is sown in the earth is subject to decay, what rises is incorruptible. What is sown is ignoble, what rises is glorious. Weakness is sown, strength rises up. A natural body is put down and a spiritual body comes up. . . . This is what I mean, brothers:

Flesh and blood cannot inherit the kingdom of God; no more can corruption inherit incorruption (1 Corinthians 15:35–38.42–44.50).

Paul admittedly tells us more about what, in his view, the resurrection is not than what it is, but at the same time he tells us enough to dissuade us from dismissing lightly the testimony of his senses, which he joined to the witness of his tradition. Here was a man quite conscious of the validity of what are sometimes thought to be modern and scientific objections to the idea of resurrection; a man convinced that something had occurred that he could only call resurrection while regretting the inadequacy of the concept. Paul was as prepared as anyone today for demythologizing, but he was not prepared to disallow any fact out of his inability to explain it. Rather than deny the fact, he preferred to retain the myth with all its attendant ambiguities.

If we accept Paul's faith as our own we can hardly act otherwise than he did. Whatever statistical, "objective" details may once have been recoverable from the tales of appearances of a risen one and of the finding of an empty tomb, they have never been recoverable within the recorded history of a Christian belief in the mystery that gave rise to the tales. We can always, if we wish, devise alternative explanations of how the tomb became empty. The materials at hand for these explanations, however, as experience has consistently shown, lie in the genius of imaginative speculation rather than in the resources of historical reconstruction. And whether or not they strike the imagination as plausible, it is difficult to agree that they can ever add to or detract from what is central to resurrection faith; Paul's own example might serve to corroborate. We may, if we choose, determine on *a priori* grounds that the tellers of the appearance stories were mistaken; but we should not try to have it both ways by accepting the stories as something they are not. For all their mythical and legendary elements they are evidently attempts to give an account of witnessed events; in no way do they resemble anything else, such as the effects of some mystical experience. The *a priori* that would judge their account mistaken was also apparent to the teller of the tale, and nevertheless the tales were told. What they told was highly unlikely, but to paraphrase the great detective, when the impossible has been eliminated whatever remains, however unlikely, must be the truth. In this spirit the tellers told their tales.

Contemporary history has provided us with many martyrs to social and political causes whose mystique death and assassination have been powerless to extinguish: "—— lives!" has been the frequent and profoundly true testimony to an influence that continues undiminished or even in greater strength from beyond the grave. The witness to the resurrection, however, affirms and claims much more than this, much more than the "Z" scrawled on Peloponnesian walls. It claims not only that a life continued but that a person continued in a new life, and that because of a unique act of God. Because that act transcended all human experience, it could not be defined, but the fact that it cannot be defined offers us no excuse to rob it of meaning by squaring it with alien models that are definable. No other claim has ever been made that is really like this one, and we respond to its challenge either by accepting or rejecting it but not by affirming another and easier option in its stead. In the same proportion, to accept the claim is to affirm of Jesus what has never been claimed for any other man. Such has been the christological import of the resurrection from the beginning and such has ever been its christological presupposition, for of a nobody great things are not claimed.

To conclude: The "physical" character of the resurrection is not an object of profitable speculation. Like many other phenomena that have occurred in or on the fringes of human history, the resurrection is an event that can be effectively examined only in its effects. One of the chief effects, we have already seen, was the revelation of the meaning of the cross, the significance of the life and death of the Jesus of Nazareth, who through the resurrection came to reign in the church as Lord and Christ. Though chronologically the doctrine of the cross was by no means the earliest christology to emerge from resurrection faith, it will better satisfy our sense of logical development—which was ultimately the sense of logical development canonized in the New Testament—if we now turn immediately to this supreme question, to which the New Testament authors returned only by degrees. Who was the Jesus of Nazareth revealed by the resurrection and whose character presupposed it? The answer to this question involves, to the extent that we can recover it, Jesus' own awareness of his place in the providence of God, as the groundsill of the place later assigned him by the church and New Testament theology. We are, therefore, impelled to an investigation of the historical bases on which the written gospels raised their reconstruction of the earthly Jesus who had become the Christ of faith.

2. HE DIED FOR OUR SINS

Christ Without the Cross

We have said that the doctrine of the cross with its concern
for the circumstances of the historical Jesus was not the earliest christology to be developed in meditation on the meaning
of the resurrection. (Neither, of course, were the circumstances of the historical Jesus of equal importance to all who
shared the doctrine of the cross; here Paul and the gospel
traditions stand in marked contrast.) To set that development
in better perspective, it may be useful to examine now a passage that professed a different kind of christology, which was
only later assimilated to that of the cross, even though in
doing so we must anticipate a number of significant themes
and facts that will come up elsewhere in their own right.

In the second chapter of his letter to the Philippians Paul
exhorts his readers and hearers to a life of love and mutual
forbearance such as befits those whose claim it is to have
been shaped and formed by the Christ-event. The mention of
Christ Jesus in this context prompts him to cite a hymn that
had celebrated the one

6   who, though he was in the state of God,
did not think it should be lusted after
to be equal with God,

7   but rather emptied himself,
taking the state of a slave,
appearing in the likeness of men, [or;]
and revealed in human shape; [or,]

8   he humbled himself,
becoming obedient unto death
[even to the death of the cross].

9   Wherefore God highly exalted him
and bestowed on him the name
which is above every name,

10   that at the name of Jesus
     there should bend every knee:
     celestial, terrestrial, and infernal,
11   and every tongue should confess
     Jesus Christ is Lord!
     to the glory of God the Father.

Though by the addition of the words we have bracketed in verse 8c Paul (or the Pauline redactor of the epistle; the difference, if any, is not important to us) has superficially adjusted the christology of the hymn to his own, the theology of the original text is not really Pauline, nor is its language. We have in it an early attempt to account for the death of Christ not, as Paul would usually have it, as a saving event in itself, "for us," "for our sins," but rather as simply the culmination of a life of obedient humiliation that has been more than counterbalanced by his exaltation as universal Lord. This cosmic exaltation, too, is the high point of the hymn, not the resurrection itself, which is not mentioned, but which for Paul is the essential exemplar of the resurrection hope of those who acknowledge Christ as Lord of the church. The passage takes its place as one of a series of hymns or hymnic fragments elsewhere cited in the New Testament, similar to this one both in content and in form, and usually beginning, as here, with the relative introduction "who" (see, for example, Colossians 1:15–20, 1 Timothy 3:16, Hebrews 1:3). By some modern scholars they have been given the name homologies, that is to say, confessions of the person of the redeemer along with his titles, in distinction to creeds, which are confessions of faith in what the redeemer has done. They were, it seems, acclamations of the object of the church's worship, having as their most likely original setting a function in a baptismal or eucharistic liturgy. (We are reminded of the younger Pliny's report to the emperor Trajan on the repression of Christianity in Bithynia, quoting the Christians' protestation that they were guilty of nothing more sinister than "to gather before dawn on a stated day and to sing a hymn to Christ as God.")

How old the christology of these hymns is and how old the

hymns are themselves can be debated. The one used in Philippians is, obviously, older than the A.D. 56 or 57 when Paul presumably wrote his letter(s) to the church at Philippi; but this is a fact that does not tell us a great deal. It would be much more interesting if we could know the sort of church in which it originated—specifically, whether that church was the primitive, Aramaic-speaking Christian community of Palestine. Ernst Lohmeyer, who was one of the earliest of the modern critics to study the hymn scientifically, did "retranslate" it into Aramaic; and while, for various reasons, he has not been generally followed by others in his hypothesis, he did at least show that it could be done, contrary to the still expressed view of others who hold that it cannot be done. (The contention that such and such a phrase or expression "cannot" be retroverted into a putatively original language is usually based on a certain amount of critical bluff; it is rarely more than a strongly expressed opinion about literary proprieties.) The best that we can say regarding the provenance of the hymn, whether its original language was Aramaic or Greek, is that it contains nothing that is incompatible with early Jewish Christian authorship. Such "foreign" elements as we believe it possesses, that is, thought forms derived from sources other than the Old Testament, had already been made part of the patrimony of Judaism in the syncretic world into which Jesus and the Christian church were born.

It will have been noticed that the translation that appears above is uncertain of the proper punctuation of verse 7. What is at issue is whether verse 8 is to be taken as appositional to the entirety of verse 7, or does verse 7d introduce a new thought that is completed only by verse 8. In other words, does the subjection unto death of verse 8 simply envisage, as does verse 7, man's mortal condition, in which case the first half of the hymn contrasts the two states, divine and human; or are there three stages in a drama, corresponding with the traditional gospel categories of pre-existence, incarnation, and ministry? In the latter interpretation, of course, the hymn would evince considerably more interest in the historical life of the Savior than we have been willing to credit to it. It would also support the view of those for whom the "slave" of verse 7b evokes the theme of the "servant" of the Lord, the figure of redemptive suffering best known from the songs of the Second Isaiah. As we have already made clear, in our opinion the hymn employed by Philippians had nothing to do with such an idea.

When the New Testament alludes to the servant of the Lord, as it often does, it calls him *pais* and not, as here, *doulos,* which we have translated "slave." The hymn thinks of the human state as one of slavery, not to denigrate it in contrast with the divine but to express the common conviction of man's subjection to the demonic powers that rule his world (1 Corinthians 2:6–8, etc.). Of the same sense is the word we have translated "obedient" in verse 8b: This word (*hypekoos*), rare in the New Testament, implies subjugation; in the Greek Old Testament it refers to people who are subject to forced labor (Deuteronomy 20:11, Joshua 17:13). Death is the very epitome of the servitude into which man has been sold (Hebrews 2:14). It was to such a state that he humbled himself, this divine being who emptied himself of godlike rank and ambition in order to share the lot of man, including death itself. In the paradox of divine grace, however, the very powers who put him to death must now join in the universal chorus of acclamation that hails him as Lord, for God has exalted him over all.

If we ask on what model this christology was formed, we will find that there were many to hand, none of which necessitated more than a minimal acquaintance with the life of Jesus. All that was involved was some conception of divine pre-existence, the human estate leading to death, and exaltation to divine lordship presumably signaled through the resurrection. One model might have been the typology, or antitypology, of Adam as first man, a subject that captivated the speculation of both Palestinian and Hellenistic Judaism and has made other appearances in the New Testament. The hymn celebrates one who, like the first man (cf. Genesis 1:26f., Ezekiel 28:12–15), was the image of God stamped with the seal of his perfection, but who also, unlike the first man (cf. Genesis 3:5), did not strive to be equal with God:

his way of obedient renunciation is the antithesis of the way of disobedient Adam (so also in Romans 5:12–21). The Jewish Adam speculation easily melded with the theme of primordial man in the popular philosophical religion of Hellenism. There were myths of Man to whom the Father of all gave birth, in his image and like to himself, who descended from the heavens to reveal to nature below the beautiful *morphe* of God (*morphe* we have translated "state" in Philippians 2:6a); myths of his return to the Father as redeemer, a gnostic redeemer of those who are deified through having acquired the knowledge of God. There were other similar myths, and without the myth but in an analogous pattern of thought was the Jewish tradition of the hypostatized and redeeming wisdom of God, of which we shall have much more to say in a proper place. Perhaps none of these models provides a total explanation of the composition of the Philippians hymn, but possibly all of them have contributed to it. What is evident is that an early christology—and a "high" christology at that—could be inspired by the resurrection and pieced together from commonly available images without venturing an interpretation of the death of Jesus.

Jesus and the Romans

Because such a christology did not interpret Jesus' death, neither did it concern itself with his life as a human history. Resurrection faith here had gone so far and no farther. Among some groups in early Christianity it probably never did go any farther, particularly among those who found the syncretistic religious thought of the age congenial to their personal understanding of the Christ-event, or who saw in it a ready outlet for the universalism inherent in the event. Those, too, of a gnostic or docetist disposition, for a christology of this kind could the more easily degenerate into heresy because of the tenuous contact it could maintain with an event that was at base historical. Still, as we have already pointed out, the entire thrust of the resurrection experience was to force attention back to the death and life of him who had been raised: to the historical person, in other words, and not simply to the ready-made soteriological category into which this person's memory could be conveniently fitted. The Pauline addition to the Philippians hymn reacted to this thrust in what must be thought a small way, by remembering the cross. Other New Testament authors would not feel it necessary to remember even that much, but most would remember far more. We shall now take a look at the more that they finally remembered, beginning where they began. As we have quoted Brandon above: The most certain thing known about Jesus is that he died at the hands of the Romans as a rebel against their rule in Palestine.

Because the thing is so certain, as a matter of fact, there has always been a disposition—shared, to some extent, even by the gospel traditions—to take the Roman accounting of Jesus fairly much at face value as one that must be either affirmed or rejected in toto. Since the beginning of the study of the New Testament without doctrinal presuppositions, there has been built up a critical tradition disposed to the view that Jesus was a Zealot leader or, as Brandon would now prefer it, the leader of a movement that converged with the Zealots in revolutionary action; the Romans presumably would have been insensitive to the scholarly distinction. This tradition is overhauled from time to time and fed with new arguments and evidence, but it always goes back to the solid gospel datum of a Roman execution ordered by a Roman governor. Alternatively, Christian apologists long felt obliged to decry the Roman verdict as a mistake of the first order, a miscarriage of justice whether connived at or merely blundered into, a façade masking uglier designs with more obscure motivation against the life of Jesus: all this because he had preached a kingdom not of this world which had nothing to do with the political scene in Palestine. The critical explanation, despite protestations to the contrary, leaves the origins of Christianity not only unexplained but unbelievable; but the apologist construction can be worse, especially if it ignores facts in favor of the mythical Christ of an escapist gospel.

Our own times have shown us that a state of far more be-

nign cast than the Roman can systematically destroy its own
citizens, even while recognizing them to be its most valuable
assets, not out of malice or evil intent but with a definite kind
of reluctance, and with the observance of every legality.
There is an inexorability to society's way of getting rid of
prophets, even when it knows its need of prophets, since its
instinct is for survival above all else, and its tolerance for
deviation is small. There is an inexorability as well to the
prophet's way, which is deviant by definition and always
larger than the life which society can normally sustain. When
confrontation takes place it is not easy to assign the roles of
hero and villain, not when the real antagonists are that ano-
nymity which a Pauline author knew as the cosmic powers
(Ephesians 6:12) and for which a less adequate contemporary term is "the system." We presuppose that when the
Romans had closed the case of Jesus of Nazareth, the usual
number of unresolved ambiguities remained, as they remain
in the gospel evidence to this day. It is no simple thing to
reconstruct the circumstances of Jesus' death without myth
and without caricature, but this we must do if we would have
the meaning of his life, equally without myth and without
caricature.

What feeling did Jesus have towards those Romans who
eventually took his life? It is impossible to believe that in a
career such as his he could have avoided, even supposing him
to have been so disposed, an expressed attitude with regard
to the Roman occupation; and it is difficult to imagine that the
expression of that attitude has vanished without a trace from
the tradition. A saying that comes perhaps first to mind is the
one contained in the Synoptic story concerning the census tax
(Mark 12:13–17, Matthew 22:15–22, Luke 20:20–26):
"Give to Caesar what is Caesar's, but give to God what is
God's." It is likely, too, that the saying does go back to a
setting in Jesus' life not unlike the one described in the story,
involving the coin of the tribute. What is less likely, however,
is that the pronouncement originally had the import that it
now has in the gospel structure: the compatibility of the
kingdom of God with the kingdom of man because of the
difference of interests. A concern of this kind meant much to

the church of the written gospels, a church whose destiny it was to survive in a Roman world of yet several centuries of hardly diminished vigor; of the same character is the direction in which the gospels have headed the story, as a further instance in which Jesus outwitted Jewish adversaries who were seeking to entrap him by various means. However, it would have hardly been the concern of Jesus in his eschatological preaching. The sense he gave to the words was, most probably, the same all-or-nothing urgency he attached to his other proclamations of an imminent coming of the kingdom (see Luke 9:57-62, for example). Leave the dead to bury their dead, give Caesar back what is his, for these are no affairs of yours; your affair is the kingdom of God alone. His reference to the Romans was, therefore, probably little more than a declaration of their irrelevance.

Still, something about Jesus is revealed in this saying, for it is not one that could have been uttered by a Zealot. The Zealots also were awaiting the coming of the kingdom of God, the consolation and triumph of Israel—but by destroying the Romans, not by leaving them to or for heaven. There were undoubtedly political and national implications to the kingdom as Jesus proclaimed it, for it was in political and national terms that the hope of the kingdom had been cherished. The gospels make it quite clear that he conceived of his mission as exclusively to Israel and that he imposed the same limitation on the activity of his disciples. He was able to enter into the conventional Jewish disdain for the arrogance of the Gentile power structure (Luke 22:25), and he had nothing but harsh words for that creature of the Romans, the tetrarch Herod Antipas (Luke 13:32). It is even admitted that within the most intimate circle of his disciples there were Zealots, or those who had been Zealots. (In the traditional listings of the Twelve, one disciple is explicitly called *zelotes*, or *kananaios*, an Aramaic word meaning the same thing. The sobriquets *barjona* and *iscariot* may have had a like significance.) It is only to supply this fact with its proper context, however, to recall that one of the Twelve disciples has been listed as a *telones*, one of the toll-gatherers who were an especially hated symbol of Roman rule and of Jewish acquiescence therein. There are numerous obvious analogies under which Jesus and his followers can be associated with contemporary nationalist movements and their brand of political messianism; but there are many more discordances that separate them and forbid an equation.

We do not propose to debate *sul serio* or at any length the proposition that "the pacific Jesus" of the gospels is either the figment of a colossal mistake or a fiction created through deceit successful beyond all parallel. If the teaching that enemies are to be loved and evil-doers not resisted does not go back to Jesus, and if he did not bless the peace-makers, then we are left with no accounting for the noblest challenges ever proposed to the spirit of man. They are found to be without genealogy, the casual devisings, even unintentional devisings of unknown and unremarkable men who nevertheless proved to be press agents of awesome powers. Nor is it at all understandable why Jesus should have been remembered for such extraordinarily wrong reasons, if the right reasons restore him to a routine category in which he had neither masterfully prevailed nor spectacularly failed, as one among many others who had played the same game with far greater style and flamboyance. It is not to deny the demands and the need of historical criticism but simply to acknowledge the demands and the need of common sense, when we take it as a working principle that Jesus, like most men who have impressed themselves on history for good or for ill, has been remembered mainly for what he truly was. We have long known how wrong was Coleridge's definition of Christianity as "an Essenism that succeeded." It succeeded as Christianity, which was a very different thing from what Coleridge imagined Essenism to have been. Similarly, Jesus was not a Zealot, or a para-Zealot, "who succeeded."

Jesus and the Jews

If the gospel portrait of Jesus is accepted as having been drawn on mainly reliable lines, we are afforded a reasonable accounting of his place in history, of a person remembered in his own right. The authenticity of the portrait is urged by the variety and contrariety of the lines that converge into the representation of someone unlike anyone else. It is the portrait of one, we have said, who could attract Zealot idealism without succumbing to the Zealot hatreds of Gentile or Samaritan, who did not shrink from violence as the inevitable response to his revolutionary preaching ("not peace but the sword"), yet whose preaching was entirely against violence. And, if this portrait is right, neither can Jesus be fitted neatly into any other of the ordered or orderly categories—social, religious, or national—that constituted the types proper to his time and place. If his ministry was to a nation and a people, as had been the ministry of the great prophets before him, yet it was never nationalistic nor exclusivist: In the openness with which he proclaimed the kingdom, the seeds of the church's later mission to the Gentiles had already been sown. His Judaism was basically the normative one of any Pharisee, imbued with reverence for the Law as the Father's will and a light to men's feet; nevertheless, some of his harshest words were reserved for the Pharisees and their Scribes for having preferred law to people, the common good to the good of man. If he could, like Jeremiah, disparage the temple of God lest it be made an idol and a symbol of vain hope, he could also find it an important enough symbol to be made a place of confrontation with the Jewish establishment (the "cleansing" of the temple attested by all four gospels); and, just as simply, he and the first Christians after him could take the temple quite for granted as one of the normalities of daily religious life (see Matthew 5:23), a thing that the doctrinaire sectarians of Qumran emphatically could not do. The revolutionarism of Jesus consists in his remaining undefined by any of the known categories of his time, the revolutionary included, though it is in virtue of all of them that he becomes recognizable.

It is at this point that we find ourselves constrained to the view that only when the gospel picture of Jesus is accepted as basically reliable does his death become understandable. Nothing else really makes a great deal of sense. There was in his career enough identification with the national aspirations of his people to account for the Romans' taking an interest in him and terminating his activity; but it does not appear that there was enough there to have attracted their attention all of itself. There were other vested interests which his career ran athwart more consistently and more continuously than it did the Romans': Even a minimal acceptance of the historicity of his teaching and activity, as set forth in the gospels, suffices to commend as a picture taken from life their portrayal of him in periodic conflict and controversy with the Jewish men of power. Because this inner-Jewish hostility has through the ages been misunderstood by Christians and turned by them into an occasion and excuse for anti-Semitism, a modern reaction has been to play down Jewish complicity in the death of Jesus, even to the extent of eliminating it entirely as a fiction created by the gospel traditions. Such efforts, however, we find to be self-defeating, since they attack the credibility of the very event they presuppose and seek to explain. The issue of credibility is an entirely historical one, independent of whatever honesty and integrity one cares to ascribe to the gospel accounts. If Jesus has, indeed, been remembered for substantially the right reasons, confrontation with both the scribal profession and the priestly hierarchy must have been inevitable. The confrontation that the gospels describe squares with what we otherwise know about the internal tensions within Palestinian Judaism, which provided the climate for it.

In this contention we do not seek to deny that the gospel narratives of Jesus' suffering and death are in the first place theological documents, and only secondarily historical; further, that one of their theological interests has been to heighten the degree of Jewish involvement in these events. The spectacle of a just man persecuted by his own brethren—the situation of Jesus—invited comparison with classic instances of the same situation in sacred literature, like those found in Psalms 22 and 69, for example; and once the typology had been established, there is no doubt that the similarity was made much closer by using the psalms as a model for the gospel stories. Many of the originally historical motifs in the stories have doubtless become obscured through a progressive lack of concern over the data and consequent vagaries in their transmission. On this score may be explained a number of incidental discrepancies about times and places and persons, and also some more important discordances as well. Detailed historical reconstruction has thus been rendered very difficult by both negative and positive factors at work in the traditions underlying the gospels.

Some of the more consequential difficulties surround the chronology and other pertinent statistics of the arrest of Jesus and the judicial process that preceded his execution. It seems impossible to settle the chronological question to everybody's satisfaction: It is necessary to choose between the Synoptic and Johannine traditions, which are irreconcilable. Both of them knew that a Jewish Passover figured prominently in the activities, but each has gone its separate way in exploiting the occasion for theological purposes. In the Synoptic view of these events Jesus' last meal taken with his intimate disciples has become a Passover celebration. Joachim Jeremias, who has devoted a good deal of his scholarly life to the study of the eucharistic words of Jesus, eventually concluded that the Synoptic version was historically accurate in this identification. Many others, however, the present writer included, feel that the Synoptic chronology, in this respect as in others, is a piece of early Christian eucharistic symbolism, not unlike the third-day chronology later attached to the resurrection which we discussed in our preceding chapter. Only in a superficial way, as a matter of fact, have the Synoptic accounts transformed the Last Supper into a Passover meal: the bread, for example, is designated throughout *artos,* the common, leavened bread of an ordinary meal, never as the unleavened *azymos* of the Passover, while the one indispensable ingredient of the Passover of that day, the lamb, is never once mentioned. The Johannine chronology is also theologically colored, but it contains enough neutral details to make one suspect that it has preserved closer contact with the statistical facts. It situates the crucifixion of Jesus on the day before the night of Passover, and, interestingly enough, it coincides in this intelligence with one of the rare bits of information that may have been preserved about Jesus in the talmudic traditions of the Jews:

> On the eve of Passover Jesus [the Nasorean] was hanged, though a herald had preceded him for forty days (saying): "This man shall be stoned because he has practiced sorcery and deceived Israel. Anyone who knows a justification for him, come and make it good for him." But no man found a justification for him, and so he was hanged on the eve of Passover.

A few things need to be noted about this passage. It is from a *baraitha* (b. Sanh. 43a) of the second century: a *baraitha* is a tradition "outside" the *mishnah*, the primary collection of early rabbinical traditions, but of equal age with it and of the same provenance. (The Talmud proper is *gemarah*, which is commentary on the *mishnah* and reconciliation of it with *baraitha*.) The Jesus in question—Jesus, we must recall, was an extremely common name among Jews at the beginning of the Christian era—cannot be identified with complete certainty. Another *baraitha* (b. Sanh. 107b) places him within the reign of the Hasmonean king Alexander Jannaeus (102–76 B.C.), but in this respect the tradition may have understandably erred, substituting for the Herods of gospel times the name of the despot who had anticipated them a century before in every unsavory way; yet another *baraitha* (b. Sota 47a) speaks unequivocally of this Jesus as "the Nasorean." Nasorean is the conventional transliteration of a title (*nazoraios*) applied by Matthew, Luke, John, and Acts to the Jesus of the gospels and also (by Acts 24:5) to the first Christians, synonymous with another title (*nazarenos*) favored by Mark (Luke uses both terms). By Matthew 2:23 the title has been brought into conjunction with Jesus' native town of Nazareth, though this may not have been its original sense, or only sense. Whatever the original sense, it is the Greek form of the Hebrew *nozri* (Aramaic *nazraya*) found in the Talmud and other Jewish literature in identical usage, a name for Jesus and Christians alike, and a name for nobody else. If the term belongs in the passage we

have cited above, there is no doubt that it referred to Jesus of
Nazareth.

By far the most arresting feature of this text, however, is its
curious blending of death motifs: Jesus was hanged, it says,
and yet the herald had proclaimed that he was to be stoned
to death. "Hanging" would be the Jewish expression for the
Roman practice of crucifixion, though it could also, perhaps,
refer to the exposure of a dead body on a gibbet following
execution (Deuteronomy 21:22f.). What we seem to have,
nevertheless, is an apologetic for some half-remembered fact,
concerning a man who had been crucified yet rightly con-
demened to death by his own people. "Deceiver" was an
epithet applied to Jesus by the Jewish leadership according to
Matthew 27:63; and Mark 3:22–27 records their attribution of his extraordinary influence to diabolical or magical
powers (parallels in Matthew 9:32–34, 12:22–30; Luke
11:14–23; and John 7:20, 8:48,52, 10:20). A half century
or so later, after the composition of the gospels, Justin Martyr
will be using the same language in his dialogue with Trypho
the Jew, quoting the latter to the effect that Jesus was a
"sorcerer and deceiver of the people," and in yet another hundred years very like expressions will turn up in the anti-Jewish
polemic of Origen against Celsus. The Jewish antagonists of
Christianity during the first few centuries of our era may have
been no better informed than their Christian counterparts
about the actual circumstances of Jesus' death, but they seem
never to have questioned the fact that it was a death in which
Jews had been deeply implicated. And indeed, as we have
said, it would be hard to imagine it to have been otherwise.

The Trial of Jesus

Seen from this viewpoint, the gospel accounts of the arrest
of Jesus display an interesting development. Mark, followed
by Matthew, speaks of "a crowd" armed with knives and
clubs, sent by "the chief priests, the scribes, and the elders"
to apprehend Jesus more or less by stealth. Those responsible
for this action are obviously thought of as the members of the

Jerusalem Sanhedrin, the supreme council of Jewry, though it also seems to be taken for granted that it was a Sanhedrin operating secretly and irregularly, a conspiracy or cabal within the council rather than the council itself. On this point the various traditions are in essential accord: John's designation of the Jewish principals as "the chief priests and the Pharisees" may reflect the looseness of language consonant with a farther remove from the Palestinian scene, or it may, as has been recently suggested, be the result of a deliberate adjustment of the tradition to fit the circumstances of Jewish-Christian tensions within the Johannine church. Mark and Matthew, in any case, appear to be describing a mob action, a hastily organized rabble of troublemakers, strangers to Jesus who had to have him pointed out to them through a prearranged sign given by the traitor Judas. (To the same end it should be noted that "the crowd," which according to Mark and Matthew was incited to demand Jesus' blood before Pilate, was also made up of strangers to Jesus, who had assembled for an entirely different purpose. In John's gospel, and probably in the original form of Luke's as well, there is no crowd at all, merely the same Jewish leaders who had condemned Jesus and dragged him to Pilate.) In Luke's version of the story of the arrest, the mob is also under the guidance of Judas, but it has taken on a more official character: Luke notes the presence of the temple police. Accordingly, for Luke the kiss of Judas has ceased to be a sign of identification and remains only as a gesture of perfidy. In John the progression has gone further afield and in another significant direction, for Judas has with him not only the *hyperetai*, the Levitical temple police, but he is also accompanied by and in the first place the *speira*, a word used conventionally to translate the Latin cohort, and its commander is explicitly named the *chiliarchos*, a Roman tribune. Many conflicting implications have been read into these redactional phenomena. The point has been made, probably validly enough, that like all traditions, this one has succumbed to the tendency to particularize and regularize into established categories a situation that initially was more obscure and opaque, both as to motivation and machination. What can hardly be maintained, however, is that the tradition has tended either to turn the affair into an exclusively Jewish intrigue or to broaden the base of Jewish guilt. (The exception to this rule stands in a Matthean redaction of the tradition: the added verses of Matthew 27:24f. have converted the crowd into "the whole people" of Israel, which assumes responsibility for the blood of Jesus.) Finally, John's insistence on early Roman intervention in the arrest deserves historical investigation in its own right.

Similar complexities are involved in the story of how Jesus came to be denounced to the Romans by Jewish agencies. This denunciation, attested not only by the gospels and early chapters of Acts but also by the oldest New Testament document that we possess (1 Thessalonians 2:14), in the gospels takes the form of a trial held over Jesus by the Sanhedrin in which he was condemned to death. Was there ever such a trial, or is the story merely an instance of Christian romance? That Jesus had given provocation to priest and scribe alike in his interpretation of what was necessary to the proclamation of the kingdom of God, we have already seen. Was the provocation so severe, however, as to arouse on their part murderous designs against his very existence? Under what title could the Jews have condemned him to death, if indeed they did so, and were they in fact empowered under Roman law to pass any such sentence? These and other questions of plausibility are raised by the very stories that tell the tale.

We cannot answer many of the questions, for they appear to be insoluble on presently available evidence. There can hardly have been a trial as Mark and Matthew describe it, though it is possible that they had an authentic memory of a trial that they mixed up with the night harassment of Jesus in the quarters of the high priest Annas, of which we are told by John. This theory is the more likely if we assume that Matthew, helpfully putting a name to the high priest who presided over the "trial" in the Marcan story that he adapted, hit upon the wrong one. John's omission of any motif of a Jewish trial is theologically motivated, and is no argument that there was none. Luke's independent account of a morning trial in the council chambers includes no peremptory notes of antihistory. It distinguishes the trial carefully from the extralegal abuse which, then as now, is the instinctive response of guardians of the peace to anyone who does not fit into the accepted categories, and it helps to explain some otherwise puzzling details in the passion narrative. *En revanche,* it does not tell us what, if anything, was the capital charge that could be brought against Jesus. After the trial, according to Luke, they brought Jesus to Pilate and denounced him as a "man subverting our nation, opposing the payment of taxes to Caesar, and calling himself the Messiah, a king" (Luke 23:2). These were charges that a Roman governor could understand and fear, charges that put Jesus on a par with the outlawed partisans, and they sound realistic enough to have been taken at the letter from a dismissorial brief; but they are not charges that would have swayed or adversely affected a Jewish court, nor—with the exception of the messianic claim, which we shall have to examine in its own proper place—do any of the charges figure in the Lucan account of the proceedings against Jesus. Nowhere in this account, significantly, is there a hint of the capital crime of blasphemy of which Jesus stood condemned in the story as it was told by Mark and Matthew.

It seems that we are unable to reconstruct exactly what took place. Some kind of trial there undoubtedly was, but under what official auspices and with the preservation of what legalities it would now be impossible to determine. To the satisfaction of those Jews who sat in judgment on him, Jesus was deemed worthy of death. Had he been denounced and was he condemned as a blasphemer? It is quite possible, but again it cannot be shown from the gospel stories, for the titles to which he responds in these were in reality bestowed on him by the early church and had no explicit expression during his historical life. However, when we investigate these titles in subsequent chapters we may well discover that behind them lie words and deeds to which Jesus did give expression in his lifetime—the implicit christology to which we have referred—which his Jewish contemporaries would have construed as blasphemous. Nevertheless, we should by no means overlook what is suggested by the Johannine account of the council taken against Jesus (John 11:47–53). That suggestion is that there was less concern about securing a Jewish condemnation of a popular healer and teacher than there was over his popularity as a provocation to the Romans. By this reasoning the merits of the case were entirely secondary; it was primary that Jesus be delivered up as a voluntary sacrifice of the Jews lest the Romans be left to take more drastic action, possibly, in their own eventual time. We cannot say that it all happened this way, but if it did, it was a piece of cynicism not without precedent, nor has it remained isolated in human annals ever since.

The whole question of Jewish-Roman complicity, if any, in these proceedings has been further clouded by the gospels' rather curious treatment of the character of Pontius Pilate. Unless their traditions were acquainted with a side of Pilate otherwise unattested in history—and such, of course, is always a remote possibility—we must put down to a known bias and *Tendenz* the passion for disinterested justice that he exhibits in the story they tell. The known bias, we are already aware, is that of the New Testament writings in general, which had as one of their interests to persuade a not-yet hostile Roman empire of Christianity's peaceable intentions, especially in view of the growing Roman-Jewish hostility which finally exploded in revolt and pogrom. The reasonable Pilate of the gospels is without doubt at least partially a fiction created by the *Tendenz:* like the Gallio (also an historical personage) of Acts 18:12–17, he has been cast in the role of the single-minded secular power totally disinterested in purely religious squabbles that held no threat to the state—precisely the posture desired of the Roman authorities by Christians when they found themselves cast out of the Jewish community and thus per se deprived of the legal protection that had so far been extended to Judaism as a tolerated religion. The resulting narrative read back as sober history inevitably becomes a caricature of the facts. The caricature turns pernicious the farther it is removed fom the gospel context, when it is made into the source of apocryphal legends and misguided Passion Plays ancient and modern, or even of *cultus* (Pilate is venerated as a saint in the Coptic and Ethiopian churches). In the gospels it is merely annoying to anyone who is trying to get at a history it has succeeded in hiding from him.

Why Did Jesus Die?

However unsatisfactory and elusive the details, we are left with a discernible substratum of fact of which we can be reasonably sure, namely that Jesus was put to death by the powers of his world in direct consequence of his fulfilling his mission as he understood it. What exactly that mission was, we shall try to see in our following chapter. We have already seen enough, however, to recognize that his predictions of passion and death in the gospels need not be without historical foundation in his life. The two variant versions of the saying ascribed to Jesus in which self-destruction and crucifixion are seen as the lot of his disciples (Mark 8:34–37 with parallels in Matthew and Luke; an older, Q version in Matthew 10:38=Luke 14:27) may be nothing more or less than a dedicated man's acknowledgment of his being on collision course with destiny. Of the same character may be the Johannine saying about the laying down of his life as the supreme proof of love (John 15:13). There is nothing at all out of the way in the thought that Jesus understood to the full the consequences of the vocation he had assumed and that obedience to it would entail even death, just as the hymn in Philippians 2:8 said.

Jesus' preaching of the imminent coming of God's kingdom was an act of polarization: "Do you think I have come to establish peace on the earth? I assure you, the contrary is true; I have come for division. From now on, a household of five will be divided three against two and two against three; father will be split against son and son against father, mother against daughter and daughter against mother, mother-in-law against daughter-in-law, daughter-in-law against mother-in-law" (Luke 12:51–53; cf. Matthew 10:34–36). It would require no special gifts for him to perceive that his own life, along with the lives of his followers, might be a necessary forfeit to the cause with which he had identified himself. Lesser prophets have known that much. Did he know, or claim, anything more than that, that his death might be more than a by-product, more even than a *sine qua non,* of the coming of the kingdom he had proclaimed? To answer that question we need to explore further what he thought of his role in relation to the kingdom. For the present we are interested in the theology of the New Testament sources as it developed probably without any connection with a knowledge of Jesus' self-awareness.

It may be begging the question at this point to insist that there was no connection, since if connection there was, it would only show that Jesus had no appreciation of his death except that it was fated. As we have seen, the earliest New Testament christology made no attempt to interpret his death, which presumably it would have done could it have laid claim to any explicit word of his relating to the subject. Furthermore, even when the interpretation came to be made, it was made on the analogy of various models, each with its own degree of salvific immediacy. Some of these models we will understand better under other titles, where they more properly belong; once having arrived at a conviction of the saving efficacy of Christ's death, the church of the New Testament did not universally maintain it as a paramount theology, but often assimilated it to more dominant ideas. Here we ask simply how and why Christians first came to believe that Jesus of Nazareth died "for our sins."

In the biblical languages as well as in modern English the "for" of our formula can be patient of many senses, some banal and some pregnant with meaning. (Several different prepositions are used in the Greek of the New Testament, but apparently interchangeably.) That Christ died for, that is, as a result of, or because of our sins, because of the sinful world into which he was born and of which he became a part, this, for example, is a banality that the New Testament took for granted. While taking it for granted, it did so in a matter-of-fact way and with a minimum of mythology. If they had only known the truth of the gospel, said Paul, the rulers of this age "would never have crucified the Lord of glory" (1 Corinthians 2:8). Luke and John, for their part, may have routinely ascribed the passion and death of Jesus to the machinations of Satan (Luke 22:3; John 13:2.27), but Satan not only makes no appearance at all in the passion story of Mark and Matthew, in their context he is represented as striving to frustrate the sacrifice of obedience that led to the cross (Mark 8:33=Matthew 16:23). Here we are introduced to the pregnant meaning of the expression, which the New Testament truly intends: If Jesus Christ died for us, for our sins, he did so on our behalf, in atonement for our sins, and even in place of us, as one who suffered and died in our stead for sins that were not his own but are ours. How did such an idea develop in the primitive Christian community?

We conceive that it developed, not at once but at length, from the contemplation of the death of Jesus now reviewed in the light of the resurrection—the kind of review that the Fourth Gospel defines as the Spirit-guided interpretation of the teaching of Jesus (John 16:13). As we know, the resurrection summoned men's attention forward as well as backward, and probably forward earlier than backward. When it did summon attention backward, the result was the gospel forms. And when these gospels forms sought expression, they fell back on existing models, just as the earlier christology had done. The difference is that while the gospel forms more or less hewed to the line of Old Testament thought, the older and parallel christologies of the epistles explored other currents of thinking of the contemporary world.

Redemptive Suffering

The idea that the sufferings of a just man and the death of a martyr somehow have a redeeming value for the sins of others, that is to say, the idea of vicarious atonement, was already well accepted in the Judaism of Jesus' day and would later become even more widely accepted and applied. It was not an idea that had come easily to the Old Testament, which through most of its long history inclined to the common-sense view of suffering and death as physical evils that should be avoided or postponed to the extent possible. A deeper experience of suffering, however, particularly in consequence of religious persecution, confirmed for the Jews as a nation a conviction that had already formed in the minds of sensitive individuals. The easy equation of suffering with personal guilt, a doctrine comforting to anyone who has never suffered much, especially if he is disposed to a bit of self-righteousness over his good fortune, never entirely disappeared from Jewish (or from much non-Jewish) thinking, but it had to yield to subtler evaluations of the mystery of evil to which Jeremiah and the author of Job, to name but two, had ventured suggestions. Confronted by the terrifying immensity of the burden and enigma of human suffering, thoughtful men through the ages have been moved either to deny the existence of a just and merciful God who can tolerate such enormities, or to postulate for them a role in a divine economy that transcends clinical examination. For its part, and as one explanation it offered among others, the faith of Israel postulated the myth of vicarious atonement for sins. Myth it may be called, in the most acceptable sense of the term, but a myth whose efficacy has been repeatedly verified, possessing a true power to bestow life. At the bier of the murdered body of Dr. Martin Luther King, Jr., a Canadian priest pronounced the only words that were utterly right: "May your death heal my sins." And while this language was undoubtedly influenced by the Christian precedent that was the inspiration of Dr. King's life, there is other testimony as well. A famous American rabbi did not hesitate to canonize the same event with the sacred phrase: "He was wounded for our transgressions." Centuries before, a Jewish martyr had offered his death as an expiation of Israel's sins: "Like my brothers, I offer up my body and my life for our ancestral laws, imploring God to show mercy soon to our nation. . . . Through me and my brothers, may there be an end to the wrath of the Almighty that has justly fallen on our whole nation" (2 Maccabees 7:37f.). "Through the blood of those pious men," went the Jewish witness, "and through their propitiatory death the divine providence saved the sadly oppressed Israel" (4 Maccabees 17:22).

The best-known expression of the myth in the Old Testament, though obviously not the only one, occurs in the so-called Servant songs ascribed to the exilic prophet whom we know as the Second Isaiah. The Servant songs (usually isolated in the passages of Isaiah 42:1–4, 49:1–6, 50:4–9, and 52:13–53:12) celebrate a figure, probably prophetic in character, who is chosen by God to be an instrument of salvation, which he accomplishes, as the song is finally sung, through an ignominious passion and death. We may debate without much profit to whom the poet may have been indebted for some of his details: The Babylonian ritual myth of the king as the annually dying and then rising god of new life in the fertility of the land may have exercised an influence, and we should indeed be surprised did it not, given the influence of Mesopotamian thought forms during the exile. Another debate would involve the identity of the Servant in the mind of the prophetic author. One prevailing interpretation, and probably the right one, took his meaning to be that the Servant was Israel itself, the just and innocent Israel atoning by its suffering for the Israel deserving of divine wrath. It is difficult to assess later Jewish interpretation, since much of it was doubtless formed in reaction to Christian identification of the Servant with the Lord of the church. Nevertheless, the collective interpretation of the Servant as Israel did not preclude but rather facilitated the attribution or extention of the figure to other corporate or individual persons, both in Christian and in Jewish exegesis, accordingly as they were found to be appropriate. (Paul, for example, without in the least derogating from the Christ whom he called Lord and Savior, seems to have thought of himself as Servant of the Lord.) The early chapters of the Wisdom of Solomon described the just Jew oppressed by his apostate neighbors in the explicit language of the Servant songs and with the precise details that make them sound like models for the passion stories of the gospels (see especially Wisdom 2:12–20 and 4:20–5:5).

Jesus is identified with the Servant of the Lord in the specimens of the early Christian kergyma preserved in Acts 3:13.26 and 4:27.30. The identification was not made first by Luke, the author of Acts, or by any of the other evangelists, all of whom have their own preferred theologies of Christ. It had impressed itself on the gospel traditions, however, on the Marcan tradition utilized in the Synoptics, on the separate traditions brought in by Matthew (8:17, 12:18–21) and Luke (22:37), and on the Johannine tradition as well. It is an early attribution, very likely presupposed in the primitive resurrection tradition cited by Paul in 1 Corinthians 15:3 ("Christ died for our sins in accordance with the Scriptures"), and certainly accepted by Paul (Romans 4:25, 15:21), even though not much employed by him. Just possibly the earliest 53:12 in the manner of the Jewish reworking of the Wisdom of Solomon, has been caught up by 1 Peter 2:22–25, a passage that formally resembles the homology we have previously recognized in Philippians 2:6–11. (In the translation that follows, we have readjusted certain pronouns of the last two verses and indicated the change by bracketing, presuming that the second person plural of epistolary address was originally the first person plural in the hymn.) As in Philippians, the author of this letter celebrated the example of one

22 who did no wrong,
    nor was deceit found in his mouth;
23 who when insulted did not insult in turn,
    when suffering uttered no threats,
    but committed himself to the One who judges justly;
24 who himself bore our sins
    in his body to [or, on] the cross,
    that, dead to sin, we might live for righteousness;
    by whose wounds [we] were healed.
25 For once [we] were straying like sheep,
    but now [we] have returned
    to the Shepherd and Guardian of [our] souls.

Though the word "servant" nowhere occurs in this text, there is no doubt about the systematic exploitation of Isaiah's imagery. We might add that a basis for the church's attribution to Jesus of the Servant title may very reasonably have been founded on the precedent of his own words and deeds, in his perception of himself as God's servant in another but not unrelated sense. One of the characterizations of his ministry that he no doubt would have most readily accepted as congenial with his own self-awareness was response to a prophetic calling; and in the language of contemporary Judaism, prophet and servant of God were established synonyms.

The Metaphors of Salvation

As we have been attempting to show, however, the Servant role as developed by the Second Isaiah is far from being the sum and substance or the only mold into which New Testament theology chose to cast the meaning and significance of the mystery of the cross. It was, rather, a concept, an analogue, that the church first eagerly took up and then largely abandoned—the latter, we may surmise, because it proved to be too much a Jewish "thing," too much dependent on an inner-Israelite history that did not say a great deal to the Gentile world. There were other Old Testament figures of greater plasticity that took its place.

One of these was the concept of ransom, along with the associated idea of redemption. A Marcan saying picked up by the gospels (Mark 10:45=Matthew 20:28) credits Jesus with defining his mission as to give his life as a ransom (*lytron*) for (*anti*) many persons. The parallel formula has been preserved by 1 Timothy 2:6 out of what is probably another early hymnic fragment: The man Christ Jesus gave himself as a ransom (*antilytron*) for (*hyper*) all men. The corresponding notion of redemption through Christ (*lytrosis* or *apolytrosis*) is found in Luke, Paul, and sub-Pauline literature, Hebrews, and elsewhere. What was meant by such expressions?

The terms are, of course, commercial in origin, borrowed from the world of affairs common to Israel and the nations, a world of buying and selling, of the redemption of pledges, human or material, given in gage (in the modern world there is no pledging of men, or any that is acknowledged as such, but we have retained the nonliving, the *mortgage*). The ransom is the price that must be paid to buy back the pledge, to recover the pawned object or to liberate the slave. It is in the last acceptation that the complex of terminology has been recruited by the christology of the New Testament: Christ is the price of redemption, the payment that has bought mankind out of the bondage of sin.

The terminology was recruited, however, in metaphor, as should always have been obvious. Unfortunately, it is an observable law of human life that succeeding generations tend to reify the poetry of their fathers, betraying thereby the demise of imagination and ushering in all manner of confusion. The Fathers of the postapostolic church wasted their time fretting over the question to whom Christ's death was a ransom that had to be paid, inventing in the process a concept of the "rights of Satan" over men's souls that could be quitted only by a blood sacrifice; they ended by turning the metaphor into a not merely foolish but also harmful mythology. A more sophisticated version of essentially the same theology tried to demythologize it by making God himself the recipient of the ransom. This refinement, however, ignored the terms of the biblical metaphor, according to which God was the one who *performed* rather than accepted the *apolytrosis* in Christ Jesus (Romans 3:24f.). It also, incidentally, succeeded in imagining a God of somewhat lower standards of benevolence than were confidently expected of his servants: a God who would not forgive men freely but only after the exaction of a price. In the eleventh century, St. Anselm of Canterbury came up with a way out of this self-made cul-de-sac by devising a solution that determined the scholastic theology of a millennium. Arguing from a framework of Roman law, he reasoned that payment for sin had to be settled neither with Satan nor with the divine honor but with justice itself, a justice that by its very nature demands compensation and requital independent of any subjective dispositions toward mercy, divine or human. There is something to be said for this rather modern, libertarian, and high-prin-

cipled conception of nature's laws, the presupposition alike
of the Protestant ethic and of *tanstaafl,* and it is certainly a
valuable contribution to any civilized comprehension of the
psychology of crime and punishment, sin and atonement. But
it also has little or nothing to do with the biblical categories
that it purported to explain.

Neither, seemingly, did Adolf Deissmann, in the first decade of the present century, discover the clue to the biblical
metaphors where he thought he had, from his profound study
of the nonbiblical everyday Greek writings of the age that
gave birth to the everyday Greek of the New Testament.
There was in this age a practice common among religious
pagans by which through a legal fiction a god could be said
to have purchased or ransomed a slave. The slave desirous of
purchasing his freedom, once he had eventually acquired and
saved the required amount, instead of handing it over then
and there to his master, would go with him to a temple
where, in the course of a religious ceremony, the master was
considered to have sold his slave to the god for the money he
now received. Henceforth the slave was regarded as having
been freed by the god, and the god as having paid the ransom price. The formula was: "The god X has brought Y unto
freedom." Deissmann thought that such a rite lay at the
background of the soteriology of Paul: "Christ has brought us
back from the curse of the Law . . . it is for freedom that he
set us free" (Galatians 3:13, 5:1). The coincidence of language is interesting, but hardly more than that. The christology of the New Testament sources undoubtedly had another
inspiration.

The commercial terms of this christological language in all
probability owe their parentage to the Greek Old Testament,
the Bible of the earliest Christian communities. There the
same terms turn up, again in a context of salvation, but obviously to refer to a work of divine mercy and no business
transaction. The psalmist called on God as his *lytrotes* (Psalm
19:14, cf. Psalm 78:35) not in any literal sense as a ran-
somer, but as one who would save him, deliver him from evil.
(In the same sense, Acts 7:35 calls Moses the *lytrotes* of
Israel.) God is frequently said to have bought, acquired,

purchased, ransomed his people, singly or collectively, to have performed an act of *lytrosis* (Psalm 49:8, for example, or Isaiah 63:4), but always in such a way that the metaphor was evident—there was no real "price" to be paid for the liberation of Israel from Egypt or Babylon, or for the deliverance of the just man from his persecutors. We have no cause to think that the New Testament intended to press the metaphor any farther than the Old Testament had. The metaphor means, to be sure, that there is more to sin and forgiveness than some sort of arbitrary amiability on God's part that he bestows or withholds at will, that sin is truly a bondage and a sentence to death and destruction, and that it therefore "costs" God much to forgive and to deliver. Having conveyed this much, it has conveyed a great deal, and its value is only obscured when the metaphor is doggedly tracked down through alien paths it never meant to go. That Christ is a "ransom" for man, that his blood was the "price" that was "paid" to "redeem" man—these are, or were, meaningful categories by which the New Testament sought to illustrate its faith in the risen Lord as one whose life and death had somehow served God's purposes in bringing about the salvific happening that was now being confidently proclaimed. They did not really pretend to be able to define that happening as having literally followed the rules of any particular human mechanism.

The Metaphors of Sacrifice

Very much associated with these figures and subject to the same kind of interpretation is the cluster of disparate patterns according to which Jesus' death is related in one way or another to the various forms of Old Testament blood sacrifice. We may, perhaps, agree with Rudolf Bultmann in his contention that blood sacrifice under any form is a superannuated myth as far as modern man is concerned—though it is also possible, as we suggested earlier, that both the prevalence and the relevance of the myth nowadays might deserve fresh examination. At all events, and before discussing the need to demythologize the New Testament, we should try to ascertain the extent to which it has really been penetrated by myth. Specifically, what did the New Testament mean when it represented Jesus as having become a "curse" for us, as having, to various effects, "shed his blood" for us, or as having been made our "expiation" or "propitiatory"?

The easiest case to handle is that of the "curse." This construction depends on a single verse of the New Testament, one we have already cited above, in which Paul told the Galatians that "Christ has bought us back from the curse of the Law by himself becoming a curse for us, as it is written: 'Accursed is anyone who is hanged on a tree'" (Galatians 3:13). The scriptural quotation that Paul included is that of Deuteronomy 21:22f.: "If a man guilty of a capital offense is put to death and his corpse hung on a tree, it shall not remain on the tree overnight. You shall bury it the same day; otherwise, since God's curse rests on him who hangs on a tree, you will defile the land which Yahweh, your God, is giving you as an inheritance." (The same Deuteronomic law is alluded to in the passion narrative of John 19:31 to explain the precipitate removal of Jesus' body from the cross on the eve of Passover.) Anyone at all familiar with the Pauline methodology recognizes a usual ploy, Paul's own form of paradox, which mixes proper and improper senses of the same word in order to make a point vigorously. Up against the wisdom of God comes the "wisdom" of men, in light of which the cross is "folly"; but "since in God's wisdom the world did not come to know him through 'wisdom,' it pleased God to save those who believed through the 'folly' of the preaching of the gospel" (1 Corinthians 1:21). Saved from the slavery of sin, Christians are now "slaves" to the obedience of faith—that is, they are in freedom (Romans 6:16). The "law" of the spirit of life has freed them from the Law, which is the sign of sin and death (Romans 8:2). In the same pattern, the one who by definition of the Law became a "curse" as an executed criminal, in reality saved men by his death from the curse of the Law.

The New Testament, then, is not guilty of superstition sometimes indulged by later Christian theology, which imagined Jesus to have been truly cursed by God, an object of wrath laden with the sins of all mankind, whose dying quenched the divine lust for retribution. This grotesque and primitive substitutionary construct travesties the idea of vicarious atonement and corresponds to no Old Testament model of expiatory sacrifice. The only correspondent it could have in the Old Testament is that of the scapegoat. The scapegoat (Leviticus 16:20–28) is featured in a curious rite typical of the Levitical law, which has absorbed a good number of barely assimilated pagan rituals into its liturgical canon. In this rite, which was doubtless an ancient one, a goat is indeed burdened with the sins of all the people, whereupon he is driven away into the desert, "to Azazel," there to die. The goat was not a sacrifice, for his highly unholy state excluded such a character. Whatever Azazel may have meant to the Levitical author who pulled together the rites for the postexilic Day of Atonement, there is hardly any doubt that he was in the original acceptation some kind of demon: Desert places were thought to be in a peculiar way the abode of demons. (A persuasion, incidentally, which accounts for the favored resort of the early Desert Fathers of the church, who by their lights went out to face up to evil, not to get away from it all.) We need not explore the subject farther, for Christ is never likened in New Testament christology to the scapegoat of the Old Testament.

Neither was atonement in any naïve substitutional sense the intent of those Levitical blood rites to which the New Testament does liken the passion and death of Christ. "Without the shedding of blood there is no forgiveness," said Hebrews 9:22, echoing Leviticus 17:11—an exaggeration, since other means of atonement were provided. When blood sacrifice was the means, however, it was precisely in the blood that atoning efficacy was sought, not in the death of an animal, which often was quite incidental to the rite. (We do not deny the possibility that older and grimmer mythologies may underlie the Levitical practices; but we are concerned only with the theology that the Bible retrieved from them.) By a tradition far more ancient than the Old Testament, blood was held to be a purifying element, consecratory and sacred (cf. Deuteronomy 12:23). Such was thought to be its function in all the Levitical rites that the New Testament has brought into conjunction with the blood, that is, the death of Christ: the purification of temple and people on the solemn Day of Atonement, done in blood, as well as the sin- and guilt-offerings of "the blood of goats and calves . . . and bulls" (Hebrews 9:12f.). Really of the same nature, then, though associated with a different kind of sacrifice, is the representation of Jesus' death as providing "the blood of the [new] covenant" in Hebrews and the eucharistic saying of the gospels (Mark 14:24, Matthew 26:28, Luke 22:20). The allusion is to the enactment of the covenant of Sinai in blood according to the Elohistic narrative of Exodus, chapter 24: the blood of a peace offering, not of a sacrifice of expiation. In sum, while the Old Testament sometimes thought of God as a wrathful deity who had to be appeased— the prevalent view of deity in the pagan world—it was not under that anthropomorphism that the New Testament chose to illustrate the sacrificial death of Christ. Rather, and whatever the specific term, whether expiation or ransoming or propitiatory (Romans 3:25: note, Christ is a propitiatory constituted *by* God, not a propitiation offered *to* God), the figure is universally one of a merciful and loving God who has provided for men a power of grace that they might escape the bondage of sin. "Yes, God so loved the world that he gave his only Son, that whoever believes in him may not die but may have eternal life" (John 3:16).

When we survey the divers images under which the christology of the New Testament has emblemized the death of Christ, we must conclude that it has been less a weaving of theology out of available myths than it has been a search through them for familiar and acceptable patterns to give utterance to a belief that was quite independent of them. The church's conviction that Jesus' death had been a saving act was born neither out of an Old Testament ransacked for suggestive texts nor even from a world that hungered for deliverance and gave voice to its hunger in a poignant language that could not be denied; it was born of the church's certain knowledge that the new life that it experienced was entirely due to the dead and resurrected Christ. "He was handed over to death for our sins and raised up for our justification" (Romans 4:25), Paul could say, because "the Spirit himself gives witness with our spirit that we are children of God" (Romans 8:16). The life-giving spirit working in the church, Paul also recognized, was the resurrected Christ himself (1 Corinthians 15:45).

When we recognize the doctrine of the cross for what it is—the church's response to the invitation of the Spirit to discern the ultimate meaning of Jesus' life and death in the face of what his resurrection had brought—the question of Jesus' own prior understanding of this mystery can be relegated to death as a substantive part of his mission, but also cast himself in a role like that of the Servant of the Lord, as Joachim Jeremias, for one, has long held? It is probably impossible to prove either that he did or did not, though we have brought to the fore certain considerations that weigh on the negative side. The fact that has validated belief in the atoning power of Jesus' death is not the psychology of Jesus, but the atonement itself. Jesus did not profess to reveal himself but only God, and the fullness of God's revelation in Christ was accomplished through the experience of him as life-giving spirit. The testimony of Christian men who professed their lives to be God's gift through a crucified Savior thus established the "fact" of vicarious atonement in a way that Jesus' premonition of it could or did not.

In the twelfth chapter of John's gospel the evangelist tells a story about some "Greeks"—to him they represented the catholic church in which he lived and for which he wrote—who came up to Jerusalem with the desire and request that they might see Jesus. What they "see," through the mediation of the apostles, is the glorified Christ acting in the church, the message of the cross as John understood it: "Unless the grain of wheat falls to the earth and dies, it remains just a grain of wheat. But if it dies, it produces much fruit. The man who loves his life loses it, while the man who hates his life in this world preserves it to life eternal" (John 12:24f.). This is Christian faith, to embrace the paradox and folly of the cross as alone offering the true meaning of life, as saving man, therefore, from sin, from a meaningless existence and from the worldly powers that will otherwise enslave him. The evangelist leaves us in no doubt of its inspiration when he quotes from the last of the Servant songs: "Lord, who has believed what has reached our ears? To whom has the might of the Lord been revealed?" (verse 38). The acceptance of this revelation with its demonstrated transforming power is at once the reiteration and perpetuation of the atoning sacrifice of one who gave himself for our sins.

3. LORD AND CHRIST

The Enigma of the New Testament Christ

The one sure bit of historical content that every New Testament scholar, skeptical or credulous, will concede to the preaching of Jesus of Nazareth is his proclamation of the kingdom of God. The kingdom is the major subject of his parables, in which he appears in the familiar guise of a prophetic herald speaking in familiar thought patterns, and also—though in a transmuted form—of his Sermon on the Mount or of the Johannine discourses, in which he appears in the totally different guise of a magisterial figure utterly superior to that of a prophet. In whichever character, there is no doubt that he was unconcerned about the comfortably remote future, that area of predilection for the safe and cautious prophet who never intends to be brought to book by common-sense rules like those of Deuteronomy 18:21f. His preaching, like the preaching of John the Baptist, which he continued, was of a kingdom that *engiken:* "is near," "is at hand," "has come to pass." The only really relevant question that rises in connection with Jesus' proclamation of the kingdom is whether he thought of it as coming very soon or as in some fashion already begun. Both interpretations have been and are fiercely defended, with many consequences for New Testament exegesis—and, among others, Martin Dibelius has insisted that the key to the proper understanding of Jesus' message can be found only when it is recognized that he entertained equally well both purviews, each of which is sustained by the gospel sources. For the present moment we need not decide one way or the other: Whether the eschatological kingdom of God had already taken hold or was still in the immediate offing, its prospect was enough to polarize the enmity against Jesus, which the gospels impartially distribute between the Roman bureaucracy and the Jewish hierarchy.

What is far more important is to try to ascertain the

grounds on which Jesus has been identified by the gospels, and by the New Testament in general, with the Christ, the Messiah, the soteriological or at least eschatological figure who in Jewish thought was corollary to the kingdom. And here we are brought up short by a paradox: that the title that Jesus not only never used to identify himself but even, seemingly, actively repudiated, has become the one applied to him by the church ever after in preference to all others. The paradox increases when we consider its implications. Already with Paul in his writings, therefore some twenty years after the crucifixion and resurrection, the Messiah title in its Greek form *christos*, Christ, is found together with or in place of the name of Jesus on precisely the same footing, simply as a proper name. Paul will say Jesus Christ or Christ Jesus with apparent indifference, except to the exigencies of Greek syntax (the case endings of "Christ" indicate the function of the word in a sentence as those of "Jesus" do not), and only in one or two instances is it evident that he intends Christ to be read in its original titular sense of Messiah, though he was of course well aware of that sense. This means that the church first bestowed on its risen Lord, doubtless not without some misgivings, a title he himself had found unacceptable, a title highly charged with a particularist Jewish content, which it then speedily emptied of virtually all content, and all this within the passing of a short generation. This would seem to add up to a rather extraordinary state of affairs, and yet it also seems to be the way things happened.

So extraordinary is the situation that one could easily be tempted to imagine that the designation of Jesus as Christ was originally an act of acquiescence on the part of the church rather than one of design. The "Christian" name, after all, came about in just such a fashion, if we may believe Acts 11:26. Such a name would have occurred only to Gentiles, not Jews, and only to those who assumed that the unusual Jews with whom they had to deal were the partisans of a man called Christ. There is an honorable history of nomenclature derived from alien and even hostile sources that has afterwards been proudly borne: Quakers, Lutherans, Melchites, Gothic, Huguenots, among many other instances of the kind. Jesus had been put to death, as we know, under the title King of the Jews, which could only be the Roman equivalent of the Hebrew or Aramaic Messiah, the Anointed [king], the Christ. What more natural then than that one who had borne the title, however unintentionally and even unjustly, should ever after find it to be the name under which he had passed into history? And, this having occurred, why could not the church have accepted the popular term as a *fait accompli* and made the best of it? In other words, why could not "Messiah" or "Christ" have been for the earliest church as equally a no-content index to an historical person—not to his character or function—as it obviously was for the church that wrote the canonical New Testament? There is much to be said for a reconstruction of this kind, which could help to explain why the New Testament can so often say of Christ what a Jew would never have said of Messiah.

What militates against the reconstruction, however, are the traces left in the traditions of a development in the Christian application of the title, together with the obvious unease that they manifest over its propriety. The gospel traditions are of two minds concerning the whole matter. On the one side they represent the messianic claim as a mistaking of Jesus' mission and a temptation that he rightly spurned; yet on the other side they do definitely make the claim, in a quite literal sense, which they attempt to justify in meticulous and often surprising detail. It becomes obvious that when the church decided to call Jesus "Christ" it did so not desultorily and by default, but only after considerable soul-searching and by a theological exploration that convinced it that the title was clearly right. Mark's gospel has been charged with first having manipulated the tradition in order to invest Jesus with a messianic character, and there is some truth in the allegation, for Mark evidently wanted to square the church's practice with a prior history that in part spoke against it. However, the issue is far more complicated than Wilhelm Wrede thought when he correctly discerned the "messianic secret" to be a leitmotiv of the Second Gospel. Before we consider the complexities, it might be just as well for us to recall what Messiah signified in the age of Jesus and why it was a designation that he would not likely have assumed.

The Jewish Messiah

As an eschatological figure, the Messiah is largely a product of postexilic Jewish hope and expectation, though its roots are planted deep in the soil of Israel's history. They drive and search even more deeply than Israel itself, as a matter of fact, into that *Mutterboden* of myth and human urging beneath which lies only bedrock, the single earth of the commonalty of ancient man, when the King was truly the man of the kin, the embodiment, for better or for worse, of a whole people, of whom he was at one and the same time representative, ruler, justicier, and mediator, who incarnated the people before its gods and in turn was the visible presence of the gods before the people. Messiah is the Jewish residue, the transmuted and even denatured metastasis, of the ancient mystique of kingship. This mystique, the myth of divine or semidivine kingship, because of Israel's distinct kind of monotheism was never digested outright by any of its theologies, but we need only read the "royal" Psalms 2, 45, 72, 89, or 110, to name only one Old Testament genre, to recognize how much it had influenced some strains of Israelite religion. These psalms later Jewish and Christian exegetes knew could not refer in any literal sense to an existing human being, and so they tended to throw them into the eschatological future, in the Christian instance into an eschaton thought to have been realized in Jesus Christ. But in their original acceptation they sprang from a life situation in which the king was celebrated not in his mundane but in his mythical character: In Psalm 45:7 he is actually called a "god," and even though an Israelite would have expected to make some necessary distinctions that an Egyptian or a Babylonian would not, still he would also have been made aware that the king was somehow an avatar of the divine. There was even a peculiarly Israelite version of the myth brought into the national history, the Nathan oracle that underlies the story of 2 Samuel

7 and the liturgy of Psalm 89, which prophetically proclaimed the principal scion of the house of David to be God's
son.

It was in this Davidic form that the myth survived and
was inherited by Judaism as the messianic hope, in an age
when Jews and Christians recoiled before the divine titles
that the Gentiles persisted in laying upon their kings, and
died rather than acknowledge their validity. The Davidic dynasty died in fact during the Babylonian captivity, and while
many Jews reconciled themselves to this reality and looked
for the continued well-being of their people through other of
God's dispensations (so, for example, Sirach 45:25), many
others yearned for a literalist fulfillment of the spacious language of the ancient oracle: "Your house and your kingdom
shall endure forever before me; your throne shall stand firm
forever" (2 Samuel 7:16); "I will make his posterity endure
forever and his throne as the days of heaven" (Psalm
89:30). In such a fulfillment they looked to see the coming
of age of other mystiques that had been nourished at the
same wellsprings of national religion and ethos—of Jerusalem
the navel of the earth (Psalm 48:3), the instructor, ruler,
and guide of all the nations of the earth (Isaiah
2:2–4=Micah 4:1–3). All peoples must be indulged these
fancies, which by no means have vanished from human
calculations, since they are the basis of every colonialist and
imperialist design. Israel's at the time might be indulged
more readily in that an objective eye would probably concur
in viewing its disposable spiritual goods as having better
value than the wares of the Gentiles with which it sought to
compete. Nevertheless, the aspiration remained a nationalist
one throughout, and therefore an imperialist dream, however
laughable may have seemed the material resources on which
it could rely for implementation. Doubtless the mystique
grew stronger and bolder as the former realities melded into
legend and the way was made open to the vision of a golden
age that might yet return. Doubtless, too, the apocalyptic
mentality, with its practical disregard of the controls pre-
scribed by historical probability, hastened the development
of the messianic idea. Immediately after the exile there was

an attempt to restore the Davidic dynasty in a real sense, in the person of Zerubbabel, the grandson of the last of the Davidic kings in the direct line. The movement was abetted by the nationalistic prophets Haggai (2:20–23) and Zechariah (6:9–15 in the original text; consult the translation of the *New American Bible*). But it was short-lived and came to nothing, probably because of the vigilance of the Persian authorities who then called the tune in Palestine. What remained was a nationalist hope that waned and waxed at various times. It left its mark in the Old Testament by the redaction and rereading of Psalms and Prophecy, but its major literary expression was by way of apocryphal writings that never made their way into the canon of Scripture. The hope was very much alive in Roman times, as we know, and was nurtured by Roman intransigence. The gospels correctly represent it as an integral element of Pharisaic piety. Its last serious expression occurred in the A.D. 132–35 revolt of Simeon Bar Koseba—who was not, as it happened, of the stock of David, though he was proclaimed Messiah by the leader of Palestinian Pharisaism—which ended in complete disaster for the Jewish cause.

This brief résumé might be enough to underscore some of the incongruities that become apparent when Jesus is identified simplistically by the Messiah model. If we are right in maintaining that the gospel traditions have portrayed Jesus basically as he truly was, it is not at all hard to understand why he would have deemed such an identification inappropriate, and it is correspondingly harder to understand why the church should have found it to be so right. This is said not to deny that the Messiah hope was capable of loftier ambitions than the pure nationalism of Bar Koseba; it was. Nevertheless, Joseph Klausner put his finger quite accurately on the point at issue when he insisted that what is recorded of Jesus in the gospels very often "cannot be imagined in the mouth of a *Jewish* Messiah, not even a Messiah of the more spiritual type portrayed in the Psalms of Solomon." (The Psalms of Solomon are a Jewish apocryphon dating from sometime after 63 B.C., when the Romans conquered Palestine. They exemplify Pharisaic piety at its best and depict the coming

Messiah, the Son of David, as one who will be the power of
the spirit of God to eradicate evil within and without Israel
and to make righteousness prevail. Though they were included in the Greek Old Testament that the church inherited,
they do not seem to have much influenced early Christianity.) There are other important data to be considered,
moreover, which serve to heighten the sense of incongruity.

Jesus' Attitude Toward Messiahship

As we have implied all along, Messiah was by no means
the sole or, for the most part, the dominant title under which
Israel first and Judaism later subsumed their soteriological
hopes. The mystique of kingship, when it entered into Israel,
encountered grave protest, as is evidenced by the early
chapters of 1 Samuel: The antimonarchical bias that made
itself felt at every stage of Israelite history was not born simply of the sad performance of kingship in Israel (Deuteronomy and the Northern experience in general) but was
rooted in a theological principle that had from the beginning
rejected the kingly ideal as an aberration from covenant faith
in Yahweh as King and Savior. Even when the myth was accepted in a more or less historicized form, it was always the
object of serious reservations. The great prophets were
usually at best lukewarm toward kingship if not actively hostile to it, and very little foundation was laid in the original
strata of the prophetical books for the later doctrine of messianism. Thus the irony of so much misdirected Christian
apologetics of a bygone era, which imagined the Old Testament to be a tissue of "messianic prophecies" marvelously
fulfilled in the person of Christ. Of the pre-exilic prophets
only Isaiah ascribed a providential role to the perdurance of
the house of David, as part of his singular reliance on the
traditions of Jerusalem in preference to the Mosaic traditions
favored by most other prophets. And even Isaiah has carefully desacralized the kingly ideal in contrast with, say, the
"royal" Psalms. Jeremiah and Ezekiel, to the extent that they
made room for a Davidic ruler in their visions of a restored

and purified Israel, did so only perfunctorily and without enthusiasm. Ezekiel 21:30–32, in fact, the prophet's doom-
oracle against the cringing and ineffectual Zedekiah, seems to
be a sarcastic reversal of the language and sense of Genesis
49:10f., in which a Yahwistic author had once hymned the
destiny of the tribe of Judah: not David, but Nebuchadnezzar the Babylonian will inherit Jerusalem! In Isaiah 45:1 an
exilic prophet proclaims the Lord's Messiah—the one clear-cut
instance of the "messianic" use of this word in the Hebrew
Old Testament—who turns out to be no Israelite at all, but
Cyrus, king of the Persians! The messianic sections of the
prophetical books are mainly the interpolations of postexilic
redactors who reread the Old Testament in light of their own
theology. They are witness to an authentic Israelite and scriptural belief, surely, but to one that must also be balanced
against the others that opposed it.

Against this background, the refusal of Jesus to be recognized as the Messiah of Israel is not hard to understand, for it
fits into an honorable tradition every bit as worthy of the
heritage of his fathers as was the standard Pharisaism. Refuse
he did without doubt, though the gospels have obscured the
fact in view of their divided interests.

For one thing, the gospel traditions never represent Jesus
as himself laying claim to the messianic title either in so many
words or by one of its recognized surrogates such as "Son of
David" or "Son of God"—the latter taken for granted in the
gospels as having a messianic import, though beset by certain
historical difficulties, as we shall see. (We must exempt in this
attempt at reconstruction most of the traditions absorbed by
the Fourth Gospel, whose Jesus is the gloried Lord and
Christ of the church speaking the language of Christian
faith.) It is true that the gospels do show him accepting the
title—sometimes—when it was proffered by others, but invariably there is an earlier non- or even antimessianic hue to these
stories that becomes perceptible with more patient scrutiny.
In the story of Jesus' interrogation before the high priest, for
example, Mark (14:61f.) allows him to acknowledge that
he is Messiah. But in the parallels (Matthew 26:63f., Luke

22:66–68), Jesus' answer is noncommittal and somewhat mysterious: Mark has by now unveiled his "messianic secret" and rendered the title proper for Jesus' use. In the similar situation of Pilate's interrogation when the Roman governor puts the same question in Gentile terms: "Are you the king of the Jews?," neither Mark (15:2–5) nor Matthew (27:11) allow a simple affirmative answer, and in Luke (23:3f.) the answer is clearly taken to be a denial. The crucial gospel passage involving Jesus' attitude to the messianic title is Mark 8:27–33 and parallels Peter's confession and its dénouement, the watershed of Mark's gospel, in which Jesus is seen to embrace the vocation of the Christ as the church later defined it, as the dying and rising Son of Man—therefore not the Jewish Messiah at all! The passage is, of course, redactional. Originally Peter's "confession" was followed not by the prediction of Jesus' passion—this, we have seen, represents the theology of a later Christianity, even though with some probable foundation in Jesus' own experience—but by the immediate repudiation of Peter for having given voice to a satanic temptation (Luke, pursuing his own thoughtful way through the gospel traditions, omits this episode). So reconstituted, the narrative corresponds perfectly with a paradigm elsewhere evidenced in the traditions. It is, after all, the *demons* who have been hailing Jesus as the messianic Son of God (cf. Mark 3:11, 5:7, and parallels). In the famous Q narrative of Jesus' temptation at the outset of his mission (Matthew 4:1–11, Luke 4:1–13), the devil tries to persuade Jesus to declare himself Son of God precisely in this sense, to be the Messiah as Peter understood Messiah. And the Johannine parallel to the Synoptic story of Peter's confession (John 6:67–70) may at one time have had the same import (in verse 71 a Johannine redactor has interpreted the "devil" to mean Judas Iscariot); it was set in the context of an attempt on the part of the Jews to declare Jesus king=Messiah (verse 15), an attempt from which he fled. The gospels recall, therefore, an historical tradition older than the church's theology that had revealed Jesus in a vigorous antimessianic stance.

The Christian Messiah

Nevertheless, the Christian community almost immediately began to confess Jesus as Messiah and speedily gained for the title such general acceptance that it could be retrojected into the traditions of his historical life. We conceive that what made possible for the church the thing that had been impossible for Jesus was that which made christology possible in the first place, namely the circumstances of his death and resurrection. In view of those circumstances, which were totally alien to the Jewish messianic tradition, there was no question at all that the Messiah Jesus would be equated with the nationalist king of a triumphalist Israel. Thus in its application to this new event in human history the title was thrown into a new perspective and given an entirely new meaning. Why it should have been chosen as an appropriate title despite all the incongruities is more difficult to explain, yet certain hypotheses may be advanced. It was, after all, a name that had given heart to generations of pious Jews who had been looking for the kingdom of God to come into the world, and it was undoubtedly the single name that rallied the eschatological hopes of the best (as well, unfortunately, of the worst) of the "standard" Jewry of the time of Jesus and the earliest Jewish church. It was also, even though wrongly and in ignorance, the title under which Jesus had suffered and died. The combination of these motives may account for the fact that Jesus came to be "called the Christ" (cf. Matthew 1:16, 27:17.22) by Christians as well as by pagans. At all events, he was given the title in its proper sense to begin with, though in the very act of ascription the process was already under way by which the Christ of Christian usage would come to signify something altogether different from the Messiah of which the Jews continued to speak. In fact, it is likely enough that only in its translated and therefore per se "ecumenical" form of Christ was the name of Messiah bestowed on Jesus by the early church (and, therefore, presumably by the Hellenistic rather than by the Aramaic-speaking

Jewish church of Palestine). If Messiah in its Semitic original had ever been widely used of Jesus, one might expect that it would have left some traces in the tradition, the way that other Hebrew or Aramaic titles and appellatives have left their traces: Maran, Cephas, Abba, Boanerges, and the like. Only in two Johannine passages (John 1:41, 4:25), however, does the word appear in its Semitic form in the New Testament, and these are probably instances of deliberate archaizing rather than witnesses to authentic tradition.

The catechesis ascribed to Peter in the third chapter of Acts has been thought by many scholars to have preserved one of the earlier stages of christological development, older than the theology of Luke, in whose work it is now found. Though other scholars have questioned this thesis, there is much to be said for it. Peter says of Jesus:

13 The God of Abraham and Isaac and Jacob, the God of our fathers, has glorified his servant Jesus, whom you handed over and disowned before Pilate when he was ready to release him.

14 You disowned the Holy and Just One and preferred instead to be granted the release of a murderer.

15 You put to death the Author of life; whom, however, God raised from the dead, and we are his witnesses. . . .

18 God has brought to fulfillment by this means what he announced long ago through all the prophets: that his Christ would suffer.

19 Therefore, reform your lives! Turn to God, that your sins may be wiped away!

20 Thus may a season of refreshment be granted you by the Lord when he sends you the Christ he has already appointed, Jesus.

21 He must remain in heaven until the time of universal restoration, which God spoke of long ago through his holy prophets.

22 For Moses said: "The Lord God will raise up for you a prophet like me from among your own kinsmen. . . ."

26 When God raised up his servant, he sent him to you
first, to bless you by turning every one of you from
your wicked ways.

The passage contains late elements: It seems to presuppose
the standard passion story of the gospels, even though the
passion is still viewed more as an unpleasant fact—albeit a
prophesied fact—than as having a positive salvific value. Also,
the Christ of verse 18 is the construct of a christology
rather than of a messianology. Only after Christ and Servant
of the Lord had been combined in one person, a thing that
did not occur in Jewish thought, could "all the prophets" be
imagined to have announced a suffering Christ. But the interesting details begin with verse 20. In this christology Jesus
appears to have been regarded as the Christ not of the past
or present but of the future: Christ is a truly eschatological
title reserved for the *parousia,* the end-time. Until this ultimate revelation Jesus remains in the glory of God, having
triumphantly fulfilled his earlier mission as Servant of the
Lord.

Another interesting feature of this passage is its illustration
of how the concept of Christ became transmuted in Christian
usage. Here, in keeping with the Servant motif asserted in
verses 13 (=Isaiah 52:13), 14 (=Isaiah 53:11), 18, and 26,
the models against which Jesus' messiahship has been measured are neither royal nor Davidic but prophetic throughout.
The Author of life of verse 15 is probably a prophetic
term: the sense is that he is author of the way of salvation (cf. Acts 5:31, Hebrews 2:10, 12:2). In Acts 7:27
virtually the same language is recalled of Moses (=Exodus
2:14), evidently with the intimation that he was a type of
Jesus; and, indeed, the way of salvation into which Jesus is
conceived to have been author or leader doubtless had for its
pattern Israel's exodus into freedom under the prophetic
leadership of Moses. There are prophetic associations to the
themes of "refreshment" and "restoration" of verse 20f., and
especially to that of the "appointed" Christ who is to be sent;
the last is an allusion to Exodus 4:13 (in the Septuagint),
concerning another who is to be sent as prophet in the stead

of Moses. All of this builds up to an appropriate climax in verse 22, when the Christ is explicitly identified with the eschatological prophet-like-Moses who was awaited in post-exilic Jewish expectation as the fulfillment of Deuteronomy 18:15. Though Jesus' role, or coming role, is characterized by use of the Davidic title, therefore, in this catechesis there is no longer any residue of royal messianism, which has been completely replaced by a prophetic soteriology.

There is no doubt that the coming of an eschatological prophet figured prominently in Jewish soteriological expectation, and that this prophet was thought of variously as a second Elijah, a second Enoch, especially a second Moses, or perhaps all of them together. Second Isaiah's Servant of the Lord, according to some scholars, had Moses for a prototype. Both in Hellenistic and in Palestinian Judaism the name and career of Moses exercised an almost magical influence on eschatological imagination. The Taheb (probably "restorer") of Samaritan and Galilean hope who corresponded to the Judean Messiah was a prophetic, and doubtless a Mosaic, image of redemption. Similar images abound in Philo of Alexandria, in Josephus, and in the apocryphal Jewish literature. There is likewise no doubt that most if not all of this Mosaic speculation has found its way into the New Testament applied to Jesus, far away from and beyond the example we have seen in Acts 3. The flow of such ideas into early Christianity was constant and pervasive: it has affected the structure that Mark first gave to the written gospel as well as the theology of all the gospels, and it is responsible for countless allusions in the New Testament by which Jesus is connected with one or another prophetic figure. We should also remember a point previously made, that Jesus would probably have experienced little difficulty in accepting the name of a prophet and that in the popular estimation he was almost certainly held to be a prophet during his own lifetime.

A Prophetic or Priestly Messiah?

It seems to be a mistake, however, or at least a loose use of language, to speak of Jesus as having realized the ideal of a

Prophet Messiah. The Prophet and the Messiah were discrete strands of Jewish aspiration, even as they are carefully distinguished in John 1:20f.25. Without better evidence to the contrary, prophetic messianism is best seen as a Christian invention that came into being after the church had recognized in Jesus Christ, in one person, the fulfillment of hopes that had once been separate and parallel. Prophetic messianism is a concept that was made possible by Jesus Christ. Nor did it come about simply by chance, because for one set of reasons Jesus had been designated the Christ, and for a quite different set he was proclaimed the Prophet. Rather, as Acts 3 might indicate, it seems to have been the result of a deliberate effort to redefine the meaning of Christ. It is as though, having felt itself compelled to adopt the messianic title despite its known shortcomings, the church quickly set about giving it a new content, not satisfied with the merely neutralizing influences that had been at work on it, which we have already mentioned. The same kind of revisionism may be apparent in the catechesis of Acts 2, to which we have referred more than once before, another passage that betrays a stage of theological development older than that of its Lucan redactor. In this version of Jesus' messiahship, contrary to that of Acts 3, the title of Christ seems to be one that he has won through the resurrection rather than a distinction awaited in the *parousia*, and there is no question about the Davidic associations of the title, as is presupposed in the gospels and the other evidences of the first kerygma (Romans 1:3, 2 Timothy 2:8, Revelation 3:7, 5:5, 22:16). But even so, it is significant that Jesus is said to have been *made* the Davidic Messiah, not to have inherited the status by right of birth, that as in the Pauline preaching of Acts 13 he is one who supplanted David and is therefore his superior, one prophesied by David and not just his descendant. "Son of David," in other words, despite its earlier quasiautomatic certificatory value, has become at best an irrelevancy and at worst a detriment to true messiahship as the New Testament now understands it. The same kind of idea seems to have been picked up by Mark when he decided to permit Jesus to call himself Messiah in the gospel sense. This could only be possible once it was made clear that the Messiah is really Lord, and therefore no simple son of David (cf. Mark 12:35–37 and parallels). Consistent with this purpose—for Mark was a superb craftsman—is the treatment that the Second Gospel accorded one of those rare traditions preserved by all four gospels, the story of Jesus' entry into Jerusalem before the last Passover, when the people were shouting:

Matthew 21:9	Mark 11:9	Luke 19:38	John 12:13
Hosanna to the Son of David!	Hosanna!		Hosanna!
Blessed is he who comes in the name of the Lord!	Blessed is he who comes in the name of the Lord!	Blessed is he who comes a king in the name of the Lord!	Blessed is he who comes in the name of the Lord,
	Blessed is the reign of our father David to come!		and the king of Israel!
Hosanna in the highest!	Hosanna in the highest!	Peace in heaven and glory in the highest!	

Though the honors may be fairly evenly divided, Mark appears to have shown the greater sensitivity in preserving Jesus from the connotations of a triumphalist messianism. Of the same quality is the application made to Jesus on this same occasion by all of the gospels (implicitly by Mark and Luke, explicitly by Matthew and John) of the prophecy of Zechariah 9:9f., possibly the most spiritualized example of royal messianism to be found in the Old Testament. (Even so, the messianism of the passage is further tempered in the citation by Matthew and John, who mingle with it an allusion to the Servant of Second Isaiah.) It is also significant that despite the acclamation "Son of David" that Matthew allows, Jesus is ultimately identified by the same crowds as the Prophet (Matthew 21:11). That early christology fretted so much

over Jesus' Davidic associations may indicate that they were
known before theology sought to make them known.

It is also probably misleading to claim, as many scholars
do, that there was in Judaism a priestly form of messianism
that prepared for the New Testament Christ. Actually, the
characterization of Jesus as a priest is fairly marginal in the
New Testament; it is chiefly the idea of the author of the so-
called Epistle to the Hebrews, and therefore it hardly domi-
nates the New Testament theology of the Christ. However,
there is more to be said in favor of a priestly than of a prophetic messianic conception in Jewish expectation prior to the
Christian church. In the postexilic community the high priest,
who assumed many of the functions and some of the mystique of the king who was now only a memory, was called in
his place the Anointed. The transition to this changed condition was signaled by Zechariah 4:1–3.11–14 where both
the Davidic scion Zerubbabel and the high priest Joshua
were portrayed as anointed (not, however, as "messiahs"),
then by Zechariah 6:9–15, where a once symbolic crowning
of Zerubbabel was rewritten—possibly after some debacle involving Zerubbabel—to apply now to Joshua. As a consequence, when salvific expectation took an eschatological and
apocalyptic turn, it was inevitable that a priestly figure would
loom large in the hopes of many, sometimes as a companion
to the Davidic Messiah, sometimes as a substitute for him.
None of this, however, precisely adds up to a Priest Messiah.
The sectarians of Qumran, who certainly set a high price on
the priesthood and thought of themselves as constituting a
proleptic priestly kingdom, possibly looked forward to an
eschatological Anointed of Aaron, a priest; but their Messiah
was the standard, royal, Davidic one. What is true of the
Qumran documents is generally true of the intertestamental
literature as well. (The priestly messianism that appears in
the Testaments of the Twelve Patriarchs, ultimately a work
of Jewish apocalyptic stemming from the fervor of Mac-
cabean times, is rightly judged to be due to the extensive
Christian interpolation that the work has undergone.)

The one sustained celebration of priestly messianism, or

better, priestly christology in the New Testament is, as we have said, that of Hebrews, where Christ is likened to Melchizedek. Like the Enoch of Genesis 5:21–24, the Melchizedek of Genesis 14 and Psalm 110 was a mysterious and fascinating character who challenged the imagination and ingenuity of Jewish speculation, and Hebrews' typology is a Christian version of it. It was, obviously, originally at least of a totally different inspiration from that which led to the idealization of the priesthood we have seen above. Melchizedek was represented in legend as a king who was also priest—thus a figure ready-made for the Christian adaptation of the Christ title—not as a priest who acceded to kingly estate. Hebrews is quick to point out that in the normal development of events Jesus, of the Davidic tribe of Judah, could never have been thought of as a priest (Hebrews 7:14). Hebrews has produced its own midrashic commentary on Psalm 110 and Genesis 14 brought into relation with Christ, just as other commentators like Philo of Alexandria brought Melchizedek into relation with various other traditional figures. A recently published text discovered at Qumran *may* indicate that some Jews identified Melchizedek both with the prophetic messenger of Isaiah 52:7 and the anointed leader of Daniel 9:25. (The latter, in the mind of the author of Daniel, was undoubtedly Cyrus the Persian. Who he was for the Qumran artist, or might have been, is anybody's guess; but in any case the meaning of the text is uncertain.) There seems to be no recognizable connection between Hebrews and the known non-Christian Jewish treatments of the Melchizedek myth; they are parallel and independent elaborations of a common and popular theme. Christ became Melchizedek for the author of Hebrews because he thought of him as a priest, but he did not become Christ because he was first a Melchizedekian priestly Messiah.

We return, then, to the view we have held from the outset, that Christ is the primary faith-formula devised by early Christianity to designate its Lord and Savior, a formula it chose because none other would do and yet was so inade-

quate to the purpose that it had to be filled with new content.
The explanation of this extraordinary state of affairs is undoubtedly the extraordinary personality of Jesus himself,
which escaped all the usual categories. Jesus impressed his
contemporaries variously as rabbi, prophet, and teacher, and
all these impressions have been registered by the gospels. In
registering them, however, the gospels also confessed that
they were approximations which, if pressed, would belie
rather than define what had occurred in his proclamation of
the kingdom of God. Within that dimension no rabbi had
ever taught like Jesus, no teacher had ever so prophesied,
and no prophet had ever laid claim to such an immediacy of
the Spirit. In the words of Ernst Käsemann, "no prophet could
be credited with the eschatological significance which Jesus
obviously ascribed to his own actions." Christ, the name that
signaled the irrevocable ending of one age and the certain
beginning of another, wholly new, was the only one that
could capture the genuine excitement of what had been
revealed in Jesus, and even it would not be serviceable till it
had taken in other affirmations that were likewise implicit in
the preaching of the Prophet of Nazareth, though utterly in-
congruous with what had been awaited of a Jewish Messiah.
No matter that Jesus had never used these terms of himself.
To quote Käsemann again:

> The predication Son of Man must have reflected the chris-
> tology and the apocalyptic of post-Easter Christianity and
> from there must have found its way into the Jesus tradition
> which today includes so many pronouncements of Christian
> prophecy, originally uttered as the voice of the exalted
> Lord. But if this really was the case and Jesus never
> expressly laid claim to messiahship, it would be extraor-
> dinarily characteristic of him. He would thus have differen-
> tiated himself equally from late Jewish expectation and
> from the proclamation of his own community. He would
> not have projected a picture of the future but done what
> needed doing in the present; he would have placed not his
> person but his work in the forefront of his preaching. But
> his community would have shown that they understood the

distinctive nature of his mission precisely by responding to his proclamation with their own acknowledgment of him as Messiah and Son of God.

Käsemann's conclusion is, in this instance, also ours.

If an aside may be permitted, we might pause a moment to reflect on the New Testament church's handling of the Christ image as paradigmatic of a faith-formed wisdom which the church of later times has seldom been able to muster when confronted by essentially the same kind of problem. To be specific, Jesus certainly took it for granted that in respect to what would later be termed church order and authority, his disciples would find other models than the power structures of the current age (see Mark 10:42–44 and Synoptic parallels, also John 13:4f.12–17). The reinterpretation of the Messiah tradition by the primitive church continued and completed the desacralizing of the royal mystique begun long before by Israelite belief and practice. Just as Israel knew that it must assert its own peculiar dynamism in the face of the nations that surrounded it, or else be lost and absorbed in them, so did the first Christianity, when it made over a nationalistic watchword into a sign of universal redemption. Neither in its Catholic nor in its Protestant expressions, however, nor in the expressions tributary to these, has the church of latter days succeeded to perfect mastery over the forces that always threaten to be its master, whether they emanate from the polity of a Byzantine despotism or a New England town meeting.

Lord and Master

"Both Lord and Christ" Acts 2:36 affirmed of the resurrected Jesus. Like Christ, Lord was obviously a credal articulation of the church, a title by which the church sought to specify the faith it held concerning its risen Savior. Unlike Christ, however, Lord had nothing particular to say about the *Heilsgeschichte* that Jesus had inherited or in which he had played a part. It was simply, then as now, a title of the utmost esteem and of universal acceptance, an acclamation of who Jesus was quite independently of what he may have done. It was, as far as we can ascertain from certain significant texts (Philippians 2:11, which we have seen above; also 1 Corinthians 12:3, Romans 10:9), a confession formula employed in the liturgy. The same would be indicated by the traditional expression "baptism in the name of the Lord Jesus" (Acts 8:16, 19:5) or simply "the name" (cf. Philippians 2:10) found more frequently in the same context (see also Ephesians 4:5), and by the Aramaic acclamation *maranatha* preserved by Paul in 1 Corinthians 16:22. Whether the latter be divided *Marana tha*, "Our Lord, come!," or *Maran atha*, "Our Lord is coming!" it is readily recognizable as a proclamation of the faithful either in a eucharistic or a baptismal setting, both of which equally celebrated a salvific reality and awaited a salvific fulfillment. Lord, after Christ had been reduced by the very breadth of its compass into nothing more than a proper name—though a unique proper name belonging to one only—remained the distinctive title that said most about Jesus; The traditional "Christ the Lord" illustrates both of these developments admirably. Lord thus survived as the most content-filled of the New Testament christological titles, and the most meaningful. When Paul utters his frequent greeting, "grace and peace from God-our-Father-and-Lord-Jesus-Christ," there is no doubt that he invokes a single source of divine benison and that for him God and Lord share a common sphere of being and activity.

It would seem natural, then, to ask: How, in contrast with the known vicissitudes associated with the attribution of the Christ, did such an exalted name so speedily—in the Aramaic-speaking Palestinian church!—come to be that of Jesus of Nazareth, lately executed as a common felon? It is a very good question which, not surprisingly, has called forth absolutely contradictory answers.

In the first place, as scholars have portentously observed and as anyone with an Aramaic dictionary can verify, Jesus was undoubtedly in his own lifetime called *mara or mare* (master), *mari* (my master), *maran or marana* (our master),

etc. The terminology corresponds with the more familiar *rab,
rabbi*, etc., the Hebrew equivalent, which sometimes appears
as such in the gospels but more often has been translated into
the Greek for master or teacher. To establish this fact is not
difficult, and it is even easier to parody it. In today's Israel
every mister is a *mar*, just as in today's Greece he is a *kyrios*,
the climactic name given to Jesus in Philippians 2:11. A
progressive democratization, which was already at work in
New Testament times, has further rendered these titles innoc-
uous of the connotations of deity and majesty. (In reverse
English, the word lord, which originally meant only the loaf-
ward, the master of the household, has taken on those connotations, even when bestowed as a courteous fiction by grace
of an Honours List.) To prove that Jesus was known as
master, however, does not explain why he came to be known
as Lord, regardless of or even precisely in view of the functional ambiguity of the same Aramaic or Greek word, which
could refer to both. The *maranatha* of the Palestinian church
(in addition to 1 Corinthians 16:22, the expression also
occurs in the ancient Christian writing known as the Didache
or Teaching of the Lord Through the Twelve Apostles, in a
eucharistic context) obviously had nothing to do with a rabbinical distinction allegedly owned by the historical Jesus but
was the confession of a veritable Lord, of one whose coming,
already or in the awaited eschaton, embodied the presence of
the only God.

This last is admitted also by those who believe that it was
the Hellenistic rather than the Palestinian church that first
began to call Jesus Lord. Rudolf Bultmann, for example, concedes the antiquity of the *maranatha* acclamation and its
roots in Aramaic Christianity, but insists that it was
addressed to God, not Christ, and that it was only later extended to Christ when for other reasons he was now named
Lord. That name he and many others think the church extracted and assimilated from the syncretic religious world
into which it moved to preach the gospel, a world in which
there were "many gods and many lords" (1 Corinthians
8:5). "For us," wrote Paul, "there is one God, the Father
. . . and one Lord, Jesus Christ" (verse 6). His words have

been compared with those of Hellenistic inscriptions, e.g., "There is one Zeus-Serapis, and great is the Lady (*kyria*) Isis." The divinized kings of this world were lords, of course: It has often been remarked that the confession of John 20:28, *ho kyrios mou kai ho theos mou,* my lord and my god, might well have been lifted from the pedestal of a statue to Augustus. Proponents of the Hellenistic origin of the title likewise have a telling argument for their position in the recognized fact that combinations like "Christ the Lord" and "the Lord Jesus Christ," which are characteristic of the usage of the term in the epistolary of the New Testament, could have been put together only after Christ had at length become a proper name and ceased to be a descriptive title in its own right.

Nevertheless, it is more probable that the title does indeed go back to the Palestinian church. What the contrary evidence might indicate is that Lord, like Christ, was attributed to Jesus at different stages and with different nuances by the several churches: as a messianic designation looking to the *parousia,* as the epitome of all that was believed about the Christ reigning with God, and so forth. Translation into the *kyrios* of Hellenism did undoubtedly affect the sense of the church's acclamation because of the new connotations it brought along with it. One of these not yet mentioned is the *kyrios* which in the Greek Old Testament rendered the name of Yahweh, the God of Israel (hence the LORD or its equivalent in most modern versions of the Bible). It has been learnedly objected that in pre-Christian copies of the Septuagint the divine name was most probably not written *kyrios,* but rather the letters YHWH appeared, usually in the ancient Hebrew script. Manuscript evidence supports this irrelevant detail, which has been accorded immense religious significance by the Jehovah's Witness. What is certain, however, is that when the Septuagint was read aloud—and it was to this means that the vast majority of Greek-speaking Jews and Christians owed their acquaintance with the Bible—it was *kyrios* that was heard and not the no longer pronounced Yahweh. The impact of this coincidence in names ("The Lord said to my Lord . . .") has been well brought out in the gospel passage already alluded to, regarding the enigma of the Messiah (Mark 12:35–37 and parallels).

The Exalted One

Lord with full overtones of its divine associations was a name given early to Christ, not later, and not through the fortuity of functionally ambiguous words. The high christology of the Philippians homology, with which we began our Chapter 2, is proof of this. It is true that some highly important considerations germane to the christology of the hymn remain so far unexplored by us and will have to wait their turn in a later chapter; but we have seen that the passage is old, and conceivably Palestinian in origin. There is no reason whatever, other than pure guesswork, to imagine that the confessional formulas of 1 Corinthians 12:3 and Romans 10:9 were not in complete harmony with the *maranatha* of Palestinian Christianity even as Paul, who knew Palestinian Christianity, evidently thought them to be. The "Come, Lord Jesus!" of Revelation 22:20 is also best understood as a translation of the Semitic *maranatha*. The expression "the brothers of the Lord" (1 Corinthians 9:5, cf. Galatians 1:19, "James, the brother of the Lord") may have some connection in the Palestinian church, where Jesus' relatives were known, and it would indicate how soon Jesus had become for that church "the Lord." It is unlikely, to be sure, that Jesus was acclaimed Lord in the proper sense before the resurrection, though it is not impossible. The gospels are full of the word, of course, but we may safely assume that when they situate it within the historical ministry of Jesus they are either anticipating the language of post-Easter faith or exploiting the irony of an historically plausible *rabbi*, teacher, master, even the sir (*kyrios*) of the Samaritan woman in John 4:11. If not in his historical life, however, at least very soon thereafter, and not without close reference to his historical life, he was indeed both constituted and named Lord. What that meant in a contemporary Palestinian scene we may judge from an Aramaic text from Qumran, in which Abraham prays to the "Most High God, Lord (*mari*) of all worlds . . . Lord (*mara*) and Master over all and Master of all the kings of the earth. . . . My Lord (*mari*), you are the Lord (*mara*) of all the kings of the earth. . . ."

Because in contrast with Christ, Lord has no real "history" to be examined, we must rather determine its content in relation to Jesus through the imprint he made on the earliest kerygma that preached him as Lord. How the impression he made was expressed by the kerygma we have already seen in part, but the major investigation lies before us and will occupy our attention, especially in the following two chapters. There we shall be dealing in the process with other titles that did very definitely have a history, because of which the name of Lord was proclaimed of Jesus, and failing which the proclamation would undoubtedly have been inconceivable.

Another aside may be ventured, however, as we pass on to this history. Perhaps the most instructive resolution of a survey of this kind is the homily it preaches on the delicacy of the theological task. The church that produced the New Testament, a church comprising more free spirits than the church of any other age, our own included, and without the blessing of ancestral errors on which it could improve, nevertheless approached the central issue of christology with a degree of responsibility hardly equalled since and achieved a proportionate success that we can only envy and certainly not surpass. What was entailed in both trial and result was a complexity of thought, and of the balance and counterbalance of conflicting thought, which the reader of these pages may often understandably find tedious in the telling, but which any professional student of the New Testament will assure him has been highly simplified for his easy reading, if not at the same time oversimplified and therefore distorted. It is no defense to protest that the church of the New Testament set the standards, to or from which a later church could only adjust or deviate. The protest is valid, to the extent that later Christianity has taken the New Testament canon for its *norma normans,* the measure by which the genuine is to be segregated from the deviant. But it is also invalid if it ignores the principle of credibility, which is age-old and from which the Christianity of the first century is not exempt, that a message proves its true value only when it can successfully pass the test of translation and appeal to the understanding even if not to the sympathy of an alien age and language. New Testament theology achieved these qualities, and not all subsequent Christian theology has.

We do not intend to denigrate here or elsewhere in this book forms of piety, including christological piety, which have comforted the human soul, even when their theological credentials have been markedly dubious. It is easy to agree with Karl Pawek that while a kitsch flower vase is only a lapse in taste, a kitsch Sacred Heart is also a lapse in theology; but it must also be said in extenuation that there are more important things than theology, one of which is man. However, theology is not unimportant for being less important than man, and since theology is our subject it does seem necessary to institute or at least to imply comparisons from time to time. In the course of this chapter we have implied some: that Christ the Lord, for example, says to this day and to us men of this day what Christ the King has tried to say in this day, but less thoughtfully and in terms that were already dated. Christ the King at least had the virtue of using biblical language, though not carefully. It is the element of care, another word for theological concern, we suggest again, that characterizes the christology of the New Testament.

4. SON OF MAN AND SON OF GOD

The Son of Man: Another Enigma

Son of Man is not the title that springs most readily to the lips of a modern Christian seeking to express his faith in the Lord of the church. This is hardly surprising, since it probably never was at home in any church liturgy and figures in New Testament theology mainly as an anachronism if not in a transmuted and no longer recognizable form. At the same time it is surprising, for no title has been more associated with Jesus and quoted of him by the gospels than this one. Christ and Son of Man thus make a perfect pair of foils: the one rejected by Jesus but eagerly adopted by the church, the other integral to his message but quickly and definitively abandoned by his followers. Statistically, Son of Man is a title found only in the gospels (the exceptions are Acts 7:56 and Revelation 1:13, 14:14), where it always appears in an utterance of Jesus and is never uttered about him by an evangelist (in the Fourth Gospel, of course, Christ's words are indistinguishable from John's); and it never turns up in the epistles or the sources utilized by them.

To sharpen the paradox, it is beyond question that of all the New Testament titles ascribed to Jesus, that of the Son of Man is the most unmistakably and ineluctably Semitic, incapable of having had an origin in any other milieu. If it has a strange and exotic sound in English, so did it have in Greek. It sounds natural only in a Semitic context, where "son" is simply a means of attribution: son of god or of the gods=a divine being; son of perdition=one doomed to die; son of oil=an anointed one; son of the prophets=a prophet, and so on. Therefore, son of man=a man or, merely, man (perhaps the meaning in Mark 2:28, asserting that man is superior to the Sabbath law and not blindly subject to its control). The usual New Testament expression, it should be observed, is not *a* Son of Man, which would not necessarily mean anything more than man, a human being—though perhaps saying it more solemnly than usual, a dignified way of referring to oneself in the third person—but, rather, *the* Son of Man, which translates into an expressly designated Man, a significant Person. The underlying Aramaic was *bar nasha.*

Scholars have long divided the Son of Man sayings of the gospels into three categories, and it is convenient and useful to retain the distinctions. There are, first of all and most significantly, those sayings in which Jesus refers, in the third person, to a future Son of Man coming as eschatological judge. Secondly, there are sayings in which Jesus clearly identifies himself as a present Son of Man active in his ministry. The most obvious explanation of at least some of these uses of Son of Man might seem the one suggested above, that it was a self-deprecating way of naming oneself. However, it seems to be the agreement of most experts on the subject that there was no such common usage of *bar nasha* in the time of Jesus, and in any case there are too many instances of this form of Son of Man in the gospels for it to be merely a clumsy translation and not a proper title. Finally, there is a group of sayings in which Jesus speaks of himself as a suffering, dying, and rising Son of Man. It is regarded as significant that this third category of sayings occurs only in the Marcan material of the synoptic gospels and not in the older Q source. Examples of all three types of sayings are numerous. Of the first: "Then [in the eschaton] men will see the Son of Man coming in the clouds with great power and glory" (Mark 13:26 and parallels). Of the second: "The foxes have lairs, the birds in the sky have nests, but the Son of Man has nowhere to lay his head" (Matthew 8:20 and Luke 9:58, a Q saying). And of the third: "The Son of Man must suffer much, be rejected by the elders, the chief priests, and the scribes, be put to death, and rise three days later" (Mark 8:31 and parallels).

Though some critics will not allow it, holding all of the Son of Man sayings to be the creation of early Christian theology, it seems clear to us that in one form or other they do put us in real contact with an emphasis of Jesus' own preaching. The alternatives to this view appear to be truly incredible.

We would have to believe that a Jewish church invented a christology whose internal complexities indicate that it passed through various stages of development, which managed to saturate the gospel traditions while leaving all others strangely untouched, for some unaccountable reason restricted itself to words it put on the mouth of Jesus, then disappeared leaving hardly a trace. It is, to say the least, somewhat easier to imagine another sequence of events as better explaining the known phenomena. But regardless of the decision we are called to make in this regard, it would appear that a primary and preliminary task ought to be to determine the provenance of the Son of Man figure in the New Testament. Whence did it arise, this name that obviously meant so much to Jesus, to the first Jewish Christians, or to both together?

Not unnaturally, the Old Testament has been searched for possible leads in the direction of an answer to this question, and not without some suggestive results. Psalm 8:5f., for example, affords a good beginning when "the son of man" (the parallel shows that simply "man" is meant) is put on a near level with God; the Hebrew text is more straightforward here than the Greek Septuagint, for while the latter affirms that the creature man has been constituted "slightly less than angels," the Hebrew has it "a little less than *elohim*," that is, God or gods, supernatural beings. The psalm is a paean to the majesty of God's creation in man, not the celebration of any particular Son of Man, let alone an eschatological figure; but Jewish and Christian exegesis of the first century often paid less attention to the historical meaning of a text than to the plasticity of its language to fit other meanings. (Compare the use made of this passage by Hebrews 2:6–8, which may prove to be a partial exception to the rule we stated above concerning the absence of Son of Man in the epistolary of the New Testament. Hebrews has no Son of Man christology, but a recollection of such a christology may have dictated its choice of the Psalms text.) Certainly Psalm 8:5f. would not alone account for the Son of Man of the New Testament, but it could have contributed to the construct once it had been built of other materials. The same might be held, perhaps to a smaller extent, of the other Psalm passages in which Son of Man occurs. In Psalm 80:18 it appears as a metaphor for Israel the people of God, the vine that he planted, "the man of your right hand." In Psalm 144:3 it signifies the transitoriness of the human estate, a sense presumably approximating that of its use in the book of Ezekiel, where it is the habitual (some ninety times) salutation of the prophet by the Spirit of God. It is possible that some of these associations have penetrated Son of Man christology as it finally achieved its full complexity: prophet, embodiment of Israel, heir to human frailty. But they can hardly explain the figure as a whole or even its most essential features.

The Apocalyptic Son of Man

It is agreed that that part of the Old Testament that sheds the most light on our problem is the Aramaic seventh chapter of the book of Daniel, a book and a portion of the book that have heavily influenced the New Testament. The chapter is an apocalyptic vision of divine judgment, in which Daniel the seer is transported into the presence of the heavenly court. There

9 thrones were set up
    and the Ancient One took his throne.
  His clothing was snow bright,
    and the hair on his head as white as wool;
  his throne was flames of fire,
    with wheels of burning fire.
10 A surging stream of fire
    flowed out from where he sat;
  thousands upon thousands were ministering to him,
    and myriads upon myriads attended him.

After the court is convened, condemnation is decreed for the successive world empires that have menaced Israel's future, symbolized by four hideous and horrendous beasts. Then into the divine presence appears

13 one like a son of man (*bar enosh*) coming
  on the clouds of heaven.
  When he reached the Ancient One
  and was presented before him,
14 he received dominion, glory, and kingship;
  nations and peoples of every language serve him.
  His dominion is an everlasting dominion
  that shall not be taken away,
  his kingship shall not be destroyed.

The son of man of this vision is a human being, the better
to contrast with the apocalyptic beasts. He stands, quite
evidently, for Israel: the glorified, triumphant, vindicated
people of God (cf. verse 18: "The holy ones of the Most
High shall receive the kingship, to possess it forever and
ever"). He is not yet, therefore, *the* Son of Man (*bar nasha*).
He comes on the clouds like the Son of Man of the gospels
(Mark 13:26, for example, cited above), yet not so much as
judge as one who receives favorable judgment. It is plain
enough that the gospel Son of Man and the one like a son of
man in Daniel share a common thought pattern and have
been turned to a common apocalyptic wavelength, but it is
not equally plain that the one is in direct succession to the
other.

The missing link in the line of succession must doubtless be
sought in the intertestamental period between the last of the
Old Testament and the first of the New. For some scholars
the link is ready to hand in documented form, in the text of
the so-called Similitudes of Enoch, part of the Jewish apocryphal Book of Enoch that is extant only in an Ethiopian version. In the Similitudes we encounter a Son of Man who is a
full-fledged eschatological judge and redeemer (the translation is basically that of R. H. Charles):

At that hour that Son of Man was named
in the presence of the Lord of Spirits,
and his name before the Head of Days.
Yes, before the sun and the signs were created,
before the stars of the heaven were made,

his name was named before the Lord of Spirits. . . .
And he shall be the light of the Gentiles,
and the hope of those who are troubled of heart. . . .
For from the beginning the Son of Man was hidden.
And the Most High preserved him in the presence of his
    might,
and revealed him to the elect. . . .
And all the elect shall stand before him on that day.
And all the kings and the mighty and the exalted ones
    that rule the earth
shall fall before him on their faces,
and worship and set their hope upon that Son of Man
and petition him and supplicate for mercy at his
    hands. . . .
And with that Son of Man shall they eat
and lie down and rise up for ever and ever. . . .
For that Son of Man has appeared,
and has seated himself on the throne of his glory,
and all evil shall pass away before his face,
and the word of that Son of Man shall go forth
and be strong before the Lord of Spirits. . . .
This is the Son of Man who is born unto righteousness,
and righteousness abides over him,
and the righteousness of the Head of Days forsakes him
    not. . . .
He proclaims to you peace in the name of the world to
    come;
for hence has proceeded peace since the creation of the
    world,
and so shall it be for you for ever and ever and ever. . . .
And so there shall be length of days with that Son of
    Man,
and the righteous shall have peace and an upright way
in the name of the Lord of Spirits for ever and ever.

Here we seem to have it all: The Son of Man is a pre-existent, quasidivine being, the eschatological judge of both the
good and the wicked. Anyone moderately familiar with the
gospels will be instantly reminded of numerous passages and

allusions. In particular, in one of the more recent works of commentary on the First Gospel, W. F. Albright and C. S. Mann have related this description to Matthew 25:31–46, the great scene of the Son of Man as royal judge enthroned before all nations and men. There is an unmistakable parallel, though to be sure that piece of the Matthean scenario that has doubtless been fraught with deepest meaning for Christians of every age is lacking in Enoch: the recognition of the presence of the Son of Man in this world living in the hungry and the homeless, the suffering and the repressed. Furthermore, there is a well-founded suspicion, a nagging doubt not dispelled by Albright and Mann, that the gospel evocations of the Similitudes of Enoch find their most natural explanation when they are recognized as being due to the handiwork of Christian interpolators. The disturbing fact, the more disturbing for its studied neglect by so many New Testament scholars, is that these crucial sections of the Book of Enoch—like the similar crucial sections of the Testaments of the Twelve Patriarchs mentioned in the preceding chapter—have failed to turn up among the Qumran fragments that have otherwise reconfirmed the pre-Christian Hebrew origins of both these works, as indeed they have failed to turn in any other version that would independently authenticate them. The same reservations must be held concerning an alleged Son of Man who appears in the thirteenth chapter of the Jewish and Christian apocryphon known as 2 Esdras (or 4 Ezra). The chapter may or may not be of Christian authorship and in any case is no older than the New Testament; and it amounts to little more than a variation on the theme of Daniel 7.

The Heavenly Man

If the missing link may not be certainly documented, however, it may nevertheless be firmly postulated on the basis of other evidence. The evidence does not so much enable us to trace a line of ascent of the gospel Son of Man from Daniel 7 as it rather proposes the Son of Man to have been the Jewish apocalyptic version of a soteriological motif or aspiration much more universal in its appeal. The Danielic "one like a son of man," in fact, though obviously older than the Synoptic Son of Man, may well represent a later stage of development of a parallel strand of the same tradition, one in which the central figure had been demythologized through identification with a whole people. There is, nevertheless, at whatever stage of development we come across it, always a certain fluidity between person and people in the Son of Man image, which probably rises out of the image's original genius. For though the Son of Man is, as we maintained at the outset, an essentially Semitic concept, it seems to have been conceived as a peculiarly Israelite and Jewish expression, enriched by a religious prehistory of its own, of a common and ecumenical speculation that had focused itself on man and his destiny in relation to cosmic forces whose menace was a universal human experience of the age.

In our second chapter we dwelt briefly on the variety of myth that lay open to the hymnist of Philippians 2, eager to supply him with the models for his christology of a divine hero. It is time now to look a little more closely at some of those models, and at the myth, since we believe them both to be most material to the Son of Man soteriology presupposed by the New Testament. They are related to, though not simply convertible with, the wisdom/gnosis speculation that we shall be examining in our next chapter. What they together prove is that the early Fathers of the church knew what they were talking about when they spoke and wrote of *praeparatio evangelica*, the conditioning of the world, and not only of the Jewish world, for the good news of the gospel, which appeared as the response to so many similar quickenings and yearnings and in a guise that was already half familiar.

Hellenism had a long tradition of the *theios aner*, the divine man, a concept that certainly penetrated some strains of Jewish thought, though perhaps more in word than in deed. Divine man, a combination that did not occur spontaneously in Jewish monotheism, originally meant little more to a Greek than someone of exceptional gifts or talents: inspiration, whether in the strict or an extended sense. Plato called prophets divine men, along with philosophers, poets, or plain good men, and in the *Meno* he has Socrates ascribe the same inspiration to politicians for what sounds like a perennially valid cause, that "they say many grand things, not knowing what they say." Plato was trying to demonstrate that virtue is neither innate nor acquired but rather a divinely infused instinct, and to do so he equated it and other powers with ecstatic prophecy (*mania*), a condition in which the inspired person was thought to be possessed by an oracular deity who entered into him (*en-theos-iasmos*, whence "enthusiasm" in an older acceptation). The Old Testament, to account for like phenomena, thought of ecstatic prophecy as due to a divine breath of spirit (whence "inspiration"), with other gifts and charismata similarly accounted for: "a divine spirit of skill and understanding and knowledge in every craft" (Exodus 31:3), or the "spirit of counsel and of strength" possessed by the king (Isaiah 11:2). The two theorems are evidently parallel, but already the Greek had a boldness of language that was denied to the Hebrew.

In later times they were especially regarded as divine men who mediated between man and god, whose righteous sufferings or wonder deeds set them apart from the ordinary run of man, or who were thought in some special way to show man what he might do to approach the divine. The name of Apollonius of Tyana invariably crops up in this connection. He was a neo-Pythagorean philosopher who lived in the time of Jesus, and was reputed to be a righteous sufferer, a worker of wonders, and a religious reformer. His life has been transmitted, unfortunately, in a form that was probably a conscious parody of the Christian gospels, as an attempt to challenge the uniqueness of the Christ image in the polemics of the early Christian centuries, but there seems to be no doubt that he was a genuine *theios aner*, a truly impressive human being who embodied many of the qualities that New Testament theology associated with the Son of Man. Philo of Alexandria was probably influenced by the Hellenistic tradition in his attribution of "divine" titles to Moses and other worthies of the Old Testament, and it is likely, too, that the suffering just man of Wisdom 2:18 (to whom in verse 13 is ascribed the *gnosis* of God) is styled "son of God" because he was viewed as a *theios aner*. In sum, if the divine man of the Hellenistic world did not in any essential trait exceed the limits defined for Old Testament man, he did contribute to Judaism the precious gift of new words in which to speak of man, and the right words are always necessary to the unlocking of any new idea.

Ideas also accompanied the words, however. The myth of the Heavenly Man, fruit of many varieties of gnostic speculation on the nature and destiny of man, permeated the atmosphere breathed by Jewish apocalyptic in which the Son of Man took shape. The myth must be reconstituted, it is true, from sources which in their extant form are more recent than the New Testament and which, therefore, are not immune to the suspicion of other and later influences; still, the myth undeniably existed. It accounts for the Primal Man of Manicheanism, the Gayomart of Zoroastrianism, the Manda d'Hayye (Knowledge of Life) alias *gabra qadmaya* (primal man) of Mandeanism, and the Poimandres and archetypal Man of the Hermetic literature. In its typical development it becomes a redeemer myth in which the Heavenly Man descends into the world of matter to rescue the men of earth by reincorporating them into himself, the archetype and image of God. Some of these ideas, or ideas from a like matrix of thought, have surely entered into the fanciful speculation of the rabbis over Adam Qadmon (Primal Man or Primal Adam; and into Philo's allegorizing of the two creation stories of Genesis to allow for both a heavenly man (stamped in the image of God) and an earthly (molded from the clay of the ground).

The apocalyptic Son of Man and the gnostic Heavenly Man are not the same. Though the myth ultimately presupposes something that resembles a "fall" to explain the condition of earthly man, it has nothing to do with any historical progression or redemptive events in the biblical sense. The Heavenly Man is throughout a personification of intellect, never a real person. When the myth is stripped of its deliberately esoteric rebuses and arcana, it can be reduced to some fairly prosaic assumptions and propositions. Man, in this conception of man, is essentially Mind: He was created to become pure

Mind, and his salvation lies in the purification of his intellect by assimilation into the pure Mind revealed to him from the world of light. The Heavenly Man redeemer, then, who gathers the children of light to himself, is the same Heavenly Man whose "fall" from the world of light accounts for the divine spark in man that makes him capable of this kind of salvation. All of this is a far cry from the notion of man and his regeneration entertained by biblical religion. Those scholars are perfectly right who resist easy equations in this delicate area, therefore. Nevertheless, it is important for us to know about this kind of speculation, which was going on at the same time that Jewish apocalyptists were elaborating the doctrine of a coming Son of Man, a heavenly savior who is also the embodiment and fulfillment of all man. An exclusively Israelite genealogy of the Son of Man has long been discounted—Carsten Colpe's recent postulate of a Canaanite reminiscence also seems to lead nowhere—and an extra-Israelite genealogy as the result of any direct borrowing of gnostic motifs it appears must likewise be excluded; but together the biblical and nonbiblical data we have considered may permit us to conjecture with plausibility the lineage there must have been that led into the New Testament.

A Church Designation?

When we return to the Son of Man of the New Testament, we are reminded that he is seen there in several guises, only one of which is that of eschatological judge and savior. He is also one whose lot it is to suffer and die, to fulfill the destiny of a servant of God; and he is everyman, a man with a mission, exemplaric of what men ought to be as the one who shows them the way. We are reminded, too, that in the gospels, Son of Man is invariably a self-identification of Jesus, and that for all practical purposes it appears nowhere else. Our next task, therefore, is to sort out the various uses of the title and relate them properly to Jesus, as a preliminary to understanding their significance for New Testament theology.

We have already argued that the title has been rightly

placed on the lips of Jesus and was not a fairly extraordinary theological afterthought of early Christianity. In what sense it belonged on his lips, however, is another fair question. Despite the fact that in the gospels it has emerged universally as a self-designation, the current scholarly consensus regards the title as one that Jesus did, in fact, use, but not originally in reference to himself. His sayings about the coming Son of Man, which are phrased in the third person, can easily be taken as evidence that he shared the common apocalyptic expectation, but they do not prove that he thought himself to be that Son of Man. Consider the Q saying recorded in Luke 12:8, where in fact a clear distinction seems to be registered between the Son of Man and Jesus himself: "I tell you, whoever acknowledges me before men, the Son of Man will acknowledge him before the angels of God." (The parallel in Matthew 10:32 has it: "Whoever acknowledges me before men I will acknowledge before my Father in heaven." This looks like an obvious adaptation. Neither Matthew nor Luke has a special Son of Man theology of his own.) Jesus was the prophet of the kingdom of God, and he looked to the coming of the Son of Man for the vindication of his mission. Of course, as a dutiful son of God he could have believed that he was meant to return as this Son of Man, but there is no evidence that he did so. If he had believed this—if he had, therefore, identified himself with the coming Son of Man in such a roundabout fashion—he would have had to include some reference to his death and resurrection in order to be understood. But there are no such references in this group of sayings; the sayings that concern a suffering, dying, and rising Son of Man belong to an entirely different category, with other motivations.

In this hypothesis, then, it was the church that first called Jesus the Son of Man: a recognition which, like so much else, followed the resurrection. His sayings about the coming of the Son of Man were remembered just about as he had uttered them and were thus transmitted into the gospel sources; only now the future, which Jesus had left indefinite, was narrowed to the time of *parousia,* with the awaited one the risen Lord himself. As a church designation, therefore,

Son of Man was at first a title reserved for the future, even as it had been for Jesus. With the continued "delay" of the *parousia,* however, and the consequent transfer of interest to the present life of the church, it came more and more to apply to the Lord present in power. Out of this development rose other Son of Man sayings that were ascribed to the Jesus of the ministry, some of them doubtless the words of Christian prophets who spoke in the name of the Lord (like Revelation 2–3, words of the One like a Son of Man of 1:13), though others are the result of a mechanical substitution of "Son of Man" for a pronoun and thus the introduction of the title into a saying that originally had nothing to do with it. Finally, through another development, were devised the sayings about the suffering Son of Man. Why a suffering Son of Man? For basically the same reason that we have a passion story and that the Fourth Gospel chose to portray the crucifixion as an enthronement: The choice of title under which the passion has been predicted shows the pains that were taken to profess that the Lord's *exousia,* his divine power concretized in the character of Son of Man, was not invalidated by suffering and death but, indeed, vindicated in the resurrection.

Jesus' Own Title?

The theory of development just outlined is, as we have said above, probably the averaged view of the matter by the majority of New Testament scholars today. It must be admitted that it makes a good deal of sense and that it corresponds with most of the known facts—always conceding its premises, of course. It contains difficulties, however. Had there been such an elaborate history of the church's wrestling with this title, had it been so important to devise a christology around the title only to see it fade from memory in quick time, we might expect it to have had a wider circulation than simply in sayings ascribed to Jesus. Furthermore, it is not entirely clear why the church should have felt it necessary to reinterpret of its Christ and Lord those Son of Man sayings in which Jesus had referred to another person. If Son of Man christology was indeed so transitory and the title so unmanageable in Christian thought, it might appear more logical that the sayings would either have been forgotten—as other sayings doubtless were forgotten—or else made over in more digestible forms and concepts. Hence it is that some scholars continue to find it far more likely that Jesus not only used the title but also used it of himself, and for this reason it was remembered, even as the gospels profess. They, too, would attribute to the church the construction of some of the Son of Man sayings. Those that involve a suffering, dying, and rising Son of Man—that in other words have combined with the figure of the Son of Man that of the Servant of the Lord—are the most obvious candidates. We argued in our second chapter that Jesus probably did not cast himself in the role of the Servant for his disciples. But the action of the church would have consisted in the modification and adaptation of a Son of Man christology, not in inventing one.

But if Jesus did call himself Son of Man, in what sense did he do so? Carsten Colpe thinks that Jesus spoke of himself as *bar nasha* in sayings of undoubted authenticity, like the Matthew 8:20 already mentioned, Mark 2:10, and parallels asserting his (=man's) power to forgive sins, or Matthew 11:19 (=Luke 7:34), comparing himself with John the Baptist—but always meaning simply "man" or "this man," that is to say, "me." We have already noted the objection to this theory. It is not that a circumlocution of this kind was unlikely or improbable—the Christian "man" known to Paul in 2 Corinthians 12:2 is a comparable instance—but it is unlikely that *bar nasha* would have served as the circumlocution. Colpe then projects a fairly intricate route by which a Son of Man christology developed around this nucleus, through the assimilation of other sayings and, especially, through the identity of language contained in Jesus' sayings about the coming Son of Man. In these latter sayings, incidentally, Jesus spoke as a prophet and not of himself, so that the identification of the Son of Man lay entirely outside his purview. A more probable assessment of the terrain, in our view, is that made by Eduard Schweizer, who begins with the sayings of Jesus concerning a present and acting Son of Man, specifically a Son of Man in the service of man and rejected by men. The theology of a suffering, dying, and rising Son of Man, we have repeatedly agreed, is late, an elaboration by the church of motifs that were native to Jesus' preaching along with others that were not and required rather the faith of the resurrection for their revelation. Already, however, something like a halfway house to this theology has been reached by various sayings preserved in the Q source of the gospels, which have every right to be considered authentic words of Jesus. We have already mentioned Matthew 8:20 (Luke 9:58) and Matthew 11:19 (Luke 7:34). Other such passages are Matthew 12:32 (Luke 12:10), Luke 6:22 (the parallel in Matthew 5:11, like the Matthean parallel to Luke 12:8, has changed "Son of Man" to a pronoun), Luke 11:30 (which Matthew 12:40 has made into a prophecy of the resurrection), and Luke 19:10. The common denominator of references like these is that of a servant of God, a *theios aner* whose lot it is to undergo obloquy, misunderstanding, and persecution in fulfillment of a prophetic mission. But also, as Schweizer adds:

Another series of sayings concerning his future role can be similarly interpreted. The expectation of the just man who would be proved the servant and son of God through guiltless suffering, who would be rejected by men and even killed by them, but who would also be exalted by God and appear to his enemies in judgment, was already widespread in Judaism before the time of Jesus (Wisdom 2:12–20, 4:10–17, 5:1–5). Naturally Jesus never looked upon himself simply as one man among many others but as the one in whom all the suffering of Israel would be borne finally and for all time. In this sense he is the "(Son of) Man," in whom the blindness of men to the reality of God and their very struggle against God reach their high point, and whom they will encounter again in judgment. The Kingdom of God is God's alone and will be inaugurated by him. The (Son of) Man, however, will be the one who intercedes on behalf of his own and witnesses against those who have denied God, thus the one who in fact decides the judgment. That in the later tradition he was finally identified with the Judge himself who comes on the clouds, is easy enough to understand. The same kind of development may be observed through the comparison of Romans 14:10 with 1 Corinthians 4:4f. and 2 Corinthians 5:10.

Schweizer acknowledges the difficulty of associating the Son of Man with the Sufferer, and leaves open the option that Jesus made a title of self-identification out of the Ezekielian "son of man" address. As we have conjectured the complicated history of evolution of the Son of Man theology, however, and its only partial correspondence with any of our biblical or nonbiblical literary sources, we cannot foreclose the possibility of all these ideas in the mind of Jesus as easily as they were later coalesced in the mind of the church.

The Enigma Once More

There is, we believe, no overriding objection to the proposition that Jesus thought of himself as the coming Son of Man as well as identified himself in some fashion with an existing and acting Son of Man. Jesus' concept of the kingdom of God certainly allowed both perspectives: Almost everyone will agree that the only way to harmonize his seemingly irreconcilable pronouncements on its imminence and actuality is to conclude that he was not of one mind on the subject but could view it both as a future event and as already inchoate. (The two points of view do not really add up to a contradiction, and the pronouncements on either side appear to be equally authentic.) It is hard to accept uncritically the proposal that Jesus the prophet was precluded from seeing himself in his own prophecy. If the sayings that we have in the gospels about a suffering, dying, and rising Son of Man are admittedly constructions of the church, this does not mean that the historical Jesus was oblivious to the role played by his deprivations and sufferings and, possibly, his death, as a *sine qua non* of the coming of the kingdom. For that matter, it is not even necessary to concede that he foresaw his death—and consequent resurrection, as any good Jew might—as the *sine qua non* to his being the coming Son of Man, so fluid were his ideas on the chronology of the proximate kingdom. A person who set himself above Moses, who confidently declared sins forgiven in the name of the kingdom come, who declared the end to be now—to restrict ourselves, for the moment, to only a few of his affirmations that seem to be beyond contest—was he likely to have been preaching the coming of another, greater than himself? (Greater, to the extent that Matthew 11:11=Luke 7:28 indicates that Jesus regarded John the Baptist as the last and greatest figure of the pre-eschaton, leading up to himself and the kingdom.) We have no right to answer this question with an unqualified no, but neither must we give it a qualified yes.

Whatever the answer, it would seem that we have no adequate grounds to postulate a "secret," let alone "messianic" or "secret messianic" Son of Man christology that was initiated by Jesus himself. There is evidence that he used the name, or even the title, and perhaps the title in its full New Testament sense, but the evidence is not irrefutable. It would be perilous, therefore, to venture brave historical reconstructions that would have to stride the relatively slender shoulders of our available certain facts. Nor need we. It is quite enough that we recognize the Son of Man christology of the nascent church to have grown out of genuine impulses stimulated by the life of Jesus and to have interpreted those impulses genuinely. It is also satisfying to be able to verify that it was not the offbeat endeavor of some obscure faction on the fringes of Jewish or heathen thought and speculation, but the response of an age to its experience of a person who had spoken to an age.

All the more reason for us to wonder, however, why and how such a theology disappeared so quickly from the confession of the church. We are assuming, of course, that that was the sequence: first acceptance of a theology to be developed and coped with, then its abandonment. We feel that what was abandoned was mainly the title, doubtless because its Semitic flavoring rendered it increasingly unserviceable, and

not all that the title had come to connote. Even the title survived for a time, for reasons that must have been peculiar to
the Johannine church, in the christology of the Fourth Gospel. It seems to be an inescapable fact, despite some de-
murrers, that in John's gospel Son of Man is the supreme
christological title overshadowing all others, not only running the full gamut of meanings already assigned to it
(especially, perhaps, that of the triumphal Son of Man/Ser-
vant of the Lord) but probably attracting some others as
well. In Mark, as we have seen, Son of Man has come to=the
(Christian) Messiah. Elsewhere the title did disappear, to be
replaced by whole or partial surrogates. Paul's concept of
Christ as a Second Adam expressed in 1 Corinthians
15:21–28.45–49 (which cites Psalm 8) and Romans 5:12–21
certainly owes a debt to the Son of Man tradition or a tradition kindred to it. Associated wisdom motifs such as that of
the Image of God (2 Corinthians 4:4, Colossians 1:15) we
shall examine in our next chapter. By far the greatest burden
in the absorption of the Son of Man theology, however, we
think was borne by another title which enjoyed more common
currency and tender, which had its own independent history
but which was not related to the Son of Man. That title,
inevitably, was Son of God.

Adoptive Sonship

We may begin our inquiry into how and in what way
Christ came to be called Son of God by looking at a citation
made by Paul in the introductory verses of the first chapter
of his letter to the Romans. The citation, seemingly a credal
acclamation parallel with others we have seen above, the
apostle has introduced as a doubtless familiar element to
place himself in rapport with a Christian community to
which up to this point he had been unknown. (As before, we
bracket the words we consider to be Pauline additions, using
special brackets for one phrase which may or may not be
original to the citation.) He identifies himself as one called to
be an apostle of the gospel concerning God's Son

3 who was born of the seed of David
    according to the flesh,
4 but was constituted Son of God [in power]
    according to the spirit [of holiness]
    {by resurrection from the dead},
Jesus Christ our Lord.

Be it noted, first of all, that this passage is of a piece with others that we shall see below that distinguish between what Jesus was by nature (the flesh) and what he became by grace (the spirit). It may be an easier procedure, however, to determine before going farther what the passage meant to Paul in virtue of his adaptations. (The Pauline vocabulary also knows a flesh-and-spirit dichotomy, but in a rather different sense.) In Pauline theology Christ is, of course, Son of God, but in a rich variety of acceptations. One of them, and a pre-eminent one, relates to his character as head of a new and regenerate race, communicating a new and divine life in virtue of the new life bestowed on him in the resurrection. The first Adam was created a living soul, Paul recalls from the Scripture, but the last Adam became a life-giving spirit (1 Corinthians 15:45). It is therefore likely that in verse 4a above Paul has added "in power" to specify the kind of divine sonship he habitually associated with the resurrection: in this sense the expression is Pauline (cf. Romans 15:13.19, 1 Corinthians 2:5, 4:20, 15:43, etc.), designating the divine vital activity released in the Christ-event. "By resurrection from the dead" may also have been added by him for the same reason, though it is equally possible that it was already part of the credal formulation. "Spirit of holiness," finally, could be a Semitism for "holy spirit" and thus original to the passage with which Paul was working, but it, too, is better seen as the result of a Pauline expansion that has somewhat altered the initial thrust of the assertion. Holiness, the word *hagiosyne* found here, is extremely rare in the New Testament and exclusively Pauline: It is an active rather than a passive term—"making holy."

What we are left with, then, when we return this text to its state before Paul, is an articulation of primitive faith in which

what Jesus of Nazareth was by birth is contrasted with what
he became by God's special action. The "constituted" of verse
4a, which in the New Testament almost invariably refers to a
work of divine dispensation, never appears elsewhere in the
Pauline writings. The closest parallel usage occurs in Acts
10:42, in the sermon of Peter, where the resurrected Jesus is
proclaimed as constituted by God judge of the living and the
dead. In this early christology, then, Christ *became* Son of
God at some point in time or out of time—in the resurrection,
or in the *parousia* (1 Thessalonians 1:9?), or at some stage
in his historical ministry. As regards the last mentioned, we
have to recognize that either for Mark himself or at least for
the gospel source on which he depended, Jesus became Son
of God, was declared and constituted such, at the time of his
baptism by John the Baptist (Mark 1:9–11). (The parallels
are instructive. In view of their infancy narratives, both
Matthew and Luke have a concept of Jesus as Son of God
from birth. Therefore in Matthew the function of the baptism
has been shunted into an entirely new direction, and in Luke
it has been reduced almost to an aside. John, who thinks of
Christ as Son from all eternity, omits the story of the
baptism.) An alternative tradition in the same line is that of
the transfiguration (Mark 9:2–10 and parallels, lacking in
John).

Scholars will agree that it is not strictly correct to term this
early Son of God christology "adoptionist," though for coven-
ience's sake most of them do so. Adoptionism was a much
later Christian heresy, which attempted to limit and cir-
cumscribe Jesus' relation to the divine solely in terms of an
adoptive sonship. Such is not the intent of these early formulations, which had not set themselves up in any competition
with other christologies. All they intended to do was to define
a functional christology of Jesus as Son of God. In other
words, they understood him to be one designated by God
through and for an exercise of divine power analogous to the
designation that had been made of the king as Son of God on
his enthronement, whence the frequent citation of Psalm 2:7
in this connection. This kind of divine sonship does need to

be distinguished from the other kinds that the New Testament has also attributed to Christ.

Because of the flexibility of the Son of God concept in the world of early Christianity, Jewish and Gentile, however, we doubt very much that it is or ever was possible to define a straight and unequivocal line of evolution on which the notion of sonship moved from an "adoptive" or "functional" alpha point to reach an omega point where it became "metaphysical." The variety of ways which Paul could count to call Christ or another person Son of God, in other words, from an almost nominal courtesy title through any number of intermediate stages to an utterly literal affirmation of deity, could also be counted by the first christological formulators; and their efforts, which we have inherited in the New Testament canon, are in all likelihood the mixed bag of multiple and parallel traditions rather than the residue of a single development. For the same reasons, we must reckon with the possibility that Jesus in his historical lifetime was known—and perhaps knew himself, at least in equivalencies—to be Son of God in all the ways then imaginable.

Variations on "Son of God"

In the New Testament Son of God was a Semitism no less than Son of Man, though it was one much more readily understandable and assimilable in a heathen society in which there were many gods and therefore had to be many sons of gods. In fact, and paradoxical though it may seem, the very prevalence of sons of God among the Gentiles undoubtedly made it easier for Judaism and Christianity to speak of a Son of God. Sons of God as a class of beings in relation to God, quite in the Gentile sense of a theogonic order surrounding the High God, appear in Old Testament myth and poetry with some frequency (Genesis 6:2, Deuteronomy 32:8, Psalm 29:1, Job 1:6, etc.), sometimes in translated form to adjust them to monotheistic sensibilities, sometimes in their pristine character when orthodoxy created no serious issue. No Jew of New Testament times would have wanted to read these references in his Bible in other than a diluted and redirected signification—and they have not affected christology—precisely because their original one would put them in the uncomfortable company of the Gentile myths that were an affront to his monotheism. Correspondingly, when for other motives and out of the impact of certain experiences he felt himself compelled to review the understanding of God he had entertained to this point, and Son of God crystallized the terms of his review, he was not likely, or at least he was not likely for long, to employ the title in any casual reserve but rather to endow it with exclusivism and unicity. Arguing in parallel: The Old Testament knew another class of beings who stood in relation to God and whom it called God's sons, obviously in an adoptive sense, the same sense in which it also called them God's people. "They shall be called sons of the living God" (Hosea 2:1); so also Paul of Israel in Romans 9:26. Neither in this sense, however, did it ever become normal to think of any individual Israelite or Jew as God's son. The suffering just man of Wisdom 2:13—who in any case is a type rather than a single person—is styled Son of God, we have seen, probably as an equivalent of the Hellenistic *theios aner*. By and large, this instance notwithstanding, a multiplicity of sons of God in the surrounding ambient seems to have constituted the Son of God an increasingly distinct figure.

The same tendency must account for the fact that Son of God was never a conventional Jewish title for the Messiah, despite the foundation that had been laid for it in passages like 2 Samuel 7:14 and Psalm 2:7. Citing these scriptural verses, Jewish authors could refer to Messiah as Son of God, but there is no evidence—aside from a problematical line from Qumran—that in pre-Christian times the expression ever became an independent messianic title. (Alleged instances appearing with our old friends the Similitudes of Enoch and 4 Ezra are either interpolations or mistranslations.) This avoidance was no doubt studied, proof of Judaism's desire that there be no misunderstandings. In keeping with the fact that only by undergoing transformation did the Messiah become the Christ of the New Testament, we are doubtless not to

look for any messianic origin of Jesus' being named Son of
God.

It is true that by the time the various traditions reached
the written gospels Son of God had become, among other
things, a messianic title, relating to Christ in its titular sense,
including the note of Davidic ancestry and the rest. This
much is evident from the cries of the demons seeking to
break the messianic secret, the stories of the temptations
placed under the rubric of divine sonship, and countless
other associations and identifications. We may be sure, however, that this messianism is Christian and not Jewish. Titles
that derived from diverse backgrounds have been freely combined in the person of the Christ of the church's preaching,
sometimes on the basis of a genuine relevance—Son of God
could just as easily, had the circumstances been different,
have developed into a surrogate for the Jewish Messiah—but
also sometimes quite nominally and casually. Matthew
16:13–16, which has Jesus ask about his repute among the
people as Son of Man (the parallels in Luke and Mark say
only "me"), likewise has Peter join to his confession of the
Christ the title Son of God (omitted in the parallels).
"Beyond doubt you are the Son of God!" the disciples profess
according to Matthew 14:33, but the parallel in Mark speaks
only of unbelief and lack of comprehension. Mark 14:61
followed by Matthew 26:63 makes the high priest combine
Son of God with Christ in his interrogation about the identity
of Jesus, but Luke does not repeat the combination. Jesus is
sneered at for having claimed to be Christ and Son of God in
Matthew 27:40, but only the word Christ turns up in the
Marcan and Lucan parallels. There are many other examples.

Miracles

One recurring theme in a preponderant number of the instances in which Son of God has been made synonymous with
or taken the place of the Christ name is that of the working
of wonders; thus in the demonic cries, the temptations, Jesus'
stilling of the waters, the allegation that he had boasted of a

power to rebuild the temple in three days, and so on. In light of this it is difficult to resist the suggestion that here again we have to do with the influence of the Hellenistic idea of the *theios aner*.

That Jesus was known as a worker of miracles is inescapably a part of the gospel kerygma: "a man attested to you by God with mighty works and wonders and signs." The critics of the old rationalistic "quest" of the historical Jesus who thought it possible to pare away the miraculous elements in the gospels, leaving behind a residue of authentic fact about a Galilean teacher, were victims of a faulty historical method, we now know. They considered miracles to be simply the discardable baggage carried along by the gospels in their passage through a superstitious age, and once they had typed them in relation to other stories about other contemporary men, they felt they had done with them. But even though we grant the parallels between the career of Jesus and that of an ascetic and reputed wonder-worker like Apollonius of Tyana, and concede, as we have just done, that the title and image under which a Hellenist Jew or Gentile contemplated the latter has partly determined the christological conceptuology of the New Testament, we have not thereby resolved the question of the miracles of the kerygmatic Christ. The miracle stories of the gospel are not a luxury, an additum to the portrayal of Jesus indulged by an imaginative Christian legend, which in a world informed by science and reason would have been rejected as the result of naïve exuberance and enthusiasm. They are not presented as credentials so that Jesus might be qualified in any character that he did not already possess in the kerygmatic history that proclaimed him. They are represented as signs of the eschatological message of the kingdom of God that Jesus brought, a message that defines his place in history, and failing which he does not really exist as an historical personage. More, as H. van der Loos has correctly observed, they are a functional part of the kingdom as Jesus preached it, integral to its salutary effects. We cannot choose between a Jesus of history without miracles and a Christ of faith with them. If there is a Jesus at all, if there ever was a Jesus conformable to the criteria by which anyone's place in history can be assured, he is only the Jesus who inaugurated God's kingdom both by wonder deeds and wonder words.

To agree to such a proposition is not, of course, to agree that the summation of historical faith lies on the surface of an uninterpreted gospel. We may not lightly or glibly put our hand in the hand of the man who walked on water, or quieted the sea. To do so is to court an obvious peril; the peril is obvious if belief comes to us with so little effort and thus betrays a shallow creed undiscriminating in content. We are then confounding, or running the risk of confounding by caring not over much whether we confound or not, symbol with reality and shadow with substance. Simply because miracles are affirmed by the gospel, the miracle stories are not thereby put all on a single plane; neither are we dispensed from submitting them like all the gospel stories to critical evaluation. A critical evaluation of the miracle stories demands, first of all, that we take them on their individual merits. Those merits involve, among other things, the proximity of the stories to the heart of the gospel message, or alternatively their marginal character in relation to it, therefore their exact historico-literary qualities, as well as the amount of attached presuppositions that may be subject to translation or discard. We have already briefly touched on this matter in our Introduction.

It is not within the scope of this book to investigate all of the miracle stories of the gospels, or even, as far as that goes, to pass final judgment on the historicity of any single one of them. For our understanding of this particle of New Testament christology it suffices that we recognize the extent to which Jesus was held by his contemporaries to have been a worker of miracles, and we need not enter into either a defense or an apology for their viewpoint nor seek to convert it to another. Nevertheless, some observations are called for concerning the literary form of some of the stories in order to assess properly Jesus' repute as Son of God; it is not so much a question of establishing historical credibility as it is of defining the sense of an historical belief.

To begin with, the so-called nature miracles do not, gener-

ally speaking, have the immediate connection with the gospel
kerygma that is proper to the miracles of healing. Some modern New Testament scholars will challenge this judgment,
pointing out that the distinction has been drawn by later critics and not by the New Testament authors, to whom presumably all miracles were as one. We believe, however, that the
distinction is quite valid, even though critics of the past may
have sometimes used it uncritically. The two kinds of miracle
story do spring from different motivations; or perhaps it
would be more accurate to say that one motivation fits the
nature miracles as a rule and another fits the healing miracles
as a rule, with exceptions notable on both sides and with the
added complication that the motivations may have become
mingled occasionally in the transmission of the gospel traditions. Some of the nature miracles, at least with the nuances
they may have taken on by their equation with the other miracles of Jesus, certainly have been related to the proclamation of the kingdom of God. The "elements of the world"
of which Paul wrote (Galatians 4:3.9), to which man is
enslaved but from which the Christ-event has saved him
(Colossians 2:8.20), and which are sometimes personified
as demonic powers (Colossians 2:15, etc.), form the backdrop for an interpretation of some of the nature miracles that
would reduce them more or less to exorcisms. But on the
other hand, the main thrust of the nature miracles appears to
be the apotheosis of power itself rather than of salutary
power. That was exactly the thrust of the many myths of
Canaan and Mesopotamia that celebrated the dominance and
triumph of the active God over the (divinized and rival)
forces of sea or river or land, which entered the Old Testament as so many poetic and exotic motifs praising the
might of a *pantokrator*. "Was it not you who crushed
Rahab?" asked the prophet. "You who pierced the dragon?
Was it not you who dried up the sea, the waters of the great
deep?" (Isaiah 50:9b–10a–here, too, the myth has been accommodated to the salvation history of Israel.) We have the
suspicion, at least, that one who had for a distinct set of
reasons acquired the renown of a worker of wonders of
healing rather easily attracted to himself the attribution of

other marvels that had long floated in the stream of Near Eastern poetry and legend. The working of legend is, of course, inevitable in the life that is told of any person who has widely captivated the popular imagination and whose fame, for that reason, we are wont to describe as legendary. The legend is not, usually, without all foundation, and often it is a sure index to character, since legends, as we have continually pointed out, do not collect about a colorless individual; but for all that, it is legend and must be read as such. One instance of a miracle story that could have grown from a true incident in the life of Jesus is the account of the blasting of the fig tree (Mark 11:12–14 with parallel in Matthew), with its obvious relation to the parable of the fig tree preserved by Luke 13:6–9.

Legend has undoubtedly affected the tradition of the healing miracles as well. For example, the story of the raising of the widow's son in Luke 7:11–16 has been closely modeled on, if not entirely inspired by, the story of the raising of the widow's son by Elijah told in 1 Kings 17:17–24. Not precisely legend but, from our coign of vantage at least, time-conditioned and time-limited constructs have likewise played their part in the formation of the gospel's wonder stories and can get in the way of our accepting them with proper seriousness. We are inclined to equate the exorcisms with the healing miracles, because of our presuppositions, in a rather inverse way to that in which the gospel sources, because of their presuppositions, would have made the equation. Sometimes the path is laid open by the story itself to allow the presuppositions to meld without difficulty. Mark 9:14–29 describes the exorcism of a "mute and deaf spirit" responsible for a condition that a modern clinical eye would not hesitate to define as epilepsy. The parallel in Matthew 17:14–21, while also ascribing the affliction to "a demon" (Luke 9:37–43a has "an unclean spirit"), characterizes the victim of the piece as moonstruck ("lunatic": which in Matthew 4:24 is set alongside "the possessed" and "the paralyzed"). The time is past, in most of the world at least, when mental and physical illness could be lumped together with spirit possession, and the last be made the shorthand reference to embrace all kinds of affliction, even though that time is not too long past, and it certainly long outlived the New Testament. The degree to which the presuppositions merely inhabit the surface, and therefore can be exchanged for others, or instead have penetrated into the fabric of a story and determined its essential content, obviously requires of us the same critical judgment of the exorcisms that we bring to the other miracles ascribed to Jesus.

The Manifested Son of God

We recapitulate. At various times, including his own historical lifetime but more likely in view of the salvific experiences that were begun with the resurrection, Jesus became the designated Son of God. This designation of functional sonship has been variously attributed by some New Testament authors to one or another episode in Jesus' career, when, it has been assumed, he would have become conscious of a vocation that he had not previously recognized. We cannot exclude the possibility of such happenings, but neither can we take it into serious historical account, since the sources with which we have to reckon do not really allow us to postulate a development in what used to be called the messianic consciousness of Jesus. Because of the kerygmatic nature of the gospel traditions, from first to last the Christ that they portray is one and the same, needing no warrant to call him to any higher destiny than the one he knew he already had. Perhaps, as we shall see in a moment, this kerygmatic fast also presupposes a fact of historical psychology; in any event, it has frustrated all attempts to define convincingly the pivotal occasions that the hypothesis of development demands. We are on much safer ground when we recognize this designated sonship to have been a revelation to the church, connected with various aspects of Christ's life in history or in exaltation, but always contingent on the resurrection: "We ourselves announce to you the good news that what God promised our fathers he has fulfilled for us, their children, in raising up Jesus, according to what is written in the second psalm, 'You are my son;

this day I have begotten you'" (Acts 13:32f.). During his lifetime probably, and certainly in the kerygma, Jesus was also known as Son of God or by equivalent titles because of his wonder deeds, which manifested the power of God coming in his kingdom.

We intend now to turn to another kind of sonship that the New Testament ascribes to Jesus and that likewise is based in his own experience and consciousness; but before we do, certain additional remarks are in order. The nonprofessional theologian or student of the Scripture and, for that matter, some professional theologians as well, may be inclined to value the sonship of which we are about to speak as the only "real" one, in comparison with which the others of which we have spoken are figurative and metaphorical. This, however, would be to misunderstand the New Testament in a very important respect. When the biblical authors name Jesus Son of God, they always mean what they say most literally. It is not that one form of sonship is greater or less than another, but only that it is differently asserted. Furthermore, as we have already suggested, it would be a mistake to regard the functional sonship with which we have been dealing as a provisional level of christology from which the church graduated into a higher conception of Christ's relation to God. On the contrary, the theology of adoptive or functional sonship continued throughout New Testament times to protect the truth it had first asserted, namely that the work of salvation was one of grace and not of nature, God's alone, that Christ was Savior not in virtue of the "flesh" but of the "spirit." We have observed the doctrine in Romans 1:3f. It remains for us to confirm it from the analysis of two other hymnic fragments which, though they do not use the title of Son of God, surely point to the same idea.

First, a passage from the third chapter of 1 Peter, where Christian suffering is explained in the light of Christ

18   [who] once died[1] for sins,
      the just for the unjust,
      that he might lead us[2] to God,
      having been put to death in the flesh,
      but brought to life in the spirit,

19 in which he also [. . .] preached to the spirits in
      prison.[3]
20 Who is at the right hand of God,
      having gone to heaven,
      being made subject to him
      angels and rulers and powers.

(Three necessary notes: [1] The word *apethanen*, he died, is
preferred to *epathen*, he suffered, the latter almost equally
well attested by the manuscript evidence but also probably
intruded from 2:21. [2] The word *hymas*, you, is better
attested for the reading of the canonical text, but *hemas*, us,
is doubtless original to the hymn. [3] Brackets indicate what we
believe to be the preredactional state of the hymn. The major
redaction occurs in verses 20–21, where the canonical author has introduced an involved analogy concerning baptism,
probably influenced in part by the Enoch legend.)

As in the hymn of Philippians 2, the Savior is represented
as having suffered death in consequence of a life of service
for others. There may be here an allusion to the Servant of
the Lord motif, as there is not explicitly in Philippians, corresponding to the lack of any reference to pre-existence and de-
scent, which are featured in Philippians. But in both cases it
is Christ's activity in the realm of the spirit that counts: By
his resurrection and exaltation he has been made supreme
over all the cosmic powers. So also Philippians 2:10. The
added note of this passage is that he also "preached" to the
spirits, that is, that he proclaimed his triumph over them
where they were popularly thought to reside, in the lower
parts of the heavens (cf. Ephesians 2:2, 3:10, 6:12).

The same doctrine is professed by 1 Timothy 3:16, a poetic fragment that is explicitly cited as a credal utterance:

> Who was manifested in the flesh,
>   vindicated in the spirit,
> appeared to angels,
>   was preached among the nations,
> believed in the world,
>   taken up in glory.

This intriguing series of couplets has persuaded Joachim Jeremias to look for a model in the contemporary myth and ritual of royalty: the divinization of the king, his presentation (before the court of the gods), and his enthronement. The parallel may seem a bit contrived, but even to propose it is to encourage us to cast more than a cursory glance at the three dichotomies involved. In reverse order: first, the world and the state of glory. The two are distinguished but do not conflict one with the other: The Lord reigning over the church is also the Christ of the kerygma. Similarly, the preaching of Christ to the Gentiles is the natural corollary of his triumphal appearance before the cosmic powers (cf. Ephesians 3:8–11, where the apostolate to the nations is in sequence with the gospel proclaimed to the principalities and powers of heaven). And finally, the vindication in the spirit of him who first appeared in the flesh. Again this is not contradiction but complementarity; nevertheless, there can be no doubt about the exceedingly high price that the ancient christology represented in these lines attached to the action of God in Christ. It would be a total mistake to conclude that there developed a theology of "real" sonship that rendered obsolete or inadequate the kind of functional relationship we have been considering.

"Real" Sonship

Another caveat must be registered as we take up this "real" sonship. Strictly speaking, it cannot and ought not be studied apart from the New Testament affirmations of Christ's preexistence and his incarnation, and these we find it convenient to treat only in our next chapter. Therefore what we shall be offering at present is only a partial view of a much broader New Testament prospect, albeit an essential one and one that is often not taken into sufficient account by modern theologians. There is, on the other hand, a definite advantage in approaching the matter from this angle, since it enables us both to avoid and to correct in the balance the conclusions that some theologians are accustomed to draw from the *a priori* of the incarnation and that New Testament scholars find difficult or impossible to square with the biblical evidence.

Catholic theology in particular has inherited from the Middle Ages a theory of knowledge that theologians then felt had to be postulated of the man Jesus in virtue of the incarnation, in virtue of their concept of the perfection of the humanity that must have been the possession of the One in whom divine and human natures were united. It was never anything so crude as the assumption that since Jesus was God and Son of God he therefore knew all things: No orthodox theology has ever denied that Jesus was truly man and that as man he could not think with divine knowledge. Rather, it was assumed that because of this intimate union of natures in Christ and demanded by it, there had been communicated to his human intellect knowledge like that of the blessed who are also in union with God, knowledge of God as he truly is and thus of all things as they truly are. "Christ as man through his human awareness and beatific knowledge clearly understands and certainly judges himself to be God's natural Son and true God." The theorem is Bernard Lonergan's, and he admits that without the postulate of the extraordinary knowledge communicated to Jesus it would be a false theorem.

This theory of knowledge is unknown to the Bible, which fact, of course, does not of itself render it an invalid theory. Not only the theory, however, but other aspects of this kind of theology make the biblical scholar uncomfortable. It seems too speculative by half, too disposed to decide what must be—a mental construct—on the basis of an analysis, and some would say a one-sided analysis, of a mystery, a paradox, which was by definition unique in human experience and therefore is outside the control of experience. From the biblical standpoint it also starts at the wrong end, determining what must have been the personality of Christ in light of its conception of God whose Son he was rather than defining God as he is in light of his being made manifest in Christ. It does not, a biblist suspects, share full faith and allegiance with those New Testament authors who likewise believed in Christ's pre-existence and incarnation but who nevertheless knew that "he emptied himself" (Philippians 2:7) and "was tempted in every way that we are, yet never sinned" (Hebrews 4:15). And it appears to take no real cognizance of the difference between the historical Jesus and the exalted Christ of which the New Testament makes such a point.

To say that Jesus in his earthly life knew and judged himself to be God's natural Son and very God is to assert the unprovable and, from the perspective of the New Testament, the improbable. Had Jesus known such a thing he could hardly have contained his knowledge, yet the gospels are witness that his most intimate disciples did not recognize his essential relation to God prior to the resurrection. The gospels, for all their other claims about Jesus, never hide but rather insist on his character both as a man and as a man of his age, with the limitations dictated by his human and his temporal condition. For this precise reason it is quaint and naïve to expect of them an answer to the anachronistic question: Did Jesus know he was God? Raymond E. Brown has said it very well:

From a biblical viewpoint this question is so badly phrased that it cannot be answered and should not be posed. The New Testament does call Jesus "God," but this is a development of the later New Testament books. In the gospels Jesus never uses the title "God" of himself; indeed in Mark 10:18 (a text that is almost certainly a genuine saying of Jesus) he refuses to be given a mark of respect that belongs to God alone. There are many passages in the New Testament writings that distinguish between God and Jesus. We do not mean that such passages prove that Jesus was not God; rather they reflect the terminological problem in the question that we are asking. For the Jew "God" meant God the Father in heaven; and to apply this term to Jesus who was not the Father and who had come down to earth made no sense. Later, precisely under the necessity of giving proper honor to Jesus, especially in the liturgy, it was understood that "God" was a broader term that could include both the Father and Jesus. This designation became more frequent for Jesus in the last third of the first century, as far as our evidence permits us to determine. Therefore, when we ask whether during his ministry Jesus, a Palestinian Jew, knew that he was God, we are asking whether he identified himself and the Father—and, of course, he did not.

We would add only that the circumstances under which "God" became a more inclusive and acceptable title for Jesus owe a great deal to the translation of the gospel message into the language and thought of Hellenism.

The way of knowledge, therefore, as affording an index to Jesus' recognition of his identity in relation to God, leads down to a cul-de-sac, as far as the New Testament evidence is concerned. Brown has perceptively indicated another way, however, in which the gospel traditions can be of definite help to him who would discover an implicit christology of divine sonship in the sayings and actions of Christ. That is the way of psychological awareness, the consciousness that a person has of his own being to the extent that he lives and does, and because of which he acts and speaks thus and not so.

Jesus' Awareness: Father

In adopting this approach as a potentially fruitful one for obtaining some insight into how Jesus perceived himself, we find it both convenient and philosophically sound to accept the definition which Lonergan attaches to consciousness in the psychology of man. Man's awareness, according to Lonergan, is simply the sum of his experience; the reality that his consciousness embraces is neither the examined nor the intellectualized nor the evaluated but only the experienced. All the other processes to which man can submit himself in the quest of his identity—introspection, comparison, and judgment, the Greek injunction of *gnothi seauton,* "know thyself"—obviously presuppose self-awareness and are consequent on it, but they also deal with the ego under their own specifications and formalities, which are not those of consciousness. It follows that self-awareness, which comes about through the experience of one's own actions, is a quite different thing from the ability to define either the self or the nature of its actions. Yet it is the consciousness of man, and that alone, that causes him to identify the "me" of his experience, and therefore, through his resultant conduct, to expose for the judgment of others even if not for his own the "what" as well as the "who" of the "me" that has been experienced. This kind of conscious but unreflected self-revelation we have reason to believe can be extracted from the gospel traditions concerning what Jesus said and did, despite the fact that his overt mission was to preach not himself but rather God and his kingdom. And, as we have already observed, Jesus' self-awareness, consciousness, recognition of himself, seems to have been pretty much the same from first to last throughout his entire historical career.

If Jesus was conscious of some "natural" or "metaphysical" relation to God—the choice of adjectives depends more on the theologian's literacy than on his theology—in what ways did he manifest it? Let us start first with a few of his words. Joachim Jeremias has invited ridicule from right and left by his insistence that the most certain *ipsissima verba* recoverable from the utterances of Jesus are his *Abba* in speaking to God the Father and his *amen* in certifying his own statements. Those who on the one side are unaware of or who feel they can scout the critical problems that stand in the way when we would restore the original speech of Jesus have been eloquent in their disparagement of this apparent minimalism, the *ridiculus mus* born of a mountain of scholarly labor. On the other side are those who suspect that even two words are an optimistic assessment of what might be expected from the attempt to get at a language that has passed through so many translations and reconstitutions, and that even these words, if they are authentic, do not carry the significance Jeremias sees in them. Nevertheless, we incline to agree with Jeremias against his opponents on both sides. To say that these or other "words" are to be ascribed to the historical Jesus is not, of course, merely what we have been presuming all along, namely that this or that saying can with likelihood be traced back in its substance to a real situation in the life of Jesus of Nazareth. We are now talking about words, about language in its precise sense, which distinguishes one man from another and by which a man reveals himself, knowingly or not, as he discovers himself in his own consciousness.

Abba occurs three times in the New Testament: twice used by Paul, evidently echoing a liturgical formula in which the Christian, moved by the spirit, "cries" to God as Father (Galatians 4:6, Romans 8:15), and once put on the lips of Jesus in Gethsemani (Mark 14:36). In all three cases it is a title employed in prayer. Jeremias' argument is that it was first the distinctive title that Jesus thought right and natural to use in addressing God the Father, and that it then became, in imitation of Jesus and at his urging, the title by which the earliest Aramaic-speaking Christian community was emboldened to call upon his and their God. The force of the argument lies, first of all, in the comparative rarity of "Father" as a title by which God was addressed in first-century Palestine; from this standpoint alone, early Christianity with its "Our Father" for its habitual prayer stands in contrast with contemporary Judaism. It is not, of course, that Palestinian Jews did not look upon God as their Father and call him that, but only that, out of reverence, to avoid anthropomorphism or misunderstanding (as in the use of "Son of God"), or for other reasons, they did not address him as such. Jeremias concludes flatly that "there is as yet no evidence in the literature of ancient Palestinian Judaism that 'my Father' is used as a personal address to God." The gospels, to the contrary, hardly indicate of Jesus any other address. And within this context *Abba* is a term apart. It means not merely "my Father" but something like "dear Father," a word connoting the utmost intimacy. It was borrowed from the child-chatter of the family, which results in endearments practically the same in all languages: *imma, abba,* mama, papa. *Abba* was, as we might readily expect, a very common saying in the households of Aramaic-speaking Palestine, but it was not, as far as we know, a part of the speech of any other Jew when praying to his God.

What this adds up to, then, is that Jesus experienced and acted on the experience of a familiarity with God that was his alone and to which other men of his time did not lay claim. Jeremias would like to speculate about the time and circumstances of Jesus' first becoming aware of this relationship—his baptism, perhaps, which Mark at least leaves open to such an interpretation—but we have already contended the fruitlessness of that or a like pursuit. To be sure, since Jesus was not only willing but anxious to share with all his disciples the distinct sonship with God of which he was aware (and his willingness and anxiety, of course, in this respect are integral to his being Son of God in the New Testament sense), there is no question that he had contemplated an ontological distinction that would separate himself from other men. We are reminded that we move in the area of awareness, not of reflex knowledge.

We come to the same conclusions when we examine some of those sayings of Jesus whose authenticity is little in doubt, in which he places himself in a filial relationship to God. One of these is the Q saying of Matthew 11:27=Luke 10:22, "the Johannine meteorite fallen on the Synoptic earth," once so called because it was thought to encapsulate Johannine christology, which, in fact, it does strongly resemble on the surface. As Jeremias reconstructs the saying it is not Johannine at all but rather a Semitic proverb that Jesus quoted and applied to himself in relation to God the Father. He would have said simply

> no one knows the son but the father,
> no one knows the father but the son,

meaning, obviously, that there is a family intimacy between father and son—any father and son—that outsiders cannot be expected to share. He would not, therefore, have been calling himself "the Son" in the absolute Johannine sense (though the evangelists, by the time the saying reached them, undoubtedly took the words in this sense), but he would nevertheless have been assuming for himself a condition unique in the human character, applying the proverb to himself as he

would have applied it to no one else and as it would have occurred to no one else to apply it to himself. In Jeremias'
reconstruction the passage becomes much more believable as
a genuine saying of Jesus without losing any of its force for
the christology implicit in his awareness.

A somewhat different judgment has to be rendered about
another text. In Mark 13:32=Matthew 24:36 (omission in
Luke) Jesus says, in reference to the end of this world
and/or the coming of the kingdom of God of which he has
been speaking, that "as to the exact day or hour, no one
knows it, neither the angels in heaven nor even the Son, but
only the Father." Most critics, persuaded that the church
would not willingly invent a saying of Jesus in which he admitted to ignorance in so important a matter, have long held
that it must rather be his, a true recollection of something he
had once said. (Jan Lambrecht, who is one recent scholar to
have submitted Mark 13 to a meticulous redaction-critical
analysis, makes this verse out to be Mark's own composition,
though he concedes the possibility that the substance of its
thought may be Christ's.) Here again, of course, we are
confronted by the problem of an absolute use of "the Son,"
which we do not expect in a saying earlier than the Hellenist
phase of the church (or which, if Mark's, we do not expect to
find coupled with a limitation placed on the knowledge of the
Son). As a matter of fact, "nor even the Son" is lacking in
some of the manuscript evidence and other witness to the
original state of the saying (the textual lacuna is negligible in
regard to Mark's gospel but noticeable in regard to Matthew's), and this fact has led some observers to decide
that it was not there in the beginning but later became a
scribal afterthought, possibly to smooth over the seemingly
erroneous short-range predictions ascribed to Jesus elsewhere
in the gospels (Matthew 10:23, for example). If "the Son" is
an original part of the saying, and if the saying is indeed integrally Jesus', then we must contend with an explicit claim
that Jesus made to an exclusive divine sonship. Even if "the
Son" must go, however, we are still left with an implicit
claim to an exclusive divine intimacy, of one who presumed
to pronounce on what was reserved to his Father alone.

Jesus' Awareness: Amen

This serenity, confidence, feeling at ease in a jurisdiction commonly thought to be divine, is also the christological note that Jeremias extracts from the language of Jesus in his saying *amen*. His argument:

> It has been pointed out almost *ad nauseam* that a new use of the word *amen* emerges in the four gospels which is without analogy in the whole of Jewish literature and in the rest of the New Testament. Whereas according to idiomatic Jewish usage the word *amen* is used to affirm, endorse, or appropriate the words of another person, in the tradition of the sayings of Jesus it is used without exception to introduce and endorse Jesus' own words.

The tradition varies: in the Fourth Gospel there is always a double *amen* (a liturgical embellishment?) and in the Synoptic tradition it is single, but it is always constant and consistent—thirteen instances in Mark, thirty in Matthew, six in Luke, and twenty-five in John. The thirteen instances in Mark all show signs of being primitive pronouncements closely connected with Jesus' eschatological preaching: on the forgiveness of sins (3:28f.), on his refusal to give a sign (8:12), on the imminence of the kingdom (9:1), on the cup of fresh water (9:41, cf. the great scene in Matthew 25:31–46), on the childlike in relation to the kingdom (10:15), on what must be given up for the kingdom (10:29), on the power of faith (11:23), on what it means to give one's all (12:43), on the imminence of the kingdom again (13:30), on the meaning of a present act in reference to the kingdom to come (14:9, cf. 9:41), on his betrayal (14:18), his abstinence in favor of the kingdom (14:25), and his denial (14:30). Thus Jeremias continues:

> So we have a completely new manner of speaking, strictly limited to the gospels and here again limited to the sayings of Jesus. Here the *amen* serves to replace oath-like formu-

lae, of asseveration which Jesus forbids in Matthew 5:33–37 because they are a misuse of the divine name; it is even more likely that the formula *amen* should be seen as an alternative to the authoritative prophetic formula "Thus says the Lord," which avoids using the divine name.

We have already considered, and discarded as inappropriate, the category of "prophetic" to qualify the kind of self-awareness Jesus manifested in word and deed. Though Jesus may have thought of himself in the character of prophet more readily than in any other, and though an early christology rightly recognized him to be the Prophet of God's kingdom, we have agreed with Käsemann that what he said and did set him apart from any other prophet imagined by Israel. What set him apart, which he obviously sensed even if he never articulated it, became the subject of the church's contemplation after the resurrection and through the experience of his living Spirit, and this led to the avowal of yet another title by which he could be acclaimed Son of God and—eventually—God himself.

We stated before that the New Testament concepts of pre-existence and incarnation are integral to this discussion of Christ's divine sonship and divinity, but we also noted the advantage gained in prescinding from them for a time. The advantage is not merely for sound theology by avoiding unwarranted apriorisms, but also to the better understanding of the process of New Testament theology. The church did not develop a doctrine of Christ's divinity based on its belief in his pre-existence and incarnation. Rather, pre-existence and incarnation became the models—and not the only models—in which the church framed its faith in a divine Christ. The Synoptic gospels are innocent of the notion of pre-existence and even, in either the Pauline or the Johannine acceptations, of the notion of incarnation; but they share together with Paul, John, Hebrews, and others a belief in a divine sonship that was unique to Christ, that made it right for him alone among men to be accorded even divine titles (Mark 12:35–37, etc.). It remained, which is to say it never had the intention of outgrowing, a functional sonship, in the sense that it affirmed that he was Son, God, Lord, primarily as he was Savior. But it was not, even from the beginning, purely functional: This christology was concerned with saying what Christ was and is as well as what he did or what God had done in him. Indeed, it would be hard to think it otherwise. Had the church evinced no interest in the nature and being of him whose activity had called it to life, it would have achieved something of a record in the annals of human incuriosity. The "biblical mentality" that is supposed to account for such phenomena is more often than not instead a biblicist mentality that will have them so on principle. We think we have seen enough in the course of this book to indicate the New Testament's interest in Jesus in his own right, and we think that the doctrine of divine sonship was an early expression of this interest.

It would doubtless be naïve to project a development of this doctrine simply out of the church's reflection on the words of Jesus, including the words we have cited above, even though their preservation shows that they were important in the church's reflection. Neither did it come about from some painstaking scrutiny of the acts and sayings of the historical Jesus that the church searched for deeper significance under the direction of the Spirit. No doubt the doctrine, once it had developed, shed additional light on all these events, but they did not create the doctrine. The doctrine was already in vigor while the gospel traditions were being collected, shaped, reformed, and rethought. What created the doctrine, before any gospel was ever written and before the epistles that drew from the taproots of the church's first hymnody, was the experience of the resurrection. In this sense as well as in the others we have spoken of before, Christ was proclaimed Son of God by resurrection. Here too, the resurrection authenticates and exercises a retroactive power.

Resurrectional Retroactivity

Authentication, as Wolfhart Pannenberg reminds us, is a juridical term and not an ontological one. We understand how a law or an ordinance may be given retroactive force by a subsequent decision, but we do not so readily comprehend how a later event can change or even affect a previous fact. If the church intended to affirm somehow Jesus' natural sonship with God—to say, therefore, that it was his nature to be divine—then it must have believed, to be consistent, that he was always Son of God. The resurrection could elucidate this prior fact, make it recognizable to those who had not perceived it before, even cast it into an entirely new dimension for them; but it could not cause to be in the past something that as yet had not been. The New Testament authors, or at least some of them, seem to have gone along with this line of thinking; so we may judge from the idea of the divine preexistence of Christ, which is the corollary of so much of the theology of his sonship. These considerations notwithstanding, however, we must not forget those clear and definite assertions of the New Testament concerning a real effect of the resurrection on the person of Christ, and we cannot permit any ontological presuppositions to rob them of meaning. We must therefore reconsider, and for some of us this probably means consider for the first time, what is the "nature" of which we have been speaking.

In the language of traditional piety, our ontology, like our physiology or cosmology or epistemology or logic even, is not "of faith." When we seek to better our understanding of concepts like "nature" and "person," we come to sit at the feet of the philosopher rather than the theologian. Ontology in the technical sense we do not expect of the New Testament, whose authors generally had neither competence nor concern in advocating one philosophical system over another. They did have ontological presuppositions, since man can hardly think without them, which were ultimately derived from philosophical speculation, just as the man on the average street of today has similar presuppositions to which he has rarely given much reflex attention, and which may or may not correspond with those of the New Testament authors. He who would accept New Testament faith as his own is obviously not obliged to theorize another ontology than the one he finds satisfactory, but just as obviously he has to recognize that his ontology may occasionally have to give way or adjust to make room for formulations that presuppose another ontology.

Jesus was, indeed, the natural Son of God in his earthly life and prior to the resurrection. This is a firm and sure New Testament statement, which was taken up by all the creeds of early Christianity. To deny it is to succumb to the heresy of Adoptionism, a tired and discredited route that leads nowhere and down which it would be folly to go again. It is in the same direction, really, as Jürgen Moltmann has incisively observed, that some modern theology moves when it supposes a complete discontinuity between the just man who suffered on the cross and the divine Lord who quite swallowed him up in the resurrection, between the historical Jesus and the kerygmatic Christ, in other words. Call it what one will, this is Docetism, equally unacceptable as gnostic myth in the first century or as existentialist myth in the twentieth. But Moltmann also warns against reducing the resurrection to a mere incident in the totality of the Christ-event, a divine gesture with no vitalizing power of its own. If the resurrection is only a verification of an historical life, we are left with the divinely approved radical rabbi beloved of liberal Protestantism, a later version of the ascetic, moralizing prophet of the venerable Ebionite heresy. And if, on the other hand, Jesus Christ the Lord is quite the same before and after the resurrection, with the resurrection itself reduced to a more or less dispensable protocol, then neither the abasement of the crucifixion nor the newness of the life in the Spirit can be taken at absolute face value, let alone the submission of the reigning Savior which is yet to come of which Paul speaks in 1 Corinthians 15:28. In such a case we have a species of Modalism, the heresy that removed all genuine distinctions in the godhead by diminishing its separate manifestations to a pure nominalism. To think of the resurrection as the demonstration of a triumph in which a dead God rose to life again "under his own power," as the elegant phrase has it, is worse than bad theology; it is not theology at all but a travesty of the Christian faith inspired neither by the gospels nor by the councils of the early church. It is, in fact, an unconscious imitation of the mystery religions of Attis or Mithras, which once pretended to guarantee man's salvation by asking him to assimilate an irrelevant myth.

We do not respond, therefore, to the problem of how Christ is one and true Son of God before and after the resurrection, yet with the resurrection effective as well as declaratory of his sonship, by mouthing traditional formulae in the presence of which the problem is supposed to vanish or the contrary data readjust themselves. "Nature" is indeed a venerable and valuable thought form, but it is not incantational. It means, in any age and among any people, only what has been granted to the wisdom of man to discover what it means. To an earlier mind conditioned to a static world in which everything had been fixed by decree, in its very creation, to be this or that, and in which, as a consequence, any change could only be for the worse, a deviation from the eternal law, "nature" obviously had to signify the absolutely constant, the once and for all, independent of time and of what time brings. To quote Pannenberg again, however,

There is, nevertheless, a way of thought which does not proceed from a timeless conception of being, which does not consider the essence of things to be what merely perdures through successive changes but rather what is vulnerable to the future: a future which is unpredictable and therefore irresistible. In this way of thought the future, therefore, determines what the nature of a thing is. The nature of a man or of a situation or even of the world itself cannot immediately be discovered simply from what is visible. Only the future will decide this—first must appear what the man or the world situation will be in the future. Thus it is no exception to the rule that the nature of Jesus should be determined retroactively by his resurrection, and that this determination is not only of our understanding but also of his being. Had Jesus not been raised it would then have been determined that he was not previously one with God. But on the contrary, through the resurrection it has been determined, not only for our understanding but for the fact itself, that Jesus is one with God, and retroactively, therefore, that he was also one with God before.

The Chalcedonian Formulations

If this way of thought seems initially strange to us when we apply it to the mystery of Christ, we should really wonder why. The world of static essences was the creation of Greek science in revolt against Greek myth, a necessary revolution in human thought but by no means the final revolution. The Fathers of the church were born into this world and made do with it, we shall see, rather sucessfully in responding to the questions put to them in the language of their times. Contrariwise, we still suffer from the wounds inflicted on the church's credibility by its so long stubborn refusal to join the Copernican revolution, which literally turned the universe upside down. We live now in the world created by another revolution in thought, a world in which names like Charles Darwin and Pierre Teilhard de Chardin figure among its prominent prophets, and in which the shaping power of the future on the present has been demonstrated in every area of existence. In *Future Shock* Alvin Toffler has spelled out some of the implications this "death of permanence" has for society, education, technology, science, and the rest, and he has issued eloquent warnings about the chances of survival for those whose mind-set dooms them to try to preserve a past that no longer exists and, indeed, by the verdict of the future probably never existed at all. In the opposite direction, as Teilhard de Chardin recalls it: "'Go quietly ahead with your scientific word without getting involved in philosophy or theology'—throughout my whole life that is the advice (and the warning) that authority will be found repeatedly to have given me." Advice, or warning, of that kind is obviously irrational, since it denies, or forgets, that all questions are ultimately philosophical and theological. Only a schizoid personality can be expected to inhabit simultaneously two different intellectual worlds. We do no more than assert the consistency and integrity of our God-thought, our theology, with the rest of our thought when we make room for a divine and human Christ in our world of fission and change, a world in which he ought to be quite as much at home as he was at home in other worlds now irretrievably gone.

Furthermore, we ought to point out that this notion of nature is not as much removed from traditional Christian ways of thinking as Pannenberg, and we too, perhaps, may be disposed to believe. Scholastic theologians also held that man is defined "man" in terms of the mature, fully-grown human being and not in terms of the infant. For Aquinas "nature" was that element of being that constitutes it in its possibilities of growth and development. As such, it could be defined only in view of its full actuation. Potency is defined by its corresponding act, and in this sense, therefore, the future is determinative of the present and the past, even ontologically.

What, then, of the so-called Chalcedonian formulation, the two-natures-in-one-person christology that since the fifth century has been the creed of orthodox Christianity? We think, first of all, that what we have been saying is not in opposition to this christology. Even more important, we think along with many present-day exegetes, theologians, and church historians that the formula of Chalcedon was both a necessary and an accurate recapitulation of New Testament faith in postbiblical categories, that we probably do not possess an adequate command of other categories to replace it with anything better, and that it therefore remains our protection and bulwark against alien christologies that are altogether undesirable, against the twin extremes of Nestorianism, which would split the person of Christ into two, and of Monophysitism, which would dissolve his humanity into nothing. This we can say despite the well-known philosophical objections to Chalcedon, which likewise contain their truth: "What formerly was called nature is now accepted as person; what formerly was defined as person is now regarded as nonexistent." And we say it with the warning clause that not all that fondly passes for the tradition of Chalcedon is so in fact. For example, not a little of the popular piety that has felt itself most threatened by contemporary theology and exegesis is not christological orthodoxy at all but rather Nestorianism or, more often, Monophysitism.

The Chalcedonian creed of A.D. 451 provisionally brought to a close more than two centuries of the church's wrestling with the ontic formulae of the New Testament—its statements about the being as well as the doing of God and Christ—in the attempt to solve the ontological problems they raised by applying to them terms borrowed from current philosophical categories that it found serviceable to reiterate the ancient faith in an acceptable and agreed language. Though this process had obviously not been undertaken by the New Testament itself, neither was it as foreign to the biblical mentality as it has sometimes been made out. Not only are preliminaries to it visible in the "early Catholicism" which, on the computation of those who name it so, accounts for a major part of the New Testament, like tendencies also appear in the period of the "pneumatic" Christian community. As A. T. Hanson has written of Paul: "He held at least a Binatarian theology, and, I would add, a Trinitarian theology in the making." The process, in any case, was a necessary outgrowth of the New Testament, a rationale of its problematic and none other, and a rationale that was required of the church if the gospel was to compete on even terms with other thought systems of the Greek-speaking world that also claimed to be liberating. The key code-words of the language of translation were: (1) *hypostatis* (literally, "what stands beneath"), which eventually, after many misunderstandings, came to be accepted as the equivalent of the Latin *persona*, the acting subject and center of attributions, the substance existing in the concrete; (2) *ousia* (literally, "being"), made equal to the Latin *substantia* (which *etymologically* is the same as *hypostasis*, hence the earlier confusions), the underlying reality, the essence, which makes a thing what it is and nothing else—whence the importance of calling Christ "consubstantial" (*homoousios*) with God the Father; and (3) *physis* or *natura*, which is simply what a thing or a person is. When Chalcedon confessed, therefore, that Jesus Christ the Lord is the same perfect in divinity and the same perfect in humanity, truly God, and the same truly man with a rational soul and body, consubstantial with the Father in respect to divinity, and the same consubstantial with us in respect to humanity, like to us in all things save sin . . . one and the same Christ, Son, Lord, Only-begotten, to be acknowledged as existing in two natures without confusion, without change, without division, without separation, the difference in natures being in no way removed through their union but rather the property of each nature being preserved and concurring in one person and one hypostasis, not parted or divided into two persons but one and the same Son, Only-begotten, God, Word, Lord Jesus Christ,

it was using every resource of its ideological arsenal to reaffirm the New Testament formulas, of course, but even more directly, since it was no longer sufficient simply to reaffirm, also to exclude every conceivable ambiguity by which the formulas could be made to say either too much or too little. Only one who prefers imprecision to exact speech, or who resents those who do like to mean what they say, will object to all these distinctions piled one atop the other. And, we repeat, we are probably incapable today of assembling a better vocabularly to draw the distinctions more finely. It should not be permitted us to glory in our incapacity, as though Chalcedon had done nothing worthwhile simply because we cannot equal it.

What Is Divine "Nature"?

Nevertheless, we have called the decisive language of Chalcedon code-words, for that is what they are. To take one example: There is no intrinsically sacred character to the word "person" that suited it to be the bearer of such awesome weight in the trinitarian and christological discussions of early Christianity. Originally it meant a face mask, the stylized façade worn by an actor in a drama to identify his role and mark him as either comic or tragic. And as we have just seen, "substance" was literally a translation of *hypostasis* rather than of *ousia*. The words were important only because they had come to have an agreed value as pointers to this or that reality, and for that reason alone they are still important. Far better philosophies of person, substance, and nature would be devised than that of the Fathers of Chalcedon—which, in fact, was a hazy philosophy at best, to the extent that it was one philosophy at all. Basic questions would be raised that had never occurred to them. To take one instance: What of the propriety of ascribing to God and man equally a "nature," as though this were a univocal predication? A later philosophy would recognize this objection and attempt to cope with it by positing an "analogy of being" between the divine and the human. An even later philosophy, we may be sure, might come up with an even better resolution of the problem. There is hardly a term in all the Chalcedonian formulations that is not susceptible to the improved insights that fifteen hundred years of human thought—with its vagaries as well as its limited triumphs, to be sure—have been able to focus upon it. Among them, certainly, as we have already observed, is the notion of nature as dynamic rather than static, as the laws of life later revealed themselves to men.

We have now arrived at our final consideration in this chapter, which still concerns nature, and, specifically, what we mean by divine nature. It was Immanuel Kant, building with some of the blocks shaped by René Descartes, who did the most to persuade modern thinkers of the invalidity and unreality of applying to God the natural laws and rules that man has discovered to be operative in his universe. The Kantian denial, however, as we said above, had been anticipated by the medieval theologians who sought to circumvent it by their "analogy of being." No true theologian, of course, ancient or modern, has ever claimed to be able to define God in human language. The five "ways" of Thomas Aquinas, which a rationalist apologetics later turned into "proofs" of God's existence, were rather, as Gerhard Ebeling put it, attempts to explain what the word "God" means. But how do we fill "God" with content; how do we decide the "nature" of God?

Karl Barth has said that the analogy of being is the "sure and infallible sign of the antichrist." Is this merely rhetoric, or does it tell us something about how we can and cannot know God?

Earlier in this chapter we wondered aloud whether we ask a proper question at all in inquiring whether Jesus was or is God. We can wonder, because such a question assumes that we already know who or what this "God" is with which Jesus may be identified, yet it has been the constant insistence of Christianity, beginning with the New Testament, that Christ is the ultimate revelation of God and that only in Christ can God be known as he truly is. Futhermore, the revelation of God in Christ was God's self-manifestation in the whole Christ-event, culminated in the resurrection, a circumstance that removes it from the sphere of Jesus' historical awareness while still leaving it within the sphere of his humanity. The question that is properly asked, therefore, is: Who or what is God as he has been revealed in the man Jesus Christ?

What we uncover here is the discrepancy between the God of biblical faith and the God of the philosophers; and the latter, as Blaise Pascal quite rightly said it, is no God of Christians. The New Testament does, of course, acknowledge that man left to himself will evolve some idea of what God must be—the kind of preconception that is necessary for any conception, to serve as its frame of reference—but it also warns about the inherent dangers in the process and how it can so easily get sidetracked into unhealthy byways (cf. Romans 1:18–32). From being merely otiose, what Paul sarcastically calls "the wisdom of man," ridiculing gnostic pretensions, becomes pernicious, because it speedily conflicts with the wisdom of the gospel. As A. Hulsbosch has put it, the God who has not revealed himself in man's history is both inaccessible to man and also irrelevant to him. Such is the biblical view of God, which holds that God must make the overtures if man is to know him truly and without confusion, and which for that reason and without arrogance speaks of the Gentiles as "those who do not know God."

The New Testament recognizes that God's overtures were begun in the Old Testament. (Had its horizons been broader, or its vision of them more sharply focused, it would have doubtless acknowledged other overtures to which in fact it had responded; but that is another matter.) The God of Israel's prophets, of Ezra and Pharisaical Judaism, he whom Jesus named Father, was the "frame of reference" for the revelation of God in Christ. But, as we have already seen, it was precisely this knowledge of God that precluded a simple and prior identification of Jesus in its terms, for Jesus is obviously not his Father. And so we return full circle: God, as the New Testament understands God, can be known only from an examination of the Christ-event. "Christ showed himself to be God" is the question-begging and really meaningless assertion. "Christ showed us who God is" is, on the contrary, the summation of New Testament revelation. How he showed us this was, in the only way possible for him, through his humanity.

We must accustom ourselves to a God, if we would have the God of the New Testament, who occasionally affronts our rationalism. This is easier said than done, since man is innately rationalistic and theology, which is the creation of man, has been tenaciously rationalistic from its inception. The primeval, greatest affront of all has been for God to reveal himself as man, to live, to suffer, to die—the God whom theology, left to itself, would define for us immortal, immaterial, infinite: the whole series of negations that it has extrapolated mainly by denying human existence. One might think that having accepted this fundamental assault on its autonomy, this real scandal to its integrity, the Christian mind could experience no further difficulties about recognizing its God as the man Jesus has made him known; yet in fact it boggles at almost every opportunity. One can only wonder whether the real scandal has been fully embraced and taken at its face value. What continually happens is that God as he must not be, the negative constructs of theology left to itself, comes into conflict with God as he certainly is revealed in Christ.

Let us not leave this subject with equivocations, however. The New Testament does not say that Christ revealed himself, but rather that he revealed God. It does not say that God has been revealed in man, but rather that he has been revealed in *the* man Jesus Christ. John A. T. Robinson has misread the New Testament evidence, therefore, when he defines God on its basis simply as man raised to the x power. Certainly Jesus never dreamed of such a revelation, nor did any of the New Testament authors. That Jesus was a "man for others" is incontestable, and incontestably he so revealed a work of God: "God in Christ was reconciling the world to himself" (2 Corinthians 5:19). But there is obviously more to the God- and Jesus-questions than this. "God is love" is testimony to an experience of God but not a definition of God, for "I have loved Jacob and hated Esau" (Romans 9:13). Just as Christ cannot be reduced to a function, neither can God in Christ. Although Robinson would not have it so, the New Testament did—eventually—name Jesus God as well as Son of God. How and why it did so we shall try to examine in the following chapter.

5. THE POWER AND THE WISDOM

The Wisdom Tradition

Since in God's wisdom the world did not come to know him through "wisdom," it pleased God to save those who believe through the absurdity of the preaching of the gospel. Yes, Jews demand "signs" and Greeks look for "wisdom," but we preach Christ crucified—a stumbling block to Jews, and an absurdity to Gentiles; but to those who are called, Jews and Greeks alike, Christ the power of God and the wisdom of God (1 Corinthians 1:21–24).

There seems to be no doubt that in appropriating to Christ the titles of Power (*dynamis*) and Wisdom (*sophia*), Paul was reacting against a tendency that later resulted in a Christian heresy, namely Gnosticism. Gnosticism assumed many forms and assimilated many myths, none of which was particularly important then and certainly not relevant thereafter, which had as its common denominator, however, the conviction that through *gnosis* (knowledge) or *sophia* (wisdom) was to be obtained the *dynamis* (power) by means of which the spirit could obtain salvation. The heresy was and is a real one; it still survives, plainly enough, in any conception of Christianity that permits one to think that an adherence to a catalogue of orthodox doctrines carefully spelled out in a recondite in-language is somehow the means to "saving one's soul." Paul, and the New Testament with him, insisted rather on a gospel that had to be accounted folly by any conventional wisdom; the only power he knew was the grace of God working in the gospel (Romans 1:16); and he declared the Christian body—not its "soul"—to be the temple of the Holy Spirit (1 Corinthians 6:15).

Paul was not shadow-boxing with some imaginary adversary. From passages like 1 Corinthians 2:5–9, 8:4–6, 10:1–14, and 2 Corinthians 4:4–6, it has been made evident to most scholars that he had found himself in conflict with a theology of redemption of a type that might later blossom into Gnosticism, and that he knew could not be a legitimate vehicle of the Christian message but only its implacable rival. In these texts he seems to be turning the language of gnosis against its own purposes, to discount its redeemer myth by forcing it instead to speak of the cross and resurrection. The cosmic and celestial powers that loomed with such prominence for the gnostically minded he reduces to feckless spectators or intruders upon the divine plan of salvation. Knowledge or wisdom itself he declares irrelevant unless it is to be reinterpreted as a deeper penetration into the ways of God that have been revealed in Christ. The "spiritual" understanding of Israel's sacred history, as allegorized by Alexandrian or Palestinian Judaism to fit the philosophy and *Zeitgeist* of the age, he rejects unless it can be made to typify Christ. All in all, he substitutes for the timeless, leisurely, esoteric, and elitist liberation of gnosis, or gnosticized Christianity, the catholic and eschatological doctrine of the cross, with its quick summons to hasty and irrevocable decision on the basis of "folly" and with the surety of disreputable companions in the bargain.

Paul is capable, however, of more kindly dealing with the speculation of wisdom than is warranted by the examples we have just cited. It is true that *philosophia*, a sacred word in Greece, occurs only once in the New Testament (in Colossians 2:8), and there pejoratively, but the incidence is not really significant. As we said in our preceding chapter, only when gnosis came into conflict with the gospel was it judged to be pernicious. Otherwise it might be considered otiose, but it might also be accepted occasionally for its positive contributions. Usually only indirectly and by means of more or less extensive redaction, Paul and other New Testament authors have consciously incorporated into their writings theological themes that were first put together within the wisdom tradition. Even more importantly, perhaps, they have assimilated from the basic gospel message as it had been thought upon in the churches of Palestinian and Hellenistic Judaism that preceded them christological data that were wisdom enunciations before they were anything else. In fact, it is scarcely too much to say that the oldest christology on which the New Testament has built, words and concepts alike, was the product of Jewish and Christian wisdom schools.

This last assertion should hardly surprise us, for wisdom was the natural home both in Old and New Testament times of the process that we now call theology—the process, that is, of rational reflection on the word of God and of its accommodation to the rest of man's experience. Until fairly recently biblical studies, taken up as they rightly were with the cardinal importance of *torah*, prophecy, and gospel in the religious history of Israel old and new, have inclined to minimize the function of wisdom in that history and to relegate it to the margins of the scriptural canon. Yet wisdom was never marginal. Its roots are as deep as any others in Israel; it was reacting to and being reacted upon by prophecy almost as soon as the first prophetic word had been uttered. When prophecy ceased for a while in Israel it was wisdom that filled the breach, asking the questions and supplying the answers that were needful for a faith that intended to survive in a world of new perplexities, new visions, and new gods. Wisdom, it seems to be agreed more and more, directed the development of prophetic eschatology into the apocalyptic lines that flowed into the thinking of Jesus and the early church. It is by no means an extraordinary thing, therefore, that wisdom should have leaped at the opportunity to grapple with the radically new happening that was associated with the name of Christ and to interpret it in language understood of both Jew and Gentile. This it had long done, and in doing it had accumulated a wealth of words and ideas. We can add to this the fact that the christology of which we are now speaking has been mostly transmitted through liturgical hymns. Not only had wisdom in the intertestamental period appropriated the liturgy to itself—the book of Sirach serves as an exemplification—it had also become the peculiar repository of the ancient Jewish thanksgiving hymn, the archetype of the christological homologies of which we have already spoken. (The Odes of Solomon, which are either a Christian adaptation of a Jewish work of the first or second century or a

Christian work to begin with, together with the Thanksgiving scroll discovered at Qumran, both of which are heavily "gnostic," document this last statement.)

Wisdom, we have been trying to say, was a permeating influence on the New Testament canon that cannot by any means be ignored. The myth of a lost wisdom once possessed by primeval man (cf. Ezekiel 28:3, Sirach 49:16) and forfeited through *hybris* was a thought form familiar to the entire Near Eastern world. That wisdom should return as God's gift in the guise of a prophetic teacher, or even as the divine wisdom incarnate, was an eventuality for which wisdom speculation had prepared men. Käsemann has called our attention to the elements of the wisdom teacher inherent in the ministry of Jesus, evidenced in his style of parables and the Q saying about hidden teaching (Matthew 10:26f.=Luke 12:2f.), both of which distanced him from the conventional rabbi (cf. Mark 1:22, etc.). The pregospel collection of Jesus' sayings that we call Q doubtless portrayed him as a wisdom-inspired prophet, and we have seen how this portrayal, taken as it was from a true emphasis of his ministry, has been preserved by the New Testament in several versions and at different levels of acceptance. For obviously, the wisdom motifs were not equally congenial to every canonical author. In fact, the New Testament taken as a whole would appear to stand as the considered verdict of first-century Christianity on the inadequacy of wisdom by itself to sustain the weight of the gospel. Probably no single one of the wisdom passages that we shall now have under consideration has entered the New Testament exactly as it was originally composed or as it was first encountered by the canonical author who made use of it. All of them have undergone redaction, which is to say that it was felt necessary to change them in some fashion, large or small. The point we have been trying to make, however, is that this wisdom theology was deemed basically acceptable despite—or rather, precisely because of—its having been redacted. Implied in redaction, surely, is the presence of valuable material which, though improvable, is better kept as it is than let go, to be paraphrased away or nullified by parody. We cannot agree with the view of these christological hymns that holds that they were cited in the New Testament only to be purified of their heterodoxy. We have seen what Paul did with a gnosticism he thought to be heretical or suspect: He did not attempt to adapt its hymns but rather ridiculed its pretensions by forcing its language to argue an alien cause (even as he forced the language of the rabbis on occasion). The hymns were cited, we believe, principally for what they were thought to have said well, as already possessing a kind of familiar authority, therefore, and only secondarily because by redaction they could be made to say it better. Redaction, in other words, was first and foremost a sign of approval and adoption, the validation by a later generation of Christians of an initial christology that it judged to have been essentially right-headed.

The Implications of Redaction

We have already seen verified the principle we have just proposed in the treatment of Philippians 2:6–11, which we saw at the beginning of our second chapter. What the Pauline author of Philippians did to his hymn was very little: the touch of a cliché involving the cross, together, perhaps, with a shift in punctuation which we have no way of deciding one way or the other. Meanwhile, the essentials of its christology, products of wisdom theology all, were accepted as common currency: the equality of Christ with God, his incarnation, his exaltation after death in divine majesty, and his triumph over the cosmic powers. Other passages containing the same theology that we have seen similarly handled by canonical authors are 1 Timothy 3:16 (which some believe to have been part of a baptismal hymn, of which the obviously hymnic Ephesians 5:14 may have been an introductory fragment) and 1 Peter 3:18–19.22. It is less obvious that Romans 1:3f. and 1 Peter 2:22–25, which we have also cited as homology-type credal tests, are of wisdom inspiration. It remains for us to examine a few others, however, which definitely are of that inspiration.

The most famous, most studied, and lengthiest of them

occurs in the first chapter of the letter to the Colossians. Here, too, the Pauline author has brought into his work a wisdom hymn with a minimum of adaptation (which we have indicated by the bracketed phrases in verses 18 and 20). This situation adds up to an exceptional case, in that we have reason to suspect that the original hymn (verses 15–20), of whatever origin we can no longer determine, had already, before it was adopted by the canonical author, been redacted into another, probably baptismal, liturgy (represented in the introductory verses 12–14). We cite the whole passage as a unit, since all of the verses are distinguished by style and vocabulary from the rest of Colossians. As it now stands, it has been made into an injunction to thanksgiving addressed to the Colossians (in verse 12a we have restored to the first person plural what the redactor presumably put in the second person): They are asked to have trust in the Lord for the strength that they need,

12 giving thanks to the Father who has made [us]
       worthy
    to share the lot of the holy ones in light:
13 who rescued us from the power of darkness
    and brought us into the kingdom of his beloved Son,
14 through whom we have redemption,
    the forgiveness of sins:
15 who is the image of the invisible God,
    the firstborn of every creature,
16 for in him was created everything
    in the heavens and on the earth,
    the visible and the invisible,
    whether thrones or dominations, principalities or powers,
    everything through him and subsisting for him.
17 And he is before all else,
    and in him everything continues to be,
18 and he is the head of the body [the church];
    who is the beginning, firstborn of the dead,
    that he might be first in all things.
19 For it has pleased the whole Fullness to reside in him,

20 and to reconcile to himself everything through him,
    making peace [through the blood of his cross]
        through him,
    both what is on earth and what is in the heavens.

What has been added here over the Philippians hymn is
principally the note of the participation of the redeemer in
the first as well as the second creation of man. The resurrection ("firstborn of the dead") is also more clearly referred
to, a detail that would seem to mark this hymn Christian
from the beginning, despite efforts that have been made to
find something vaguely similar in non-Christian gnostic mythology. It should be noted too that only through the resurrection is the redeemer considered to be first *in all things;*
this christology is not one of a timeless ontology, but it is
dependent on the action of God in history. Only in virtue of
this action, not simply through his being, is Christ the recon-
ciler. Reconciliation rather than triumph is the leitmotiv of
this hymn (as in 1 Timothy 3:16; in 1 Peter 3:18–19.22
we have both triumph and reconciliation). The "fullness" of
divine power of verse 19, therefore, cannot be regarded as
referring to the *mana* possessing a gnostic savior; it is the
salvific power bestowed on him who has been raised from the
dead and constituted a life-giving spirit (1 Corinthians
15:45). The redactor, whether of Colossians or prior to
Colossians, has changed the meaning of verse 18a by add-
ing the appostion of "the church"; the original sense of "the
body" was doubtless that of the cosmos, a familiar philosophical concept in the first-century world. (The discerning
reader will have observed that the punctuation we have used
above, a compromise at best, would certainly have been altered in the process of redaction.) He also introduced into
verse 20b a modification almost identical with that of Philippians 2:8c. Beyond this, nothing important has taken place
in the transition from wisdom into canon: The christology of
Colossians 2:12–20 has been accepted into the New Testament in all substance as it was first conceived.

    In Colossians 1:15a, Christ is identified as the image
(*eikon*) of the invisible God. In its present context, and in

the context of verses 12–14, which presumably testify to an earlier stage of redaction, this "image" is the incarnate Christ, the God-Man Jesus, the Lord of the church (cf. verse 13b: "the kingdom of his beloved Son"). What was the original referent of the "who" of verse 15a, the center and consistency of all creation, we cannot say for sure; but in view of the sharp break and change of pace in verse 18b, we may reasonably presume that it was the pre-existent one of Philippians 2:6, the one equal to God in the divine estate. Whether or not this is true (and we think that it is true), it is highly significant that Christians within a very short period of time were prepared to identify with the personified creative power of God (for that is what verses 15–18a seem to have had in mind) the historical person of Jesus of Nazareth, now recognized as having been raised from the dead and gloriously reigning in heaven, having reconciled the world to God (and, a Pauline author would add, "by the cross").

The model for this concept of Christ as image of God is personified wisdom, an idea that emerged as the gnostic redeemer myth but that is also very much in the wisdom tradition of the Old Testament. Wisdom is the image of God's goodness (Wisdom 7:26), was in the beginning with God and his firstborn (Proverbs 8:22), and was his mediator in creation (Proverbs 3:19, Wisdom 7:22). The same concept and model are reflected in Hebrews 1:3, another hymn fragment that a canonical author found useful for his purposes. He introduces it into his contrast of God's prior revelation of himself through prophecy with the revelation now made manifest in his Son, "whom he has made heir of all things and through whom he first created the universe," and

> who is the reflection of his glory
> and the very stamp of his being,
> sustaining all things by the word of his power,
> having brought about the purgation of sins,
> he took his seat at the right hand of Majesty on high.

We have here virtually a paraphrase of the Wisdom 7:26 to which we already referred: Nowhere else in the New Testament, and nowhere else in the Greek Old Testament, occurs the word we have translated "reflection" (*apaugasma*, possibly with a more active meaning, "effulgence"). "Stamp" here is evidently the equivalent of "image," as it is elsewhere in Greek literature. There are other resemblances to the Colossians hymn, including the mention of redemption, though it is put in terms of man alone rather than of the universe. ("Purgation of sins" may sound like a conventional assertion of Pauline or Servant soteriology, but it is not; the expression appears only here in the New Testament.)

The Johannine Hymn

We shall pass over some other possibilities of wisdom hymns whose presence we may suspect but which, if indeed they are there, cannot be extracted with reasonable certainty from their surrounding redaction. Instead let us reserve for the final text with which we shall be concerned under this heading one that is even more famous and has been even more studied than the Colossians hymn, though it is of a quite different category and, in fact, of a category unique to itself. In the prologue to the Fourth Gospel there is, it now seems universally agreed, an imbedded hymn of the same sort of provenance as those others we have seen. What makes it so different is its form, which is totally unlike an homology that we can readily imagine in a liturgical setting. No one, it seems, is much prepared to venture an opinion on what the original setting of this hymn might have been, though it is obviously a hymn, and for various reasons more probably one adapted by the author John than composed by him. If it was a hymn adapted by him, of course the next question is how much of a hymn there was to be adapted. The following verses would undoubtedly be accepted as providing at least a minimal accounting:

1 In the beginning was the word,
   and the word was with God,
   and the word was god.
2 He was with God in the beginning.

3 All things were made through him,
   and apart from him nothing was made.
4 What came to be in him was life,
   and this life was the light of men.
5 And the light shines on in darkness,
   a darkness that did not overcome it.
9 He was the real light
   giving light to every man[,]
   coming into the world.
10 He was in the world,
   and through him the world was made,
   yet the world did not know him.
11 He came to his own,
   but his own did not accept him.

We repeat that this is a minimum accounting of the original contours of the hymn. Thus far, it is by no means difficult to amass a wealth of Old Testament wisdom to stand at its background. *In the beginning was the word* (Proverbs 8:22, Sirach 1:4, 24:9); *the word was with God* (Proverbs 8:27.30, Sirach 1:1, Wisdom 8:3, 9:4.6); *he was with God in the beginning* (Proverbs 3:19, 8:27); *all things were made through him* (Proverbs 3:19, 8:30, Wisdom 7:22, 8:6, 9:1f.9); *what came to be in him was life* (Proverbs 3:18, 8:35, Wisdom 6:18f., 8:12.17, Baruch 4:1); *this life was the light of men* (Sirach 24:30, Wisdom 6:12, 7:10.26, Baruch 4:2); *the light shines on in darkness* (Wisdom 8:24–30); *he was in the world* (Wisdom 8:1, Sirach 24:3.6); *the world did not know him* (Proverbs 1:24f., Baruch 3:31); *he came to his own, but his own did not accept him* (Sirach 24:7f., Baruch 3:11f.). We do not find in this background a precedent for *the word was god,* that is, divine, one who was actually in the same *morphe* as God, as in Philippians 2:6, and therefore one who could eventually be called by God's name. For reasons we have aready dwelled on, this bold concept is not one we have a right to expect of Judaism. The language, and the shifting of mental gears that went with it, we undoubtedly owe to Hellenism. Also, whereas the Old Testament in all the parallels we have cited above predicated marvelous

things of a personified wisdom—a feminine figure both in
Hebrew and Greek—the Johannine hymn has brought them
all into conjunction with the personified word, a masculine,
the only appropriate antecedent for a christology celebrating
the man Jesus. The move from wisdom to word is perfectly in
accord with biblical thought: The word of the Lord, no less
than the wisdom of God, was synonymous with the spirit, his
creative and saving power (cf. Psalm 33:6). But the absolute
use of word, *logos*, to convey by itself all the connotations
that had been attached to wisdom, was not, it would appear,
a native Jewish development. Here, too, we probably find
ourselves tributary to the kindred world of gnostic Hellenism.

The hymn, if it is to be confined to the verses above, is
rather creational than soteriological; or, if soteriological, of a
soteriology that is incomplete and inconclusive. From this
standpoint it succeeds in saying less than most of the other
christological hymns have said with fewer words, even
though the assertion of divinity in verse 1c is stronger than
in any of the other hymns. Hence it is that many scholars
want to classify it a pre-Christian paean of the Logos, that
divine or divinized Rationale of the universe imagined by the
popular Stoic philosophy, which the author of the Fourth
Gospel adapted radically to fit his christology of a divine Savior who came down to earth to bring all men back to God.
Others believe that there was more christology in the hymn
to begin with, and therefore they ask whether it did not continue into some of the following verses even before the
Johannine author went to work with it. Passing over other
options where a dubious case can be made both pro and con,
we can grant at least a colored title of authenticity to two
subsequent verses:

14   And the word became flesh
     and made his dwelling among us.
     And we have seen his glory,
     the glory of an only Son of the Father,
     full of grace and truth.
16   For of his fullness we have all received,
     namely, grace after grace.

It is not extraordinary that we should find no precedent in Judaism for the word or wisdom of God becoming man, as in Philippians 2:7, for neither is there a precedent in Hellenism: If verse 14a pre-existed the Fourth Gospel, this was truly a Christian hymn from the beginning. The rest of the verse certainly falls in place: He *made his dwelling among us* (Sirach 24:8, Baruch 3:38); *we have seen his glory* (Wisdom 9:11); *glory of an only Son* (Wisdom 7:22–25). "Fullness" we have looked at above, in Colossians 1:19.

There is probably no way of proving definitively that these verses do or do not belong to a pre-Johannine hymn. Even if they do, and if, as we tend to believe, the Christ-event has been their inspiration, they remain within the bounds of wisdom speculation. For, as Raymond Brown writes of *the word became flesh:* " 'Flesh' stands for the whole man. It is interesting that even in the unsophisticated christological terminology of the 1st century it is not said that the Word became *a* man, but equivalently that the Word became man." Whether they were composed by John or helped him in forming his thought, these verses are in complete harmony with the theology of the Fourth Gospel and of the other wisdom hymns. The divine redeemer not only descended from heaven to earth, he descended into the human estate itself. This is not, obviously, the same thing as the myth of divinization of a man, familiar and even commonplace in the first-century world. Nor is it, less obviously, the same thing as the gnostic myth of a divine man come down to earth to recall as his own those in whom resided still the divine spark. The incarnation has no real parallel in gnostic thought and is, in fact, abhorrent to it. The children of light, in the Fourth Gospel, are everyman—everyman who chooses to believe, to welcome and know as his own the God of unconditioned love revealed in the Son of Man, that Son of Man whose nature is everyman's. It is, nevertheless, the thinking of wisdom that has been pressed into service in order to cope in understood terms with the vision of Christ as reflection in the spirit now required him to be seen. Wisdom's formulations came to be generally affirmed in the Christian churches, but plainly they were more at ease in certain theologies than they were in others. Just as plainly, in the theologies where they were most at home they displaced, in point of emphasis at least, doctrines that other theologies held very dearly to be the authentic revelation of God in Christ. To be specific, the doctrine of the cross has perforce undergone a translation in the gospel of John; it is still there, but it had to be otherwise interpreted in a conception of salvation that understood it to be communion with an ever-present God-Man. To take another example, in a rather different theological channel, we might point to a similar situation in the First Gospel, which has cast Jesus in the role of supreme Teacher of the way of righteousness—a role that, if pressed to the limit, renders superfluous both cross and resurrection, not to mention any inquiry into the character of the Savior. And this, regardless of the fact that Matthew's portrayal of Jesus, as wisdom Teacher or as Wisdom incarnate, has been clearly dictated by the same wisdom speculation of which we have been speaking.

Why the Cross?

What we now begin to understand, however, is why some of the canonical authors of the New Testament found it necessary to take into their writings only with modifications the seminal and aboriginal christology that we feel was first uttered in the language of wisdom. Why, for example, was it considered so important to specify the "death" of Philippians 2:8 as "the death of the cross"—a change that is quite negligible—or to define "the head of the body" in Colossians 1:18 by glossing it with "the church"—a substantial change indeed, which, as someone has said, has shrunk the cosmos to a rather sectarian limit? There are several observations that must be made. First of all, it is usually with Pauline additions that we are involved. Paul, and the disciples who followed him and edited his works, was advocate of a charismatic and prophetic presence in the church that could hardly outlive the first generation of its vigor. He very probably, and very properly, held suspect without further examination utterances that had emerged from the spontaneity of the liturgy (cf. 1 Corinthians 14:6–19). He may have shared, with the prophet Jeremiah and with lesser prophets like Dietrich Bonhoeffer, in fact, a prejudice against liturgy as a shaper of men's minds and the preoccupier of their thoughts. *Nur der darf Gregorianik singen, der laut für die Juden schreit.* "He alone is worthy to chant the liturgy who has learnt to cry for God's abandoned people." Just as Bonhoeffer had to fight a "flight of theology into liturgy"—that is, into a never-never land of irrelevancy, a flight that theology often takes as the easier course to judging man's confrontation with his here-and-now realities and decisions—Paul resisted any attempt to submerge the eschatological summons of the cross into a ready-made salvation that required only a new set of mind, or to trade the church where salvation is worked out painfully in fear and trembling for a once-and-for-all redeemed cosmos in which all the inimical powers and forces have been quite laid to rest. There is no doubt that liturgy, though its aim is to presentify past event—"do this in memory of me"—and to propleptecize the eschaton—"come, Lord Jesus!"—nevertheless finds its easiest expression in the present triumph: "We are one in the Spirit," "we are—not will be—sons of God," "we have been raised with him and with him we live the life of God." Its proclivity, in other words, is for a "realized" eschatology, a perfectly legitimate point of view that need not crowd out the equally important thrust of the futurist eschatology preached by the kerygma, and a point of view that is no doubt equally primitive as a response to the Christ-event. But it is a point of view, in any case, and therefore corrigible by other points of view. Paul, in all of the writings that can be certainly ascribed to him, adhered throughout to a futurist eschatology that was premised on determined events that occurred in *Heilsgeschichte.*

Nevertheless, Paul and the other New Testament authors who took up the christological hymns of wisdom theology took up along with them the conclusions that its speculation had reached. This was an essentialist rather than an existentialist understanding of the Son of God: a Son of God who must have been one with God from the beginning, equal with God, God who became man. It was not easy to reconcile these conclusions with what was otherwise evident about the man Jesus, of course. The reconciliation was to be the task of theology, and a changing task in proportion to the changing notion of the nature of God and man as well as to a changing reaction to the biblical data and their implications.

The Chalcedonian Formulations Again

In our preceding chapter we discussed the so-called Chalcedonian formulations of the patristic church and the fact that they achieved an enviable clarity in defining the meaning of Christ for their age. For all of that, they achieved it in a language that has not been bettered with the passing of the centuries, and that has remained instead a bulwark against irresponsible and unheeding heresy or merely slipshod, bad theology. It is slipshod, bad theology, we feel, that prompts some of our present-day colleagues to denigrate Chalcedon, Nicaea, and Constantinople, as though all these early councils had been excursions into an irrelevant speculation. That the New Testament itself did not evolve such formulations is not, as we saw, any argument against their necessity: The New Testament certainly invited the responses that Chalcedon gave. It is arguable that other responses could have been offered, but to offer no response at all would have been a betrayal of New Testament faith. Furthermore, that the response was four centuries in coming is as much testimony to the care and concern that went into them as it is to the confusions and bickerings that are more often remembered in their connection. William Sanday, who was a distinguished biblical scholar in his time, at the beginning of this present century, regarded the formulations as "the outcome of a long evolution, every step in which was keenly debated by minds of great acumen and power, really far better equipped for such discussion than the average Anglo-American mind of today." Sanday believed, as Reginald Fuller, Alan Richardson, and a host of other Anglo-Saxon authors have concurred, that Chalcedon was a genuine development out of the New Testament and that its conclusions, therefore, even if not its history, properly concern New Testament theology; and we believe, as he doubtless would, that its conclusions are still more faithful to the New Testament than are various alternatives more recently proposed in the name of "biblical relevance." It is not biblically relevant to try to dodge the whole issue by a retreat into archaism, "sticking to the biblical categories," for what this means in practice is to select one set of categories at the expense of others and therefore to freeze at some arbitrary stage a development that the New Testament itself began and did not complete. Nor is it particularly relevant to divert the issue into other channels by synthesizing in the academic laboratory a "modern man" whose needs are no longer met by Chalcedon but only by certain other biblical emphases that turn out, not surprisingly, to have been pinpointed better and accorded their central significance by present-day ethical and existentialist thinkers rather than by any biblical author. One thing that the "Jesus people" have shown us in recent days (we are gambling on the movement's having a long enough life to be still recognized by the time these words find print) is the perennial attraction that the person of Jesus has for the mind and imagination of our society. Whatever the disposition of Rudolf Bultmann to the contrary, it does matter to most people who are religiously minded at all what went on in the mind of Jesus. Because the "Jesus people" are so largely made up of those who are willfully ignorant of the past and therefore incapable of discerning the present, they have committed themselves to a passé Jesus whom rational criticism has rendered an impossible construct. Still, a yearning of this kind deserves better information, the sort of information that theology can provide when it is responsive to urgings other than those of its fellow club members, when it really ventures out into the street where the man for whom it professes to care is supposed to be found.

A decent respect for Chalcedon and its tradition, however, requires imitation rather than reiteration. Or translation rather than recital. We already broached this topic when we proposed that the Chalcedonian code-words "nature" and "person" are patient of a closer correspondence with an improved knowledge of the biblical realities in proportion to their ability to be rethought in terms of an improved ontology. There are other words and concepts that both can and most probably must be rethought in the same vein if they are to accord with the spirit of Chalcedon and continue to convey what they once did.

Let us consider, first of all, the concept of the unchangeableness of God, a term that figures prominently in the church's consideration of the related doctrines of the incarnation and the trinity. Chalcedon spoke of the Only-begotten of God as existing in two natures "without change." The term is an adverb here, referring to existing rather than natures, but there is no need to make a fine point of a technicality: It was taken for granted that natures would coexist unchangeably because they were unchangeable natures. Previously we examined the nature of Christ's divine sonship from the viewpoint of a dynamic rather than a static ontology, a distinction that does not challenge the principle of unchangeableness so much as it throws the underlying question into a new sphere of thought, in which the present is already determined by the future because of the retroactive power that the future possesses. Can we say something of the same thing concerning the divine nature of the triune God, or of the pre-existent Word of God who became man? More importantly, perhaps, is it ncessary that we say any such thing, is it necessary that we force Chalcedon's formulas to fit these new paradigms?

Apparently it is. The church of the Fathers had to assimilate only to a vague and accommodating philosophy the trinitarian doctrine it had inherited from the New Testament. Its ontology, to the extent that it had one, was unembarrassed by facts that the critical study of the Bible has compelled us to take into account. It did not have to submit itself to an equally penetrating analysis of historical religion. The Fathers, working from the reasonable premise that God always was what he is, experienced no difficulty at finding a trinity of persons in God revealed throughout the Old Testament, and, indeed, in not a few pagan sources as well. When it could not be found there in so many words, it was thought to be present in a myriad of allusions, hints, and prophecies. When even these failed, recourse was had to the theory of special "senses" of Scripture, according to which a secret meaning lay hidden in many texts, to be unlocked only by subsequent revelation, namely by the New Testament. All of these redoubts have now had to be abandoned, though it is remarkable how long some of them were defended—mainly, it is true, by theologians who had lost control of their primary source material. The instinct was right, however, even though the deductions were wrong. That is to say, if God has revealed himself fully at any given point of time, and if the revelation of God to man is of a constant, never changing deity, then his trinitarian character must have been as manifest in the first millennium before Christ as it became in the first Christian century.

To assert such a proposition, nevertheless, is not merely to assert what is incapable of factual proof, it is also to assert what is both demonstrably false and unbiblical, not to say antibiblical. Demonstrably false, because it is a matter of record that the trinitarian concept of God, to the scandal of other monotheistic religions like Judaism and Islam, has been evolved in the history of religions only by an early Christianity following the lead of the New Testament. Antibiblical, because the New Testament itself ties the revelation of the Son and the Spirit to definite occurrences during an historical period of Christian coming-to-awareness: "In this, the final age, he has spoken to us through a Son" (Hebrews 1:2); "there was, of course, no Spirit as yet, since Jesus had not yet been glorified" (John 7:39). The biblical documents clearly connect both the trinity and the incarnation—and the latter supposes the former—with the process of *Heilsgeschichte*.

Beyond Chalcedon

It is within such a context that modern theologians have been trying to go beyond Chalcedon while remaining faithful to its spirit and acknowledging the same biblical phenomena that it grappled with. As Piet Schoonenberg has well phrased it, antecedently there is nothing more objectionable to saying that God "became" triune than there is to saying that the Word "became" flesh. There is not, because, first of all, these are equally truths made known at definite points of time in human experience, which furnishes us with the only control that we possess over an otherwise unbridled speculation. What can man really know about God—know, and not simply imagine what he will have God be—aside from what God has revealed about himself? But the trinity, no less than the incarnation, is a matter of revelation, assignable to roughly the same period in time. The trinity, therefore, "happened" for man just as surely as the incarnation "happened" for him.

If the unchangeableness of God is supposed to conflict with such a view of revelation, we must reconsider what we mean by the unchangeableness of God. That he is indeed unchangeable is affirmed by the Scripture; but in what sense? In the sense, obviously, that he has been recognized as unchangeable through his contacts with man; for only in this way is man capable of judging any of the attributes of God. Put another way, this amounts to the constant biblical claim that God is true and faithful, that he exemplifies *emeth* and *zedek* (fidelity and mercy). The unchangeableness of God, in other words, means that he is consistent with what he has proved himself to be in the past. An abstract, timeless truth outside of God and man by which both may be measured in terms of deviation and change, is not among the Bible's affirmations. It was Wilhelm Hegel, in Pannenberg's view, who reintroduced into Western philosophical thought the notion of an absolute truth as only that which emerges at the end, toward which all the options have worked their way; a truth, therefore, that is not timeless but is achieved in time, in relation to which all other truth is provisional or proleptic.

The notion of the unchangeableness of God that was worried over in early Christianity was admittedly not consciously connected with this biblical idea of truth, but indirectly it was, since by its means the church entered the lists against the pantheistic *hen to pan:* "Everything is everything else." When the early church councils applied to God appellatives like *atreptos* or *analloiotos* (immutable), they were insisting on his transcendence of nature, his imperviousness to man's yearnings and imaginings, and his autonomy in having freely presented himself to man in man's history. Thus he is immutable, immutable to man's manipulation of nature and to nature's mutations of itself, in sovereign control of history as its Lord.

Neither as it was first proclaimed in Scripture nor as it was explicitly defined in the early councils, therefore, does the concept of God's unchangeableness come under attack by theologians like Schoonenberg and Eduard Schillebeeckx, who approached trinitarian doctrine from the viewpoint of process. There are many interrelating considerations that motivate this approach, some of which we have noticed before. Prominent among them are the new ideas about nature and personality, along with the desire to do better justice to what has actually been revealed about God as the New Testament has recorded it. As we saw when dealing with the question of Jesus' awareness, medieval theology considerably complicated the whole matter by its speculations concerning the various kinds of special knowledge that must have been communicated to the human soul of Christ. Speculations like these, however, would appear to be the inevitable consequence of any christology that follows the lines that have often become traditional in explicating the decrees of Chalcedon, which has insisted on the "and" in the God-and-man formula to the extent of postulating two distinct bases of awareness in a single person, resulting in a hypostasis impossible to imagine without the aid of elaborate and often conflicting theorizing. By this theorizing such a theology has sought to handle in a more sophisticated way the dilemmas it created for itself, stringing a tightrope on which it thought to walk above the canyon filled with the rough and ready resolutions of popular piety, usually monophysite and docetic. It has been suggested that the Fathers, untroubled as they were by this theorizing that later became so important and necessary to the schoolmen, spoke with greater conviction of the presence of God in Christ than did scholasticism eventually with its postulate of *grati creata*, the created "grace" that is the medium by which a human soul can be united with the divine essence. When all the explanations were offered and the last subtle distinction drawn, we may still wonder whether the conception of a personality "behind," "under," or "alongside" which an integrally constituted divine person is thought to dwell could ever be convincingly portrayed as possessing a genuinely human awareness, capable of development and growth. When the God-man becomes God-who-is-also-man or man-who-is-also-God, the antinomy almost invariably results in the distortion of one or the other term and to a composite that does justice to neither one. Such a posture, which Schillebeeckx has termed that of "textbook" theology, has certainly deformed the true image of authentic Christian thought and, as he has shown, is in reality opposed by not a little of it.

Therefore the new approaches. Schillebeeckx would understand the doctrine of the incarnation to mean that the divine knowledge, terminated in the Son, *became* the new Adam, just as the Scripture says; that is, it became a redeemed but entirely human awareness, the only awareness by which Jesus was able to identify himself. In this perspective it is much easier to understand how it is that the humanity of Christ is the revelation of God. Easier to understand even though it is agreed that Jesus' self-awareness did not necessarily lead him to articulated reflections on himself. The reality is present in any event, to be discerned in the totality of the human experience of Jesus. "The divine nature is irrelevant except to the extent that it exalts the human nature; to the extent that it does not do this, it has no significance for us; to the extent that it does, we are concerned with a human reality." Where, however, does this leave the wisdom christology of a pre-existent Word—the principal question toward which we have been working all along? The Logos pre-existed rightly enough, Schoonenberg will say, for he is God; but he did not exist as a separately constituted person until the incarnation. As Schoonenberg reads the evidence (others, of course, will disagree), Christian theology until the time of Origen (who died in the middle of the third century) did not deal with the Word as a pre-existent person. Subsequent theology followed

Origen's contrary lead in this, as it did not in other respects: Origen also believed in the pre-existence of all human souls. (A related concern was for the *natural* immortality of the soul, which Origen thought defensible only in terms of its pre-existence. Here again theology followed Origen's lead, and again contrary to the usual bent of Scripture, which is to treat immortality as a soteriological gift.) Finally, these and the other theologians who concur and complement would not want their propositions to be confused with the Arian formula *en pote hote ouk en:* "There was a time when he [namely, Christ, the Son] was not." Arianism's formula was meant to credalize Christ as a pure creature, created from nothing, and that is not what modern theology is trying to assert.

The Final Ecumenicism

It is not within the competency of this book to pass any final judgments on the success of these recent theological ventures, and, of course, they have not been presented as final by their proponents. (Nor, for that matter, should these be considered as constituting a "school," for they often sharply differ with one another.) We are content if only it has been persuasively shown that the biblical data, once given an appropriate home in the formulas of Chalcedon, can still provoke responses in the same tradition, which indicate that it, too, is yet alive. The survival of the tradition, which we think was integral to the proclamation of the word in the first place, in turn testifies to the continued relevance of the wisdom thought assimilated by the New Testament. It is a thought that persists in fecundating our thought, and it did not end when it had stimulated the thought of early Christianity.

This brings us to another consideration of the wisdom christology of the New Testament, one that does not belong to the tradition of Chalcedon or, strictly speaking, to any Christian tradition at all, though it may be argued that it has always lurked on their fringes. We are thinking of the wisdom/gnostic ideology itself underlying the christology, a *Weltanschauung* with which both the Old and the New Testament flirted without ever wholly sharing it. This ideology, we suspect, may hold the key to the solution of certain christological problems that were never contemplated either by the New Testament or by Chalcedon.

We persist in the view stated above, that redaction in the New Testament signified basic approval rather than repudiation of the redacted material. Therefore the New Testament itself invites us to examine this material always afresh, to consider it in the light of our own needs and opportunities, to inquire whether or not they coincide with those of the New Testament redactors. To the extent that our needs and opportunities may differ from those of the New Testament redactors, we may find it proper to make our own redaction of the material in accordance with them without violating the spirit of the New Testament canon. This, too, is New Testament relevance.

The christological hymns that have appeared in this chapter, we say again, were in our opinion Christian from the beginning; they were inspired by the Christ-event, and did not simply and superficially apply to the Christ-figure a ready-made gnostic redeemer myth. Nevertheless, they are representative of a Christianity much more *disponible* to the uses of gnostic thought than that which became the New Testament "standard"—too open, in fact, to be accepted by most of its authors without some kind of qualification. But what was deemed—and later proved in the event—to be dangerous for the Christianity of the first century may no longer be unsafe, and even may conceivably be indicated for a present-day New Testament religion that would adjust to the quite different world-view with which it must fend. The Pauline redactor who tampered with the entirely realized eschatology of Colossians 1:16.20, 2:15 by confining the *kosmokrator* of 1:18 to headship over the church, now represented as a model only for a redeemed universe, did so undoubtedly in order to bring its christology into closer accord with the historical word of the gospel. But it is possible that the original cosmic sweep of its vision might now be better suited for the proclamation of Christ, in an age when dialogue with the other world religions may be the form, or one of the forms, in which the church's mission is destined to be cast, equally important with its great commission to evangelize, if indeed it is not the modern version of that great commission. For the church must recognize, even as Paul did in other circumstances (Philippians 1:18), that in the last analysis the center of the gospel kerygma is only Christ, that Christ alone matters, even to the exclusion of the church if necessary. And if it becomes evident that the Christian church will forever play a minor role in the eschatology of future mankind, just as its role has been minor for the totality of mankind past and present, still, the role of Christ can be something else again. Only, it would then appear that it must be a role that largely bypasses a specific *Heilsgeschichte*, a particular cultural tradition, and the fulfillment of types that are doomed to remain meaningless for most men. A role, in short, very like the one projected by wisdom christology.

The world of first-century Christianity, we must remember, was tiny: The *oikoumene*, the inhabited earth, was the *orbis terrarum*, the circle of coastlands surrounding the Mediterranean—a sea whose very name testifies to the same kind of contemporary, insular arrogance that prompted the Chinese to call theirs the Middle Kingdom, an arrogance born of the ignorance of much geography or history beyond the immediate frontiers. The Mediterranean world that thought itself to be the whole world knew nothing of civilizations far older than its own that then as now had for their portion the overwhelming burden of the population of man. These civilizations included the one that six centuries before Christ brought forth the first world religion, a religion which like Christianity possessed a fierce evangelizing spirit along with an amazing ability for adaptation, which speedily took on the coloration of the cultures that accorded it hospitality and lost that of the land of its birth, where it virtually disappeared. Buddhism and Christianity both have displayed marvelous, self-renewing vigor through the centuries, but in these centuries both may also have reached the limits intended for them when the Most High assigned the nations their heritage

(Deuteronomy 32:8f.). There is always room in the economy of God for the free human spirit to find its salvation where it may, crossing over every border of language or tradition. The church acknowledges and welcomes this fact of life, which even an unsympathetic eye must see is pragmatic justification for its continued missionary activity. But the church must also acknowledge other undeniable facts of life. One of these would seem to be that the day of mass religious conversion has been spent, be it for Christianity, Buddhism, Islam, Judaism, or any other faith that now or in the past has vindicated to itself a gospel and the call to proselytize. It would seem to be a fact of life that the vast majority of mankind will always be what it has always been, neither Christian nor Buddhist nor Muslim nor Jewish, but these and many other things as well. If this is so, the Christian drive for the conquest of the world for Christ realistically must be diverted into other channels besides the traditional one of word and sacrament.

Paul, not much bothered by thoughts of this kind in the security of his smaller world, could imagine the eschatology of word and sacrament as satisfying every demand of Christian mission while the church awaited its full complement from the Gentiles, which in turn was the providential condition for the conversion of all Israel (Romans 11:25f.)—and this he evidently expected to be accomplished in his own lifetime, or very shortly thereafter. The horizons of this world would be extended in later Christian history, but not much and not very quickly: The formulator of the Athanasian Creed and Thomas Aquinas are separated by eight hundred years or more, but their *Weltbild* hardly differed at all in its basic assumptions. The gospel, in all its explicitness, which by now had become a rather Western explicitness, was thought by both to be a live option for all the human beings of the world who really counted. It is far more reprehensible that ideas premised on this world-view should have persisted long after the world-view itself became an anachronism; by proving themselves to be impervious to geography and ethnography they obviously preferred to parochialize God rather than look up from their ancient drawing boards. Yet we have known for a very long time that most men who have ever lived or who will ever live on this earth have not been destined to hear and embrace the gospel word; and this is to say nothing about other possible worlds that we do not know but of whose existence we have reason to suspect. In the face of these facts only a grossly ungenerous conception of God and of his merciful designs would conclude that salvation was intended for such a few. Dante's condemnation of the good pagans to hell, albeit a kindly hell invented for the purpose, simply because they had been born before their time, now seems to us a quaint conceit, as does Xavier's undoubtedly sincere lament over the thousands of souls doomed to torment because of the vicissitudes of sea and sickness that had prevented their baptism at his hands. It is no less quaint, however, when even our supposedly sophisticated theology chooses to ignore the implications of Christianity as forever a minority religion, one religion among many others of at least equal staying power, and will not, therefore, accept a God who by Christianity's own definition of God has interests broader than those of Christianity.

It is not only the fundamentalistic type of Christianity, untroubled by the facts of real life, that can project a gospel that offers great consolation for the select few at the cost of making it irrelevant and even repellent to most others. Liberal theology, too, can become so enamored of its own pursuits and the issues that it has engendered, so caught up in its own narcissism, that it confuses the great world outside with the thin ranks of academe. It does not even enter into its mind to inquire, usually, about that great world in relation to its pursuits. It ordinarily knows little or nothing about Asia and Africa in their religious dimensions, and one may even suspect that the Europe or America of which it does claim knowledge is in reality its extrapolation from its own unrepresentative ranks. It shows little interest in the religious character of other men, who are most men, whatever may be the compassion and charity it will extend to them as human beings; it does not often acknowledge that it has anything of great value to learn from these other men. Yet an aloofness and self-centeredness of this kind are strangely out of tune

with the spirit of the gospel; in their own way they succeed
in identifying Christianity with a tribalism, a worldly culture
great or small, just as surely as medieval Catholicism
identified it with the culture of feudal Europe, and in other
ways Boers, Ulstermen, and Keralese have identified it with
smaller tribalisms.

The Unknown Christ

The Fathers of the church, whatever their other faults,
were never guilty of this fault. Their concept of *praeparatio
evangelica* may have been naïve, but it was at least open to
the persuasion that the religious insights of man universal
had something to contribute to the understanding of the
Christ-event; they did not close off the latter as the exclusive
domain of a single and ever-narrowing cultural tradition.
Clement of Alexandria and Eusebius in the East, Ambrose
and Jerome in the West, could write with approval of Hindu
piety, as little as they knew about it. The point is that they
were interested in knowing about it and that they thought it
mattered to Christianity. They did not despise, as much modern theology has affected to despise, especially following
Wilhelm Herrmann, the way of mysticism which, like the
way of wisdom, has been the common experience of men and
women of every religion; they would not brand this ecumenical experience treason to the gospel. Had the circumstances
been other, they could as easily have accommodated the gospel to Far Eastern as to Near Eastern or Western forms and
language, to *jnana* and *bhakti* and *karma* as easily as to law
and word and righteousness. They could have found the
means, we have no doubt at all, to integrate with the Christian godhead the concept of God the Mother—no more
curious an anthropomorphism, of course, than that of God
the Father—had it been their lot to translate the gospel for the
millions to whom this revelation has been given to the
fulfillment of their spirit. (The revelation is not entirely lacking in the Bible, cf. Isaiah 49:15, the Q saying in Matthew
23:37=Luke 13:34. As we have seen, the feminine Wisdom

was the divine hypostasis preferred in the Old Testament and in Judaism to the masculine Word of Hellenism.)

In Acts 17:22–31 Luke represents Paul preaching to the Stoics and Epicureans of Athens. He preaches to them the gospel, but the gospel that has discarded its habitual thought forms in favor of those of pagan poets, and that has built on an exotic construct of deity: *agnostos theos* (the unknown god). The early wisdom christology, we feel, followed its instincts in attempting the same kind of *rapprochement*. A like instinct today, when once more we have been made aware of the many-splendored thing that is the totality of man's religious experience, may commend this christology again to a church seeking its rightful place in a world that really is, the world that has replaced, or is on the way to replacing, that ideal world whose familiar but quite fictive demands it would fain prefer and to which, alas, it often addresses itself still in its official statements. At the 1961 Faith and Order Conference of the World Council of Churches held in New Delhi, Asian delegates who had perhaps been made more cognizant of the real world than their European colleagues pleaded for an evangelization of the cosmic Christ as a corrective to the "church steeple" theology of the West that had become ineffective. And it was largely at the prompting of its missionaries that the church of the Second Vatican Council recognized for the first time the positive virtues of the other religions of man, their "certain perception of that hidden power which hovers over the course of things and over the events of human life" and their share in "that Truth which enlightens all men"; the Declaration *Nostra Aetate* cites in this connection John 14:6 and 2 Corinthians 5:18f. Raymond Panikkar has not unduly exaggerated the implications contained here when he concludes that

The Council's Declaration truly opens up boundless vistas for our eyes to behold. Jesus the Son of Man, the prophet, priest, and king, not only bespeaks bonds with the Abrahamic religions; albeit unknown there, he is present and secretly at work in all the religious forms that in one way or another trace back to Melchizedek, and in all the human forms that trace back to Abel, the primal, truly human man.

It is our own inclination to approach such a conclusion with diffidence. As anyone who has read the first part of this book will surely agree, our inclination is instinctively toward the relatively hard line of Oswald Dijkstra, who is rather skeptical of the ways of cosmic christology:

In the man Jesus God's promise became reality: God became man. He lived at a particular time in a particular country where the culture—under God's guidance—had developed the symbols and concepts which enabled Christ to make himself and his mission understood to simple fishermen. These elements are as inseparable from Christianity as the humanity of Christ is from his divinity. These elements will always be as foreign to the Christians of today in the west as well as in the east. To interpret Christ in terms of Purusha, Narayan, or Vishnu is to turn Christ himself into a symbol of man's self-realisation by removing his historical mediacy and all the elements that express it.

Nevertheless, we cannot but suspect that this view must yield to, or be sharply qualified by, the considerations we have tried to explore in the past several pages. Christ was *a* man, yes, with all the properties of time and place that distinguish one human being from another. Such is the raw material, the phenomenon to be investigated by christology. But over and above the observable phenomenon, the claim of the New Testament is that he became *man*—redeemed man, to be sure—but man, very man, in man's highest potential, which is to show forth God. The realization of that potential, as Karl Rahner has pointed out, is why Christ still is and not merely was man: another justification of the Chalcedonian formulations. The potential of man in Christ—again to rely on wisdom theology—is to rise to his full stature (Ephesians 4:13), to reach up to him as a building grows into its capstone (2:20). If this somewhat Teilhardian prospect on human destiny is to be seen through in a christology that genuinely corresponds with the historical condition of man, it would appear that it must count among its resources the varieties of man's religious experience past, present, and to come. And if this prospect leaves us with somewhat ambivalent and unresolved attitudes regarding the relation of church and of Christianity to the good news that is meant for all men, then perhaps this is yet another of the ambiguities with which we are destined to live in faith, another of the ambiguities revealed for us as we come of age in a world that grows ever more complex.

6. THE CARPENTER OF NAZARETH

The Stuff of Legend

With the conclusion of the preceding chapter we have run a course, however briefly and spottily, through what we consider to be the major landmarks of New Testament christology. We have examined the principal claims that the New Testament chose to make concerning Jesus of Nazareth, partly as they can be assumed to have grown out of his own historical awareness, but chiefly as they fructified in the church's contemplation of the meaning of his life and death in light of his Spirit testifying to his enduring presence in its midst. Doing this, we have gone down some byways of detail that many authors refuse to consider christological at all, but the pursuit of which we have been at some pains to justify in our Introduction. Nevertheless, our main focus has centered on the emergent impressions of Christ that rose out of resurrection faith, which gathered about the titles and types that explained him to the church, and which turned into theology events like suffering and crucifixion and experiences called resurrection and exaltation.

One thing we have not done, or done very much, is to probe into the redactional theology of the New Testament, into the separate christologies of the several canonical authors. Christ in the Theology of St. Paul, Christ in the Fourth Gospel, Christ in the Theology of St. Matthew, and the rest, are certainly integral to any theology of the New Testament, and in failing to deal with them in any systematic fashion we may be charged with not having lived up to the promise implied in the subtitle of this book. Aside from the fact, however, that to encompass such vastnesses in a single book is impossible, and that an attempt to do so even superficially would be an impudence, we may legitimately plead that the New Testament of our subtitle has less to do with a determined body of writings than it does with the new quickening of Spirit that was their eventual inspiration. We think that this sense and scope of our New Testament study have not been dissembled in the writing of these pages.

What we now propose is a further venture, a final venture, into fields that many scholars again will tell us lie outside the limits of christology properly so called, and this time we are prepared to agree with them. However, so much that is in them has so long and traditionally been enmeshed in our christological thinking that it is impossible to ignore them at this stage, and we would not wish to do so. We can perhaps settle for this distinction: If christology is the theology of the Christ myth, the material that we now take up constitutes the accompanying Christ legend.

Just as we trust that by now there will be no misunderstanding over our use of "myth" in connection with Christ, we may hope that neither will "legend" put anyone off the point of our distinction. Legend, that which is to be read, corresponds with saga, that which is said, as making up essentially the same genre of written or oral storying about great men by which was handed on the lore of the past. Legend has been, for that matter, the only medium by which most of the lore of the past has been handed on. It has produced the adjective legendary, which in one of its acceptations connotes information that is unreliable or at least unverifiable, and there is no doubt that legend is often unreliable and usually unverifiable. It is not for information in any statistical sense, however, that we scan the legends, but rather for their having kept alive the memory that deserved remembering. "It is the chief value of legend," G. K. Chesterton wrote, "to mix up the centuries while preserving the sentiment." The very existence of legend testifies to its truth, the only truth in which it is engaged; for without the man worthy of the song it would never have been sung, and the saga would never have been told.

Legend is often unreliable and usually unverifiable in its details. What do we make, for example, of the Lucan notion, contained in the infancy narrative adopted by the Third Gospel, that Jesus and John the Baptist were kinsmen, related through their mothers (Luke 1:36)? At the very least, we must confess that there is no hint of anything like this in the other gospel traditions surrounding these two persons and concerning their dealings with each other, and it may be argued that John 1:31 at least would tend to contradict it. It is the sort of notion easily created by legend, which loves to invest its heroes with noble genealogies and to bring them together in schemes unknown to history: Roland and the Twelve, Arthur and the fellowship of Camelot, St. Stephen at King Herod's court. It may have been created out of some half-remembered theological motivation, such as the desire to predicate a common priestly origin of Jesus and the Baptist, a thought that clashes with some New Testament christology but is also consonant with some. But it is likewise just possible that a true fact has been remembered here, to which there is no intrinsic objection and that might account for the undeniably close association of the two men. A blood relationship may have been invented to provide background for some spare facts of history, or the same facts in turn may presuppose the background. It is of the nature of legend that we can only take note of its genre and presume nothing for or against the historicity of its particulars.

What had been remembered about Jesus' preresurrection life, aside from detached sayings, parables, and other teachings, and a minimum of factual details that were frequently ambiguous, such as his baptism by John the Baptist, were chiefly situation stories of various kinds, conflicts with his opponents, instructions to his disciples. Even if we do not go along with the extreme critical view that would place all these situations in the life of the postresurrection church rather than that of Jesus, still, it is evident that from them alone no continuity could ever be gathered together sufficient to reconstruct the story of his ministry, let alone anything that lay outside it. Legend has had to supply the continuity, to provide the outline that Mark and—presumably—some of his predecessors had decided should be imposed on the gospel forms to create, in the tradition of Israel's historiography, the soteriology of recital that we know as the written gospel.

The Source of the Legend

The principal quarry of the legend was the salvation history of the Old Testament: the saving events in the life of the people and the lives of its great heroes—Abraham, Moses, Samuel, Elijah, and Elisha, among others—both as they could be read in the sacred books and as they had already entered into a legend of their own. The latter had already taken in influences from the world that was wider than Judaism. The types exploited by the legend, in other words, were the types exploited by the christological myth. The names and the incidents differ, but they come from the same sources. There is little to choose between the two, probably, as far as antiquity is concerned. They are to be distinguished only as myth and legend are to be distinguished.

Let us consider the structure of Mark's gospel. Most present-day commentators would probably concur with the interpretation suggested by many modern versions of the Bible in their division of the text, that the first thirteen verses set the scene of the gospel and establish one of its dominant motifs. Here, after his baptism—a passage through water—Jesus is represented as being in the wilderness, where he undergoes temptation. Through the remainder of the gospel he is, so to speak, on a journey through the wilderness, which is frequently mentioned, till his fateful visit to Jerusalem before the crucifixion. Along the way there is a mountain ("the" mountain in 3:13, 6:46) where or near which decisive events take place: The Twelve are chosen, the multitude is fed, there is a vision of glory in which Moses and Elijah appear. It is quite evident that the evangelist has chosen to have Jesus retrace Israel's steps of old in the wilderness, through the sea, and by the mountain, and that his outline owes less to the historical recall of a man's life than to his intention that a man should relive the formative experiences of a people.

The same kind of structure, worked out with greater artifice and in more complexity, is discernible elsewhere in the written gospels: The other evangelists followed Mark's precedent in devising schemes of their own for the telling of the new story of salvation. However, it was not only when Mark or one of his forerunners first constructed a literary gospel that these types and figures became determinants of the Christ legend; they were already in the forms in which the gospel traditions had been cast, and they had already done their share to produce the forms.

The meeting between Jesus and the Baptist, with the delineation of the role of each, looks in the Matthean version (Matthew 3:13–15) to have been modeled on the meeting of Moses and Aaron that was to the same purpose (Exodus 4:14–16.27f.); perhaps there is a hint of the same typology in the Lucan version of the events, for like John the Baptist, Aaron is both a priest and a kinsman to the principal of the story. The call of Jesus' disciples as told in all the gospel traditions with the note of their forsaking their homes and occupations strongly resembles the story of Elisha's call by Elijah with all its consequences (1 Kings 19:19–21). When Jesus' disciples inquire about fire from heaven to punish the hostile Samaritans (Luke 9:52–54), they speak the language used by Elijah to the messengers of the king of Samaria (2 Kings 1:12). We have already remarked along the way the parallel between Jesus' raising of a widow's son (Luke 7:11–17), the occasion of his being hailed a great prophet, and Elijah's similar deed (1 Kings 17:17–23): in each instance the prophet "gave the boy back to his mother." The theme of the twelve disciples judging the twelve tribes of Israel (Matthew 19:28) doubtless owes something to the story of Moses' selection of twelve princes, one from each of the twelve tribes (Numbers 13:2), just as Jesus' appointment of the seventy (or seventy-two), probably with some assistance from the legend of the Septuagint (Luke 10:1), is in debt to the appointment of the seventy by Moses (Numbers 11:24–26). Jesus' ascent of the mountain of transfiguration in the company of a select few disciples is recounted in such a way as to constitute the story a mélange of the ones told about Moses' ascent of Mount Sinai and Mount Hor. These random examples, which serve to illustrate what we mean when we speak of a Christ legend, are by no means the only ones that could be brought forth at this time and may not be universally the most important ones, though they are among the more obvious ones. They form a piece with others we have seen and are analogous to the typology of a somewhat different kind, which distributed the events of the passion tradition to agree with the details of Isaiah 53 or Psalm 22. Our chief purpose in adducing these examples has been to suggest that the infancy narratives in the gospels, which we now propose to examine under certain respects, are not altogether differentiated by their literary form from much of the rest of the narrative material of the gospels relating to the life of Jesus. If there is a difference, it is one of degree much more than of literary genre. There is a reason for this difference. The infancy narratives did not rise out of the early kerygma, which had interpreted a life and death subject to a generation of historical scrutiny; perforce, therefore, they had to rely more on the stuff of legend to fill out their meager store of facts.

Certainly the infancy narratives, both in the Matthean and in their Lucan forms, contain their full share of the legendary. Again the sources of the New Testament stories are to be found as much in postbiblical Jewish elaboration on the Old Testament as they are in the Bible itself, but the latter unassisted can still show through as their primary motivation. The Matthew story has been modeled on the Moses tradition, and the Luke story has been modeled on the tradition of Samuel. That is the simple fact of it, though the simple fact can be spelled out in tedious detail, and many other traditions have been worked into the tales in the bargain. Both stories, in fact, seem to be composites, built up by stages, with disparate interests to be served, some of them probably Hellenist as well as Jewish. Besides the figure of Samuel, the Lucan annunciations evoke memories of Isaac, Moses, Gideon, and Samson, along with the chronology and "prophecy" of Daniel 9. Matthew has joined to the Moses legend a number of other Old Testament themes and probably still others that were of more common currency at the time: The story of the astrologers and the wonder star, for example, may have grown out of the postbiblical legend of Abraham, but there is also something like it in Suetonius' *Life of Augustus,* concerning the birth of the great emperor. The emperor, we must remember, was *soter* and *kyrios* (savior and lord), and his words and deeds were for men *euangelion* (good news, gospel). His birth, according to a document of 9 B.C., "was for the world the beginning of the gospels which have emanated from him." The infancy narratives are like the rest of the gospel stories, unmistakably Jewish in inspiration, but of a Jewishness that was fully at home in a Greek-speaking and Roman world.

The Virgin Birth

It is not our intention to worry over most of the historical issues that are posed by the infancy narratives of the gospels. Undoubtedly there are authentic facts caught up in these portions of the Christ legend that deserve to be recognized or at least argued, but mainly they do not enter into the subject matter of this book. Whether Jesus was a native of Judea, as Matthew (and John, probably) would have it, or of Galilee, as Luke tells the story, may be of some consequence in the retelling of his life; but it is likely to be a question than can never be answered with complete satisfaction, and it remains to be proved that it has affected either the implicit or explicit christology of the New Testament. (That Jesus was—by birth or by adoption—a Galilean, is another thing entirely, which doubtless does have a bearing on his relation to the Jewish establishment and the Roman state. But this fact does not appear to be in dispute.) The intent of both Matthew and Luke to provide Jesus with a Davidic ancestry, though by different routes, certainly has christological implications, but we have seen that they were not peremptory for all of New Testament christology. The relation to history of magi, angelic visitations, divine intimations to shepherds and other folk, and the literary genre that we must assign to the story of these happenings singly and collectively, are legitimate questions calling for answers through literary and historical criticism; but their resolution, even supposing that we could make one, does not in our judgment alter the course of our present inquiry one way or the other. They are simply not the stuff of which New Testament christology was made. One enunciation of these narratives, however, we do have to consider at this time, since it does—whether or not it was originally intended to—very much link up with the christological thinking both of the New Testament and the later church, having entered into all the ancient Christian creeds. We refer, of course, to the assertion made by both Matthew and Luke, working independently with independent traditions, of the virginal conception of Jesus.

For many modern authors nothing is more indicative of the legendary character of the infancy narratives than the story of the virgin birth. It was, as we have just seen, fairly routine to surround the birth of famous men with wonders and portents. What more wonderful, what more portentous than a virginal conception? We are almost given the impression that in the folklore of antiquity virgin birth must have been about as common as the other kind. Not only is it legend we have to deal with, according to Pannenberg it is a maladroit and clumsy legend that contradicts the Pauline and Johannine doctrine of the incarnation of the pre-existent Word. For in this construct, he argues, Jesus was conceived and born the Son of God, but the Son of God did not become man.

The idea of a virgin birth appears only in the legend of the infancy narratives, we are assured, and there only by imposition, since some of the elements in the tradition did not know of it. The genealogies of Matthew 1:1–17 and Luke 3:23–37, which trace Jesus' ancestry through Joseph, must have originally had in mind a natural procreation, and only later were they harmonized with the story of the virgin birth by some superficial and somewhat illogical alterations. (As a matter of fact, there is some textual evidence that the conclusion of Matthew's genealogy has been disturbed, though the "as was supposed" of Luke 3:23 occurs in all the known manuscripts of the Third Gospel.) In Luke 2:27.33.43 "his parents" or "his father and mother" has been changed in some of the manuscripts to a neutral "Joseph and Mary" or

"Joseph and his mother": certainly a proof that the doctrine of virgin birth has provoked tamperings with the New Testament text, but at the hands of nervous copyists rather than of the evangelist. The same kind of nervousness accounts for the omission in some manuscripts of the "other" in Luke's reference (23:32) to the "two other criminals" who were crucified along with Jesus. Some scholars detect the influence of the doctrine on other texts of the New Testament. Mark 6:3, in the reading of the most and best of the manuscript evidence, has the citizens of Nazareth wondering about one of their own who has developed sudden pretensions: "Is this not the carpenter, the son of Mary . . . ?" A respectable number of manuscripts, however, have instead ". . . the son of the carpenter. . . ." Has the received text been changed from this latter form? Probably not. Rather, it is likely that the variant has been produced by copyists who wanted to make Mark agree with the parallel Matthew 13:55. The first authors of the New Testament documents, whatever their christological presuppositions, never displayed the passion for wooden consistency that a subsequent orthodoxy thought to be the right and due owed to its sources.

It cannot be shown, for sure, that Mark—presumably our oldest gospel—"knew" the doctrine of the virgin birth, any more than it can be shown that John—presumably our latest gospel—"knew" it; which is to say that, known or not, it has entered into the theology of neither one. Is it proper to observe in return that the far more basic doctrine of the resurrection never turns up in a recognizable form in the Epistle to the Hebrews, or in most of the earliest christological hymns? Paul Althaus once protested to Karl Barth that "there has never been a message of Christ that was not the Easter message . . . but witness to Christ and Christian faith are quite possible without the virgin birth." Is either part of his proposition literally true, or did he have the right to prescribe so arrogantly the conditions of Christian identity? Only, it would seem, if he had justly hit on a criterion of Christian belief that could narrow the New Testament canon down to some essential that the New Testament itself had not worked out.

Mark 6:3 in its most acceptable reading is straightforward:

Is this not the carpenter, the son of Mary, a brother of James and Joses and Judas and Simon? Are not his sisters our neighbors here?

What is the most obvious meaning of a verse like this, if we set aside all prejudices one way or the other? If the verse is authentic, as we have every reason to believe that it is, it does the extraordinary thing of identifying a Jewish man by giving the name of his mother rather than the name of his father. There were precedents for this extraordinary usage: the case of a bastard, for example, whose father was unknown or unacknowledged. Obviously Mark had no intention of conveying any such notion concerning Jesus' birth, and he would have been sensitive to any implication of it in his tradition. The canards about Jesus' illegitimacy and his mother as a loose woman, whch disfigure later Jewish lore, rose out of anti-Christian polemics parodying the doctrine of the virgin birth; they did not anticipate it or contribute to it. Another possible explanation for the language of Mark 6:3 is the one proposed by Ernest Renan: "This supposes that he was long known as the only son of a widow." Certainly Mark nowhere betrays any knowledge of Jesus' father, despite his fairly good information about the rest of the family, and Renan's guess may be an accurate appraisal of what he meant to say. Matthew's parallel as well as the independent tradition represented by John 6:42 make it more than likely that Mark's identification of Jesus as the carpenter rather than the son of Joseph the carpenter is the result of design and not of ignorance. Matthew could afford to call Jesus the son of a carpenter just as Luke could afford to speak of his parents, for the infancy narratives of both stood at the outset to remove all ambiguities. Mark did not have the same advantage. It is very true that the idea that Jesus had been virginally conceived never played any part in Marcan theology, but it is not equally clear that the Second Gospel had no knowledge of the doctrine and made no provision for it in its handling of the tradition.

The Brothers and Sisters of Jesus

Even though we would prefer to avoid it, we probably have to bring in at this juncture the related issue of the brothers and sisters of Jesus, if only to let the gospel be heard on the subject of Mary's alleged virginity in the whole and not after the fashion of rationalist exegesis, which tried to make myth respectable by cutting it up into historicizable and nonhistoricizable pieces. Vincent Taylor has very rightly put it that Roman Catholic interpretation of the New Testament passages surrounding this question has been "strongly coloured by belief in the perpetual virginity of Mary." "Perpetual virginity" is without doubt an inept term, but the ineptness is not Taylor's—the term has indeed been employed in tradition to express the belief, born of the New Testament itself, that Jesus was not only virginally conceived but that his conception by Mary was a unique experience in her life. Where Taylor becomes inept in his own right is in his further statement that "the simplest and most natural explanation of the references by the brothers of Jesus in the Gospels" is that they were the natural, year-by-year product of the marriage of Joseph and Mary. For emphatically the gospels suggest no such simple thing. The brothers of Jesus who appear in Mark 3:21.31 and John 7:3 seem to be a rather large group (compare "all his sisters" in Matthew 13:56), who treat him in the manner of a somewhat wayward younger relative patronized by his elders. If it be thought simple and natural to regard all these people as Mary's sons and daughters, it must be at the expense of the credibility of the other traditions which represent Jesus to have been a firstborn son. The word "firstborn" (Luke 2:7) itself, of course, as many who know better persist in overlooking, does not commit this infancy narrative to a view of Jesus as one of many children: a Jewish mother's son, even if an only son, was her "firstborn"—and surely the obvious assumption of the story in Luke 2:41–52 is that Jesus was an only child. In 15:40 Mark identifies as children of a certain Mary two of the brothers of Jesus he named in 6:3. More than one commentator has ventured, in his dogged determination to hew to "the simplest and most natural" line at all costs, to hypothesize another James and Joses rather than admit straightforwardly that a different Mary is the mother in question.

We make no claim that the gospel traditions support a belief in the continuing virginity of Mary following the birth of Jesus, but only that they do not rule it out of court. This belief, misguided or not, did not grow up among men who were illiterate as regards the biblical data—far from recondite—which later sober critics think must have escaped them. Since we are engaged with simple and natural facts, one that should not be disregarded is the extended Semitic sense of "brothers" and "sisters" to include kinsmen of every kind, including members *de la raza,* a sense that no one, certainly no American attuned to the realities of his contemporary society, should find foreign to his understanding. The Lucan legends that present Jesus as a second Samuel have no interest in speculating about other siblings. The other legends that have him an elect son harried by his brethren—as Joseph and David, among others, had been before him— are not involved with the doctrine of the virgin birth. Legend is the operative category throughout. From the standpoint of gospel tradition the virgin birth of Jesus is quite as well established as that he was a carpenter in Nazareth and that he belonged to an extensive family that included names like Joseph and Mary, whose roles can be fairly well established, and others like James and Joses and Judas and Simon and Salome, which cannot. It is not our present task to try to determine these roles, but simply to admit that they are undetermined. Or, in other words, to insist that the infancy narratives are not aberrant details hanging on the fringes of the gospel tradition but are integral and respectable parts of that tradition, and just as worthy of serious consideration as the other gospel stories.

We need to ask, therefore, though admittedly there is some less urgency to the question, what the gospel traditions meant by ascribing to Jesus a virgin birth, just as we need to ask what they meant by ascribing to him a resurrection. The questions are equally legitimate and cannot be skirted by semantic subterfuge, as though legend were somehow of smaller account than myth as a vehicle of communication.

Why Born of a Virgin?

First of all, it should be plain enough that the idea of a virginal conception was not copied from anything out of Jewish tradition, including the stories on which so much that is in the infancy narratives was modeled. Isaac, Samuel, and John the Baptist were all children of promise, born out of due time, and Moses and Abraham, the stories said, came into the world to the accompaniment of cataclysmic signs; but for none of these was the virginity of the mother ever an issue. Judaism had, quite rightly, set no store on virginity as representing any positive value in its own right; it was seen simply as a negative factor, a state of incompletion. Neither is it easy to imagine the obviously Jewish circles in which the infancy narratives grew up suddenly having been infected by the notion that a virginal conception was necessary to safeguard the Christian theologoumenon of Jesus' sinlessness (Hebrews 4:15, 1 Peter 2:22, 3:18), the sole mark by which his was to be distinguished from the usual human condition. In the first place, his mother Mary, her husband Joseph, John the Baptist, and probably others as well who figure in the same narratives were doubtless thought of as having been sinless, but without the benefit of other than natural human conceptions. Furthermore, an alleged connection of virginal conception with sinlessness is not one that would have occurred normally to Jewish minds, just as it would never have occurred to them to equate sexual union with sinfulness.

Nor is it evident that the idea of a virgin birth for Jesus was an import into early Christian thought from the hero legends of the Hellenistic or Near Eastern world. When the parallels that are supposed to have provoked such an idea are closely examined, they turn out to be less than significant for an understanding of the New Testament story. Neither Sargon of Akkad, whose father was simply unknown, nor the

Egyptian pharaohs, nor Buddha, whose virgin birth was actually a reincarnation, nor Augustus, sat for the portrait of mother and child that has been drawn in the infancy narratives of the gospels. Quite aside from the fact that the infancy narratives of the gospels are obviously intended to be the preface to a history that takes place in the world of sober reality, while the myths and legends of the Gentiles are quite literally out of this world, both the spirit and the essential meaning are quite different. The intention of the biblical narratives is not to mask the humanity of Jesus in some docetic fashion, which is what the hero legends were all about, but rather to afford a vision of the uniquely new humanity of Jesus in which God chose to reveal himself. There are no genuine precedents for the story of the virgin birth either in Judaism or in the Gentile world for the very simple reason that in neither of them had appeared a precedent for the Jesus of Nazareth who was made and manifested Lord and Christ.

The legend of the virgin birth of Jesus is a variation, possibly an older variation but in any case not demonstrably a later one, on the theme otherwise expressed by Paul in his myth of Christ the new Adam. Jesus is the son of no earthly father but only of God because with him begins a whole new creation of man, a new human race. The new Adam appears as son of God and without other father precisely as the first Adam appeared (Luke 3:38). "If anyone is in Christ, he is a new creation. The old order has passed away; now all is new!" (2 Corinthians 5:17). Paul, to be sure, understood Christ to be the new Adam of a new creation in virtue of his resurrection rather than his incarnation (Romans 5:12–21, 1 Corinthians 15:45–47). It is the resurrectional image of God, undoubtedly, in which the new Christian man has been created according to the mind of Colossians 3:9f. and Ephesians 4:24. Nevertheless, we know that Paul shared the wisdom christology of the pre-existent Christ, which proclaimed that he had always been the Son of God who he became in the resurrection. The one who in Philippians 2:6 was in the state of God prior to the incarnation, who in Colossians 1:15 was the image of the invisible God and the principle of creation at the beginning, was obviously not thought to stand in any conflict with the resurrected Christ-Savior of the dominant Pauline theology; they were acknowledged to be one and the same. To maintain both perspectives it was not necessary to subordinate resurrection to incarnation, as, among others, John and the author of Hebrews tend to do. We find exactly the same relationship between the pre-existent Son of God and him who was born Son of God by a virgin that plainly existed between the pre-existent Lord and him who was constituted Lord and Christ. That is to say, merely, that contrary to Pannenberg's view, we find no internal conflict, no either-or, just as early Christianity apparently found none.

To say this is not, of course, to insist on the historical facticity of the legend of the virgin birth. Quite patently it is far more congenial to the critical mind past and present to conclude that it is merely a wonder story, like many other wonder stories in the gospels, whose symbolic purpose exhausts its function and renders historical criticism both futile and naïve. The futility we may probably concede, but the naïveté probably not. We are in less an advantageous position to evaluate historically the details of the infancy narratives than we are with regard to many others in the gospel traditions. However, the elements of wonder and of theological symbolism—not purposeless or inept symbolism, indeed, as the universal experience of the Christmas event in all the Christian churches helps to prove—do not automatically exclude the factual plausibility of an alleged event. We have already made a point that we feel has some relevance, namely that those New Testament sources that make nothing of a virgin birth of Jesus also say nothing to rule one out, even in a most literal and unavoidable sense.

And Why Not?

We have possibly confused the original intentions of the gospel traditions that spoke of a virgin birth by asking, in our ignorance, all the wrong questions and probing into all the wrong areas. The gospel stories were not, as students of com-

parative religions have tried to pretend, modeled on the mul-
tiform myths by which the heathen had entertained the possibility of divine commerce with the human estate through
some literal kind of copulation, even in the sublimated forms
of Danaë and the golden stream or Leda and the swan. The
texts themselves witness to this. In the words of Luke 1:35:

> Holy spirit will come upon you,
>   and power of the Most High will overshadow you,
> hence there will be a holy offspring
>   called Son of God.

There is no gross suggestion that God the Father takes the
place of a human husband in generating a child, and even
less, of course, that the personified Spirit—pre-eminently on
assertion of Johannine theology—is the Father of Christ,
which would indeed be a grotesquerie of early Christian
thought. In the same manner, Matthew 1:18 says that
before Joseph and Mary had ever come together in marriage
"she was found to be with child by holy spirit," and it was
revealed to her husband (verse 20) that "what she has conceived is of holy spirit." The spirit of God means simply the
divine power. In the Greek, "spirit" is a neuter, not a
masculine. In the Semitic—always supposing the likelihood
that these stories are Semitic in origin—"spirit" is a feminine.
Without denying at all the legendary character of the stories
of the virgin birth, we must point out that they were not
guilty of the gratuitous mythology with which some later
Christian folklore has surrounded them.

The legend of the virgin birth intended to say something
about Jesus, just as the myth of the resurrection intended to
say something. Since there is no parity between the two, we
do not propose an equation but only an analogy. Even as the
idea of resurrection is easily reduced to an absurdity—Paul
was witness to this in the first Christian century, and
witnesses have not been lacking in the centuries that have
succeeded him—the idea of virgin birth can be subjected to an
equally disastrous reduction. The concept of resurrection can
be attacked on the score of body chemistry and half a score
of other sciences. The *reductio ad absurdum* of the virgin

birth was already unintentionally achieved by the pseudogos-
pels of the first few centuries, which tried to translate it into
the clinical language of the physical virginity of a woman
ante partum, in partu, and *post partum,* speculation that not
only had nothing to do with what the New Testament was all
about but that inevitably amassed a collection of statistical
crudities that later and gentler ages refused to dignify with
vernacular versions. In both cases, resurrection and virgin
birth, the pursuit of a literalist chop logic has led not to
edification of the spirit nor to the enrichment of sound doctrine but invariably to the disrepute and cheapening of the
faith that the New Testament first placed in these signs of
contradiction.

It needs to be added, in conclusion, that the New Testament doctrine of virgin birth intended neither to disparage
womankind in general nor to glorify one woman at the expense of others, not even that woman whom Christians had
already named *theotokos,* Mother of God, at a time when
they were still arguing over the Chalcedonian formulations.
It has not been our purpose in this book to discuss Marian
piety, the cult of the Virgin that is a feature of historical
Christianity both Western and Eastern and deserving of
investigation in its own right. The early mariological dogmas
were formulated, when the Fathers set about completing the
work of the New Testament, because they were necessary to
the completion of their christological elaboration. In the New
Testament itself, however, the development of thought has
not gone so far, and the story of the virgin birth intended
only to define This Man Jesus in his relation to God.

A FINAL POSTSCRIPT

Let us, now that we have come to the end of what we have had to say, recapitulate the way we have said it, in the hope that by saying it again very briefly we may commend at least its rationale, even if not the equal persuasiveness of every particular.

We began by insisting on the importance of history, a sign of contradiction for many and a value that has not always been well served by some who have praised it the most. History, as we understand it, relates to the facticity of certain events underlying faith, events to which faith has given an interpretation and which we know only through this interpretation, but events which had they not really occurred would leave faith worse than meaningless and a cruel deception. We do not pretend to be able to establish by historical method a reconstitution of those events that would either substitute for faith or "prove" it: As we put in on p. 26, "what we seek to do" in this historical inquiry "is to get at the origins of a belief." To get at those origins is, nevertheless, most important, and it is the reason for this book.

The belief with which we are concerned regards the person of Jesus of Nazareth as he came to be perceived by the church as its Lord and Savior, God's very Son. Since it was the experience of the resurrected Jesus that convinced the first Christians that he was, indeed, all these things, we felt it incumbent on us first of all to try to determine what this experience was, as far as it can be discerned in the earliest testimony, and how the resurrection is to be accepted not only as a symbol but also as a fact, in terms that do no violence either to the biblical affirmation or to the nature of realities as we know them.

The experience of the resurrection directed the attention of the church both back to the past and forward to the future—to the past as it defined the person of the historical Jesus who had lived and died and had now been raised by God, and to the future as it defined him the Lord reigning over a community of faith which lived in hope of a resurrection like his. Without seeking to establish a chronological priority in the direction of the church's attention, we chose first to look in the backward direction, to the interpretation that the first Christians were impelled to give to a life that had, inevitably, culminated in a death, but a death that had singularly given meaning to that life, that is to say, to the doctrine of the cross. To do this intelligibly it was necessary for us to dwell at some length on the historical circumstances of Jesus' death before examining the ways in which the church eventually figured to itself the salvific significance of the cross.

Following these preliminaries, we took up some of the most significant of the christological titles under which the church professed its faith in a resurrected Savior: Messiah or Christ, Lord, Son of Man, and Son of God. We tried to discover not only the original sense(s) of these titles and their development, but also to indicate what they continue to say in a church now separated from the New Testament by the gap of many centuries and as many cultures. To do this it was necessary to ask, not always with conclusive results, what went on in the mind of Jesus himself—what was the connection, if any, between his consciousness of certain realities and the later titles by which the church sought to encapsulate them—as well as to explore the cultural milieus supposed by the titles in their varied uses, the routes by which they made their way into the New Testament canon. Finally, and in particular, it was necessary to discuss the present-day validity of the formulations by which the patristic church undertook to complete the work of the New Testament by defining the sense in which Christ was to be professed Son of God, the title that rightly had come to be seen as most significant of all.

This same question of continuing relevance had to form a part of our fifth chapter, in which we discussed "wisdom" christology, a matter not so much of titles as of outlook. In this chapter, doubtless the most problematical of our entire book, we advanced the thesis that this ancient christology, possibly the most ancient christology of all, but in any case representative of a respectable strain of biblical thought, can not only continue to shed light on the meaning of the terms in which Chalcedon strove to formulize it, but can also beckon us to new ways and summon us to new voices. It can do this, perhaps, more easily than other New Testament christologies, which have produced other emphases. The fact that it can do this may also be an indication that it ought to.

Frequently in the course of our writing we had occasion to employ the term "myth," not as it is an expression of the unreal but rather of the ineffable. In the same spirit in our last chapter we laid alongside it the term "legend," not in the sense of the unbelievable but rather as the medium whereby the memory of most great men and great things has been kept alive. Our principal purpose in introducing this theme was to bring into proper perspective the church's belief concerning the virginal conception of Jesus, a New Testament affirmation certainly related to its christology. We concluded that this doctrine must be taken seriously as a definition of Jesus' character just as surely as the christological titles defined it. And in making this conclusion, we reaffirmed the limit previously assigned to our work, which has been merely to outline the constitutive elements of New Testament thinking on the mystery of Christ.

SCRIPTURAL CITATIONS

OLD TESTAMENT

Genesis
  1:26 f.   60
  3:5   60
  5:21–24   107
  6:2   137
  14   107
  22:4   44
  42:18   44
  49:10 f.   98

Exodus
  2:14   102
  4:13   102
  4:14–28   203
  19:11–16   44
  24   87
  31:3   125

Leviticus
  16:20–28   86
  17:11   86

Numbers
  11:24–26   203
  13:2   203

Deuteronomy
  12:23   87
  18:15   103
  18:21 f.   91
  20:11   60
  21:22 f.   70, 85
  32:8 f.   137, 193

Joshua
  17:13   60

2 Samuel
  1:2   44
  7:14   94, 138
  7:16   95

1 Kings
  17:17–24   143, 203
  19:19–21   203

2 Kings
  1:12   203
  20:5   44

Esther
  5:1   44

Job
  1:6   137

Psalms
  2:2–4   94
  2:7   136, 138
  8:5 f.   119
  19:14   83
  22   67
  29:1   137
  33:6   179
  45:7   94
  48:3   95
  49:8   84
  69   67
  72   94
  78:35   83
  80:18   120
  89:30   95
  110   94, 107
  144:3   120

Proverbs
  1:24 f.   178
  3:18 f.   176, 178
  8:22   176, 178
  8:27–30   178
  8:35   178

Wisdom
2:12–20   79, 125, 131 ff.
           138
4:10–17   131 ff.
4:20–5:5   79
5:1–5   131 ff.
6:12   178
6:18 f.   178
7:10–30   176, 178 ff.
8:1   178
8:3   178
8:6   178
8:12–17   178
9:1–9   178
9:11   180

Sirach
1:1   178
1:4   178
24:3–9   178 ff.
24:30   178
45:25   95
49:16   172

Isaiah
2:2–4   95
11:2   125
42:1–4   79
45:1   98
49:1–6   79
49:15   195
50:4–10   79, 142
52:7   107
52:13–53:12   79, 80, 102
63:4   84

Baruch
3:11 f.   178
3:31   178
3:38   180
4:1   178
4:2   178

Ezekiel
21:30–32   98

28:3   172
28:12–15   60

Daniel
7:9–14   120 ff.
9:25   107
10:6   38

Hosea
2:1   138
6:1 f.   43, 46

Jonah
1:17   44
2:10   44

Micah
4:1–3   95

Haggai
2:20–23   96

Zechariah
4:1–14   106
6:9–15   96, 106
9:9 f.   105

2 Maccabees
3:26–33   38
7:37 f.   78

4 Maccabees
17:22   79

NEW TESTAMENT

Matthew
1:1–17   100, 206
1:18–20   214
2:23   69
3:13–15   203
4:1–11   99
4:24   143
5:11   131
5:23   66
5:33–37   155 ff.
8:17–21   80, 118, 130
9:32–34   70

10:23	154	2:28	117
10:26 f.	172	3:11	99
10:32	128	3:13	202
10:34–36	75	3:21–31	209
10:38	75	3:22–27	70
11:11	133	3:28 f.	155
11:19	130, 131	5:7	99
11:27	153	6:3	207 ff., 209 ff.
12:6	45	6:46	202
12:18–21	80	8:12	155
12:22–30	70	8:27–33	99
12:32	131	8:31	118
12:40	44, 131	8:33	77
13:55 f.	207, 209	8:34–37	75
14:33	139	9:1	155
16:13–16	139	9:2–10	136
16:23	77	9:14–29	143
17:14–21	143	9:41	155
17:23	44	10:15	155
19:28	203	10:18	149
20:19	44	10:29	155
20:28	81	10:42–44	109
21:9	105	10:45	81
21:11	105	11:9	105
22:15–22	63	11:12–14	143
23:37	195 ff.	11:23	155
24:36	154	12:13–17	63
25:31–46	123, 155	12:35–37	105, 112 ff., 156
26:28	87		
26:61	45	12:43	155
26:63 f.	98, 139	13:26	118, 121
27:11	99	13:30	155
27:17–22	100	13:32	154
27:24 f.	72	14:9	155
27:40–63	44, 45, 70, 139	14:18	155
27:64	44	14:24	87
28:2–4	38	14:25	155
28:11–15	47	14:30	155
		14:36	152
Mark		14:58	45
1:9–11	136	14:61 f.	98, 139
1:22	172	15:2 f.	99
2:10	130		

15:29	45
15:40	209 ff.
16:1 f.	43

Luke

1:35	214
1:36	201
2:7	209
2:27–43	206 ff.
2:41–52	209
3:23–37	206
3:38	212
4:1–13	99
6:22	131
7:11–16	143 ff., 203
7:28	133
7:34	130, 131
9:22	44
9:37–43	143
9:51	46
9:52–54	203
9:57–62	64, 118
9:58	131
10:1	203
10:22	153
11:14–23	70
11:30	131
12:2 f.	172
12:8	128 ff.
12:10	131
12:51–53	75
13:6–9	143
13:31–33	46
13:32	64
13:34	195 ff.
14:27	75
18:33	44
19:10	131
19:38	105
20:20–26	63
22:3	77
22:20	87
22:25	64
22:37	80

22:66–68	98 ff.
23:2	73
23:3 f.	99
23:32	207
24:7.46	44
24:21	36 ff., 44

John

1:1–16	177–181
1:20–25	104
1:31	201
1:41	101
2:19–22	45
3:16	87
4:11	113
4:25	101
6:42	208
6:67–70	99
7:3	209
7:20	70
7:39	186
8:48–52	70
10:20	70
11:47–53	74
12:13	105
12:24–38	88
13:2.27	77
13:4–17	109
14:6	196
15:13	75
16:13	77
19:31	85
20:3–9	47
20:28	112

Acts

2:22–36	37
2:36	109
3:13–26	80, 101 ff.
4:27–30	80
5:31	102
6:14	45
7:2–53	45
7:27	102

7:35	83
7:56	117
8:16	110
10:42	136
11:26	92
13:32 f.	104, 144 ff.
17:22–31	196
17:24	45
18:12–17	74
19:5	110
20:7–12	42
24:5	69

Romans

1:3 f.	104, 134 ff.
	145 ff., 173
1:16	169
1:18–32	166
3:24 f.	82, 87
4:25	80, 88
5:12–21	61, 134, 212
6:16	85
8:2	85
8:15	152
8:16	88 ff.
9:13	168
9:26	138
10:9	110, 113
11:25 f.	193
14:10	132
15:13–19	135
15:21	80

1 Corinthians

1:21	85
1:21–24	169
2:5	135
2:5–9	169
2:6–8	60
2:8	76 ff.
4:4–6	132
4:20	135
6:15	169
8:4–6	111, 169

9:5	113
10:1–14	169
11:23–26	39
12:3	110, 113
14:6–19	182
15:3–8	39, 80
15:12–19	22
15:28	159
15:35–50	52 ff.
15:43	135
15:45	88, 135, 175
15:45–47	134, 212
16:22	110, 111

2 Corinthians

4:4	134, 169
5:10	132
5:17	212
5:18 f.	168, 196
12:2	130

Galatians

1:12–16	41
1:18 f.	40, 113
3:13	83, 85
4:3–9	142
4:6	152
5:1	83

Ephesians

2:2	146
2:20	197
3:8–11	147
3:10	146
4:5	110
4:13	197
4:24	212
5:14	173
6:12	63

Philippians

1:18	146, 192
2:6–11	57–61, 80, 173
2:7	149
2:8	75, 175

2:10   110, 146
2:11   110, 111

Colossians
1:12–20   174–176
1:15   134, 175
1:15–20   58, 191
1:18   181, 191
1:19   180
2:8   142, 170
2:15   142, 191
2:20   142
3:9 f.   212

1 Thessalonians
1:9   136
2:14   72

1 Timothy
2:6   81
3:16   58, 146 ff.,
              173 ff.

2 Timothy
2:8   104

Hebrews
1:2   186
1:3   58, 176
2:6–8   119
2:10   102
2:14   60
4:15   149, 211
7:14   107
9:12 f.   87
9:22   86
12:2   102

1 Peter
2:22–25   80, 173, 211
3:18–22   145 ff., 173 ff.,
              211

Revelation
1:13   117, 129
2–3   129
3:7   104
5:5   104
14:14   117
22:16   104
22:20   113

INDEX

Aaron, 203

Abba and *amen*, from utterances of Jesus, significance and interpretations of, 151, 152, 155–57

Abraham, 202, 205, 211

Act of faith, 13

Acts, Book of, 37, 41, 42, 45, 69, 72, 74, 80, 101–2, 104, 144–45, 196

Adam: as first man, 60; Jewish, 61; primal (Adam Qadman), 126

Adoptionism, heresy of, 159

Albright, W. F., 123

Alexander Jannaeus, Hasmonean king, 69

Althaus, Paul, 207

Annas, high priest, 72

Antidocetism, 52

Anti-Semitism, Christian excuse for, 67

Apocalyptic Son of Man, 120–123

Apollonius of Tyana, 125–26, 140

Apologetics, Christ of, 16–17, 24, 62

Apologists, skeptics and rationalists, 14, 15, 17, 25, 28, 47

Apolytrosis (*lytrosis*), 81, 84

Aquinas, Thomas, 162, 165, 193

Aramaic language, 40, 59

Arrest and judicial process preceding execution of Jesus, 68

Assumption concerning priority of Christ, 13

Assumptions on which this book is based and premised, 13, 16, 24, 30

Athens, Stoics and Epicureans of, Paul preaching to, 196

Awareness of Jesus, 150–57

Azazel, and scapegoat rite of Levitical law, 86

"Baptism in the name of the Lord Jesus," 110

Baptism of Jesus, 27, 136, 201, 202

Baraitha, 69

Bar Koseba, Simeon, 96

Barth, Karl, 13, 166, 207

Biblical theology, 30–31

Biblical word, as inextricably bound up with Christianity, 23–24

Biblicism and biblical relevance, 30–34; definition of biblicism, 30–31

Birth of Jesus, 26, 205–8; why born of a virgin?, 211–13; and why not?, 213–15

Bloch, Ernst, 51

Blood rites, Levitical, 86, 87

Blood sacrifice, Old Testament, 84, 87

Bodily resurrection, what is?, 51–55

Bonhoeffer, Dietrich, 182

Book of Acts, 37, 41, 42, 45, 69, 72, 74, 80, 101–2, 104, 144–45, 196

Brandon, S. G. F., 25, 36, 62

Brothers and sisters of Jesus, 209–10

Brown, Raymond E., 149–50, 180

Buber, Martin, 29

Buddha, 212

Buddhism, 192, 193

Bultmann, Rudolf, 16, 30, 48, 84, 111, 184

Caesar, payment of taxes to, Jesus as opposing, 63, 73

Carpenter of Nazareth, Jesus the, 199–211

Catechesis ascribed to Peter, 101–2

Catholic theology, on Jesus as God and Son of God, 148

Celsus, Origen against, anti-Jewish polemic of, 70

Census tax, Synoptic story concerning, 63

Cephas (Peter), meeting of, with Paul, 40

Chalcedonian formulations, 161–64, 183–86; beyond Chalcedon, 186–90

Charles, R. H., 121

Christ: priority of, 13–16; classic "lives" of, 14–15, 16–17, 18–19; of Apologetics, 14, 15, 16–17, 25; "new" theology of, 15–16; Paul on resurrection of, 22; of the gospels, 24–25; of the synoptic gospels, 25, 80, 156; without the cross, 57–61; as Lord of the church, 58; of the New Testament, enigma of, 91–94; as Savior, 145; the unknown, 195–98. See also all entries under Jesus

Christian: apologists, 16–17, 25, 62; faith, earliest beginnings of, 40; theology, early phase of, 40; Messiah, 100–3

Christianity: as inextricably bound up with the biblical word, 23–24; postbiblical, 24; Coleridge's definition of, 65; identified with tribalism, 195

Christians, first, 36

Christmas legend and event, 27, 213

Christology, 13, 16; New Testament christology, 15; and the historical Jesus, 23; and ecclesiology, 23; as elaboration of Christian community of faith, 26; Sermon on the Mount, 29, 91; affirmation of, 29; and docetism, 52; christological impact of the resurrection, 54, 57; and old hymns, 58–59; and interpretation of Jesus' death, 61; Son of Man christology, 129, 134; Son of God concept, 136, 137; and Christ's relation to God, 145; cosmic christology, 197; landmarks of New Testament christology, 199–200; and titles proposing faith in a resurrected savior, 218

Christus Dominus rubric, 13–14

Chronological questions regarding Jesus' arrest and execution, 68

Church, existential issues to be faced by, 14, 20–21

Church designation, and the Son of Man, 127–29

Church's later mission to Christianity, 65

Church structures, and Second Vatican Council, 13, 14

Classic and mythical "lives" of Christ, 14–15, 16–17, 19, 24

Code-words of language of translation, 163, 165, 185–86

Coleridge, Samuel Taylor, 65

Colossians, Paul's letter to, 174–75

Colossians hymn, 177

Colpe, Carsten, 127, 130

Concept of Christ, transmuted in Christian usage, 102

Confessional formula, 110

Confession of Peter, Johannine parallel to the Synoptic story of, 99

Copernican revolution, 161

Corinthians, Paul's letter to, 39

Cosmic christology, 197

Cross: doctrine of the, 57, 88; Christ without the, 57–61; mystery of the, 81; removal of Jesus' body from the, 85; message of the, as John understood it, 88; Why the cross?, 181–83

Crucifixion, barbarous technique of, 35

Crucifixion of Jesus Christ, 19, 36, 70, 75, 76–77; first interpretation of, outside walls of Jerusalem, 37; "on the third day" following, 42–46

"Curse" for us, Jesus as a, 85–86

Cyrus, king of the Persians, 98, 107

Damascus, road to, and revelation given to Paul, 41

Daniel, 120–21, 123

Darwin, Charles, 161

David, house of, and Davidic dynasty, 95–96, 97, 98

Day of Atonement, 86, 87

Death of Jesus, 27, 43, 44, 61–62, 75–77, 81, 84, 87–88, 218. See also Crucifixion of Jesus Christ; Why did Jesus die?

"Death of the Cross," 181

"Deceiver," epithet applied to Jesus by Jewish leadership, 70

Deissmann, Adolf, 83

Dei Verbum, concerning divine revelation of the Second Vatican Council, 18

Demythologizing the New Testament, 31–32, 48, 85

Descartes, René, 165

Desert places, as abode of demons, and favored resort of early Desert Fathers of the church, 86

Dibelius, Martin, 91

Didache or Teaching of the Lord Through the Twelve Apostles, 111

Dijkstra, Oswald, 197

Disciples, twelve, of Jesus, 64, 202

Divine intervention, earliest Jewish stories of, 38

Divine "Nature," 164–68

Docetism, 52, 61, 159

Doctrinaire sectarians of Qumran, 66

Doctrine of the cross, 57, 88

Dogmas of faith, often ignored by the church, 20–21

Easter, celebration of, fixed on a Sunday, 43

Easter event, faith, and tradition, 37–40, 44, 48, 49, 50, 52, 207

Ebeling, Gerhard, 23, 165

Ebionite heresy, 159

Ecclesiology and christology, 23

Ecumenism, the final, 190–95

Elijah, 103, 143, 202, 203

Elisha, 202, 203

Ellis, John Tracy, 15

Empty-tomb of Jesus, 37–42, 43, 46–47, 53

Enigma of the New Testament Christ, 91–94

Enigma of the Son of Man, 117–20, 132–34

Enoch, 103, 107, 121, 123, 138, 146

Epicureans, 196

Epistle to the Hebrews, 207

Essays in Christology, 13

Evans, C. F., 41, 49

Exalted One, 113–15, 146

Existential issues to be faced by the church, 14, 20–21

Exodus into freedom, Israel's, 102

"Eyewitness accounts" of Jesus, 28

Ezekiel, 98, 120

Ezra, 138

Faith: act of, 13; dogmas of faith, often ignored by the church, 20–21; as commitment of the total man, 21; christology as elaboration of Christian community of faith, 26; resurrection as interpretation of faith connected with empty tomb of Christ, 38; earliest beginnings of Christian faith, 40; Easter faith and tradition, 44, 48–50, 52; in resurrection, 61

First Gospel, 29, 181

Flavius Josephus, 27

Flusser, David, 25

Fourth Gospel, 42, 77, 98, 117, 155, 177, 179

Fuller, Reginald, 183

Future Shock (Toffler), 161

Galileans, as sympathizers of Jesus, 36

Gallio, 74

Gemarah, 69

Gentile power structure, Jewish disdain for, 64

Gentiles: church's later mission to, 66; as "those who do not know God," 166; myths and legends of, 212

Gideon, 204

Gnosticism, 170, 172

God, unchangeableness of, 187–88

God of the New Testament, 167–68

God's kingdom, imminent coming of, Jesus' preaching of, as an act of polarization, 75

Good Samaritan, parable of the, 35

Gospel, First, 29, 181

Gospel, Fourth, 42, 77, 98, 117, 155, 177, 179

Gospel, Second, 93

Gospel, Third, 35, 200, 206

Gospels: as myth and legend, by skeptical critics, 14–15; historicocritical study of, 17; material connecting Jesus with, 17–19, 23, 28; historical enquiry into, 19–20, 22–23; Christ of the synoptic gospels, 25, 156; infancy gospels of Matthew and Luke, 27; John's gospel, 27; narratives describing Jesus' death, 27; and story of Jesus' tomb, 38; resurrection appearances in the gospel narratives, 42; "pacific Jesus" of the gospels, 65; and climate for confrontation, due to alleged role of Jews in death of Jesus, 67, 70; accounts of, on arrest of Jesus, 70; Q source of, 131

"Grace," 188

Greek New Testament, 76

Greek Old Testament, 60, 83, 97, 176

"Hanging" (crucifixion) of Jesus, 70

Hanson, A. T., 163

Heavenly Man, the, 123–27

Hebrew or Aramaic languages of the Jerusalem Church, 40, 59

Hegel, Wilhelm, 187

Hellenism, 61, 112, 150, 154, 178, 196; and the divine man, 124, 125

Hellenistic Judaism, 60, 170

Henderson, Ian, 31
Hermetic literature, Poimandres and archetypal man of, 126
Herod Antipas, 46, 64
Herrmann, Wilhelm, 195
Historical objectivity, beyond subjectivity and transsubjectivity, as necessities of search in history for Jesus, 21–25
History: importance and priority of, 16–21; and method of examining the New Testament, 25–30
House of David, and Davidic dynasty, 95–96, 97, 98
Hulsbosch, A., 166
Hymn, adapted or composed by John, 177–78
Hymn, Colossians, 177
Hymn, Johannine, 177–81
Hymn of Philippians, 61, 146, 175
Hymns, old, and christology, 58–59
Hymns cited in the New Testament, 58–59, 60

Incarnation and pre-existence, concepts of, 147–48, 156, 158, 186, 189
Infancy Gospel of Matthew and Luke, 27, 204
Infancy narratives: of the gospel, 204; legendary character of, 206, 210, 211
Isaac, 204, 211
Isaiah, 79, 80, 98, 128, 142
Islam, 193
Israelite religion, 94
Israel's exodus into freedom, 102
Issues, existential, to be faced by the church, 14, 20–21

James, meeting of, with Paul, 40
Jehovah's Witnesses, 112

Jeremiah, 78, 97
Jeremias, Joachim, 88, 147, 151, 153, 155–56
Jerusalem church, original languages of, 40, 59
Jerusalem temple, 45
Jesus: preresurrection of, portrayed by the gospels, 17–18; historical, and christology, 23; birth of, 26, 205–8, 211–15; and the Romans, 61–65; feeling of, toward the Romans who eventually took his life, 63; "pacific Jesus" of the gospels, 65; and the Jews, 65–70; why did he die?, 75–77; preaching of, 91, 108, 118, 147; attitude of, toward messiahship, 97–99; own title of?, 129–32; as a worker of miracles, 140–43; as the manifest Son of God, 144–47; "real" sonship of, 147–50; awareness of, 150–54, 155–57; carpenter of Nazareth, 199–211; brothers and sisters of, 209–211. See also all entries under Christ
Jewish: tradition preserved in the Talmud, censoring of, 28; stories, earliest, of divine intervention, 38; Jewish-Christian church, 40, 59, 119; response to idea of resurrection, 41; Passover, 43; Sabbath, keeping of, by first Christians, 43; Adam, 60; tradition of hypostatized and redeeming wisdom of God, 61; disdain for the arrogance of Gentile power structure, 64; complicity in the death of Jesus, modern playing down of, 67; men of power, Jesus' conflict and controversy with, 67; Jewish-Roman complicity and growing hostility, 74;

Jewish Messiah, 94–97
Jews and Jesus, 65–70
Job, 78
Johannine: Johannine vs. Synoptic tradition, regarding arrest and execution of Jesus, 68, 69, 80, 101; account of trial of Jesus, 73–74; Johannine Hymn, 177–81
John: gospel of, 42; true sayings of Jesus, recognized by, 45; designation by, of Jewish principals leading to trial of Jesus, 71, 72, 73; on crucifixion of Jesus, 77; message of the cross, as understood by, 88; hymn adapted or composed by, 177–78
John the Baptist: tradition that links Jesus with, 27, 136; as kinsman of Jesus, 200–1; meeting of, with Jesus, 203; as child of promise, 211
Joseph and Mary, 206, 208, 210, 211
Josephus, 103
Joshua, 106
Judaism: Hellenistic, 60, 170; of Jesus, 66; Palestinian, 60, 67, 152, 170
Judas Iscariot, 71, 99

Kähler, Martin, 19, 25
Kant, Immanuel, 165
Käsemann, Ernst, 108, 109, 156, 172
Kerygma: primitive, of the church and Christ, 19, 28, 80; Christian kerygma about Jesus, 26, 28, 30; and Jesus as a miracle worker, 140–44
King of the Jews, The, sign of Roman derision, 36, 93
Kitsch: flower vase and Sacred Heart, 115
Klausner, Joseph, 96

Lambrecht, Jan, 154

Last Supper (Passover) of Jesus, 68, 69
Legend, the stuff of, 199–201; source of the legend, 202–5
Letter to the Colossians, Paul's, 174–75
Letter to the Corinthians, Paul's first, 39
Letter to the Philippians, Paul's, 57–58, 59
Levitical blood rites, 86, 87
Life of Augustus (Suetonius), 205
"Lives" of Christ, classic and mythical, 14–15, 16–17, 18–19, 24
Lohmeyer, Ernst, 59
Lonergan, Bernard, 148, 150
Lord of the church, Christ as, 58
Lord and Master, Christ as, 109–13
Luke: infancy gospel of, 27; Luke's story of two disciples on road out of Jerusalem overtaken by a stranger, 36–37; and Peter's proclamation to the Jerusalemites, after experience of Spirit of Pentecost, 37; and interpretation of empty tomb of Jesus, 38, 42; and tradition of Christian gathering for "breaking of bread," 42; and tradition of the "third day," 43; going-to-Jerusalem theme of, 46; forty-day interval of, leading up to a visible ascension, 52; synoptic story of census tax, 63; and the kiss of Judas, 71; on trial of Jesus, 72, 73; on crucifixion of Jesus, 77; as author of Acts, 80; tradition of, 80; two sayings recorded in, 128; Son of God concept of, 136; and miracles, 143
Lytrosis (apolytrosis), 81, 84

Mandeanism, Manda d'Hayyes
of, 126

Manicheanism, Primal Man of,
126

Manifested Son of God, Jesus
as, 144–47

Mann, C. S., 123

"Map of Palestine in the Time
of Jesus," 15

Mark: and interpretation of
empty tomb of Jesus, 38; and
his branding of the tradition
fabricated against Jesus as a
lie, 45; synoptic story of
census tax, 63; on arrest of
Jesus, 70, 71; on trial of
Jesus, 72, 73; on crucifixion
of Jesus, 77; and Jesus as a
messianic character, 93, 98,
99, 104, 105; and miracles,
143; structure of Mark's
gospel, 202–3

Martyr, Justin, 70

Marxsen, Willi, 47, 48

Mary, virginity of, 209

Mary Magdalene, 47

"Master," and other titles bestowed upon Jesus in his own
lifetime, 110–11, 117

Matthew: infancy gospel of, 27;
and interpretation of empty
tomb of Jesus, 38, 42; and
tradition of the "third day,"
42; Matthew's interpretation
of Jesus' saying about destruction and rebuilding of
the temple in three days, 45;
synoptic story of census tax,
63; on arrest of Jesus, 70, 71;
on trial of Jesus, 72, 73; on
crucifixion of Jesus, 77;
traditions of, 80; and Son of
Man theology, 128, 136; and
Son of God concept, 136;
miracles, 143

Melchizedek, 107

Messiah: Christian, 100–3;
Jewish, 93–97; prophetic or

priestly?, 103–9

Messiahship, Jesus' attitude
toward, 97–99

Messianic character, Jesus as,
93, 98, 99, 104, 105

Metaphors of sacrifice, 84–89

Metaphors of salvation, 81–84

Methodology, 30; Pauline
methodology, 85

Miracles: doctrine of, and the
New Testament, 33; Jesus as
a worker of, 138–44

Mishnah, 68

Modalism, 159

Moltmann, 159

Monophysitism, 162–63

Monotheism of Israel, 94

Moses, 83, 103, 125, 202, 203,
204; and Israel's exodus into
freedom, 102

Mount Sinai and Mount Hor,
Moses' ascent of, 203

Mythical Christ, means of pre-
venting creation of a, 24–25

Mythical and classic "lives" of
Christ, 14–15, 16–17, 18–19,
23

Myths and legends of the
Gentiles, 212

Nasorean (nazorenōs), origin
and meaning of titles referring to Jesus of Nazareth, 69

"Nature," Divine, 164–68

Nazareth: Jesus of, 36–37, 69;
the carpenter of, 199–211

Nebuchadnezzar, 98

Nestorianism, 162–63

New American Bible, 96

New Testament: christology,
15; historical examination of,
24–29; development of, 27;
affirmation of christology and,
29; demythologizing the, 31–
32, 48, 85; and doctrine of
miracles, 33; and idea of
bodily resurrection, 41; and
man's struggle against cosmic

forces in Nature, 47; and the Easter faith, 48; hymns cited in, 57–60; allusions in, to the servant of the Lord, and other translations and meanings of words and phrases, 60; some authors of, 62; and Jesus' self-awareness, 76; and Jesus' death for us for our sins, 76; and the mystery of the cross, 81; and blood of Christ, 86; enigma of Christ of the New Testament, 91–94; and divine Sonship, 137; and miracles of Jesus, 141–42; and Jesus as Son of God, 145; and "real" sonship of Jesus, 147–50; concepts of pre-existence and incarnation, 147, 156, 158; God of the, 167–68; and the Western tradition, 170; and Chalcedonian formulation, 183–86; redaction in, 191; landmarks of New Testament christology, 199–200; doctrine of virgin birth, 215

New Testament Christ, enigma of, 91–94

Odes of Solomon, 171

Old Testament: theologians and the, 30; and bodily resurrection, 41; blood sacrifice, 84, 87; and the Lord's Messiah, 98; and concept of divine "inspiration," 125; and God's sons and people, 138; on the might of God, 142; wisdom traditions of, 176; salvation history of, 202

"On the third day," tradition of, 42–46

Ontology, 157, 158, 185

Origen: against Celsus, anti-Jewish polemic of, 70; beliefs of, 189–90

Palestinian Judaism, 60, 67, 152, 170

Panikkar, Raymond, 196

Pannenberg, Wolfhart, 51, 158, 160, 162, 187, 206

Parables of Jesus, 35, 91

Parable of the Good Samaritan, 35

Pascal, Blaise, 166

Passover: Jewish, 43; of Jesus (Last Supper), 68, 69

Paul: and resurrection of Christ, 22; Paul's reinterpretation of Christian creeds and liturgies, 25; thinking and preaching of, after death of Jesus, 26; belief of, as to source of world's disorders, 31; Paul's first letter to the Corinthians, 39; meeting of, with Peter and James, 40; revelation given to, on road to Damascus, 41; theology formulated by, 43–45; Paul's thoughts on bodily resurrection, 52–53; Paul's letter to the Philippians, 57–59; on crucifixion of Jesus, 76–77; as Servant of the Lord, 79; primitive resurrection tradition cited by, 80; soteriology of, 83; Paul's concept of Christ as Second Adam, 134; and the wisdom tradition, 170; and gnosticism, 173; Paul's letter to the Colossians, 174–75; preaching of, to Stoics and Epicureans, 196

Pauline: methodology, 85; theology, 135

Pawek, Karl, 115

Pentecost, Spirit of, 37

Peter (Cephas): meeting of, with Paul and James, 40; confession of, Johannine parallel to synoptic story of, 99; catechesis ascribed to, 101–2;

and Christian suffering, 145–46

Peter's: proclamation to the Jerusalemites, following disciples' experience of Spirit of Pentecost, 37; understanding of Messiah, 99

Pharisaic piety, 96

Pharisees, 46, 66, 71

Philippians, Paul's letter to, 57–59, 80

Philippians hymn, 62, 146, 175

Philo of Alexandria, 102, 125

Plato, 124–25

Pontifical Biblical Commission, April 21, 1964, document of, 18–19

Pontius Pilate, 20, 27, 36, 71–74, 99; torture executions carried out under, 35

Postbiblical Christianity, 24

Postscript, final, 217–19

Preaching of Jesus, 91, 108, 118, 147

Pre-existence and incarnation, concepts of, 147, 156, 158, 173, 189

Preresurrection Jesus, portrayed by the gospels, 17–18

Primal man of Manicheanism, 126

Priority: of Christ, 13–16; of history, 16–21

Prophetic or priestly Messiah?, 103–9

Prophets, society's way of getting rid of, 63

Psalms of Solomon, 96

Q narrative of Jesus' temptation, 99

Q source and sayings, 118, 128, 131, 172, 195–96

Qumran: doctrine sectarians of, 66, 106, 138; text and scroll discovered at, 107, 113, 172

Rahner, Karl, 197

Raisedness and Risenness, 48–51

Ransom, concept of, 81, 83, 84

Rauschenbusch, Walter, 24

Redaction, implication of, 173–77; in the New Testament, 191

Redemptive suffering, 60, 77–81

Reimarus, Hermann S., 24

Renan, Ernest, 208

Resurrected Savior, christological title, professing faith in, 218

Resurrection: Jewish response to idea of, 41; appearances in the gospel narratives, 42–43; bodily, what is?, 51–55

Resurrectional retroactivity, 157–60

Resurrection of Christ: Paul on, 22; earliest witness to, 37–41; the "third day," 42–46; interpreting the, 46–48; Raisedness and Risenness, 48–51; what is bodily resurrection?, 51–55; christology and, 61; exaltation and resurrection, 146; and position of the church, 217–18

Revelation: given to Paul on the road to Damascus, 41; matter of, 187

Revolutionarism of Jesus, 66

Richardson, Alan, 183

Robinson, John A. T., 168

Roman derision of Jesus, calling him King of the Jews, 36, 93

Romans and Jesus, 61–65

Sacred Heart, 115

Sacrifice, metaphors of, 84–89

St. Anselm of Canterbury, 82

Salvation, 194; metaphors of, 81–84

Samaritan, parable of the Good, 35

Samaritans, hostile, 203

Samson, 204

Samuel, 202, 204, 211

Sanday, William, 183

Sanhedrin, 71, 72

Satan, rights of, concept of, 82

Savior: Christ as, 145, 179; resurrected, christological titles, professing faith in, 218

"Scapegoat" of the Levitical law, 86

Schillebeeckx, Eduard, 188, 189

Schoonenberg, Piet, 187, 188, 189

Schweitzer, Albert, 20, 25

Schweizer, Eduard, 130, 131, 132

Scroll and text discovered at Qumran, 107, 113, 172

Second Adam, Paul's concept of Christ as, 134

Second Gospel, 93

Second Isaiah, 79, 81

Second Isaiah's Servant of the Lord, 103

Second Vatican Council: and church structures and other matters of policy, 13, 14; concerning divine revelation and the gospels, 18; recognition by, of virtues of other religions, 196

Sermon on the Mount, 29, 91

Servant of the Lord, Jesus identified with, 80–81, 88, 102, 146

Servant songs, 79, 89

Similitudes, 121–22; of Enoch, 123, 138

Sins, Jesus' death for us for our, 77

Sirach, book of, 171

So-Called Historical Jesus and the Historic, Biblical Christ (Kähler), 19

Socrates, 125

Solomon: the Wisdom of, 78, 80; Psalms of, 96; Odes of, 171

"Son of David," 97, 104, 105

"Son of God," 136; variations on, 137–39

Songs of the Second Isaiah, 60

Son of Man: enigma of, 117–20 132–34; the apocalyptic, 120–23; and church designation, 127–29

Sonship, "real," of Jesus, 147–50

Soteriology of Paul, 83

Star of David, as Nazi badge o shame, 36

Stoics, 196

Subjectivity, beyond, as necessity for search in history for Jesus, 21–25

Suetonius, Gaius, 205

Suffering, redemptive, 60, 77–81

Swidler, Leonard, 15

Swinburne, Algernon Charles, poem of faith of, 50

Synoptic: gospels, Christ of the 25, 80, 156; story of census tax, 63; tradition, regarding arrest and execution of Jesus 99

Tacitus, 27

Talmud, 69; Jewish tradition preserved in, censoring of, 2

Tax, census, synoptic story of, 63

Taylor, Vincent, 209

Teaching of Jesus, research into, 28

Teilhard de Chardin, Pierre, 161

Temple: destruction and rebuilding of, in three days, Jesus' saying about, 45; polemic against association of Jesus with, 45

Temptation of Jesus, 99, 202

Tendenz, 74

Text and scroll discovered at Qumran, 107, 113, 172

Theologians: radical, 24; and the Old and New Testaments, 30

Theology: "new," of Christ, 15–16; biblical, 30; Christian, early phase of 40; formulation by Paul, 43–45; Son of Man theology, 128, 136; Pauline, 135–36; Catholic, on Jesus as God and Son of God, 148

Thielicke, Helmut, 21, 23, 38

"Third day, on the," tradition of, 42–46

Third Gospel, 35, 200, 206

Titles ascribed to Jesus, 110–12, 117, 169; Jesus' own title?, 129–32

Toffler, Alvin, 161

Tolkien, J. R. R., fairy tales of, 15

Tomb of Jesus, story of, 37–41, 42, 46–47, 53

Torah, and function of wisdom, 171

Transforming event, the resurrection of Christ, 35–37

Translation, language of, key code-words of, 163, 165, 184–86

Trial of Jesus, 70–75

Trinitarian doctrine, 185, 186, 187

Trypho the Jew, 70

"Twelve," theme of, 203

Twleve disciples of Jesus, 64, 202; twelve apostles, teaching of the Lord through, 111

Twelve Patriarchs, testaments of the, 106

Unknown Christ, the, 195–98

Van der Loos, H., 140

Vase, flower, and Sacred Heart (Kitsch), 115

Virgin birth, 205–8; why born of a virgin?, 211–13; and why not?, 213–15; doctrine of, in New Testament, 215

Western tradition, and the New Testament, 170

Why the cross?, 181–83

Why did Jesus die?, 75–77. See also Crucifixion of Jesus Christ; Death of Jesus

Wisdom, redeeming wisdom of God, Jewish tradition of, 61; of Solomon, 79, 80; traditions, 169–73, 175–76; function of, and Torah, 171

Witness, earliest, to resurrection of Christ, 37–41

Words of Jesus, research into, 28

Wrede, Wilhelm, 25, 93

Yahweh, as King and Savior, 97; the God of Israel, 112

Zealots, 35, 64; Jesus and, 62, 64, 65

Zerubbabel, 96, 106

Zoroastrianism, Gayomart of, 126

OTHER IMAGE BOOKS

OUR LADY OF FATIMA – William Thomas Walsh (D1) – $1.45
DAMIEN THE LEPER – John Farrow (D3) – $1.45
MR. BLUE – Myles Connolly (D5) – 75¢
THE DIARY OF A COUNTRY PRIEST – Georges Bernanos (D6) – $1.75
CHRIST THE LORD – Gerard S. Sloyan (E6) – 95¢
PEACE OF SOUL – Fulton J. Sheen (D8) – $1.25
LIFT UP YOUR HEART – Fulton J. Sheen (D9) – $1.75
THE PERFECT JOY OF ST. FRANCIS – Felix Timmermans (D11) – $1.95
THE IMITATION OF CHRIST – Thomas à Kempis. Edited with an Introduction by Harold C. Gardiner, S.J. (D17) – $1.75
THE EVERLASTING MAN – G. K. Chesterton (D18) – $1.95
ST. FRANCIS OF ASSISI – Johannes Jorgensen (D22) – $1.95
THE SIGN OF JONAS – Thomas Merton (D31) – $1.95
LIGHT ON THE MOUNTAIN: The Story of La Salette – John S. Kennedy (D33) – $1.45
SAINT THOMAS AQUINAS – G. K. Chesterton (D36) – $1.45
THE ART OF BEING HUMAN – William McNamara, O.C.D. (E45) – $1.25
THE STORY OF THE TRAPP FAMILY SINGERS – Maria Augusta Trapp (D46) – $1.45
ST. FRANCIS OF ASSISI – G. K. Chesterton (D50) – $1.45
VIPER'S TANGLE – François Mauriac. A novel of evil and redemption (D51) – 95¢
THE AUTOBIOGRAPHY OF ST. THÉRÈSE OF LISIEUX: The Story of a Soul – Translated by John Beevers. An Image Original (D56) – $1.25
THE CITY OF GOD – St. Augustine. Edited by Vernon J. Bourke. Introduction by Étienne Gilson. Specially abridged (D59) – $2.95
ASCENT OF MT. CARMEL – St. John of the Cross. Trans. and ed. by E. Allison Peers (D63) – $1.95
RELIGION AND THE RISE OF WESTERN CULTURE – Christopher Dawson (D64) – $1.95
THE LITTLE FLOWERS OF ST. FRANCIS – Translated by Raphael Brown (D69) – $1.95
DARK NIGHT OF THE SOUL – St. John of the Cross. Edited and translated by E. Allison Peers (D78) – $1.45
ORTHODOXY – G. K. Chesterton (D84) – $1.45

These prices subject to change without notice

OTHER IMAGE BOOKS

THE LIFE OF TERESA OF JESUS: The Autobiography of St. Teresa of Avila. Trans. and ed. by E. Allison Peers (D96) – $2.45

THE CONFESSIONS OF ST. AUGUSTINE – Translated with an Introduction by John K. Ryan (D101) – $1.75

SPIRITUAL CANTICLE – St. John of the Cross. Trans. and ed. by E. Allison Peers (D110) – $2.95

A WOMAN CLOTHED WITH THE SUN – Edited by John J. Delaney (D118) – $1.75

INTERIOR CASTLE – St. Teresa of Avila (Translated by E. Allison Peers) – (D120) – $1.75

THE GREATEST STORY EVER TOLD – Fulton Oursler (D121) – $1.75

LIVING FLAME OF LOVE – St. John of the Cross (Translated by E. Allison Peers) – (D129) – $1.45

A HISTORY OF PHILOSOPHY: VOLUME 1 – GREECE AND ROME (2 Parts) – Frederick Copleston, S.J. (D134a, D134b) – $1.75 ea.

A HISTORY OF PHILOSOPHY: VOLUME 2 – MEDIAEVAL PHILOSOPHY (2 Parts) – Frederick Copleston, S.J. Part I – Augustine to Bonaventure. Part II – Albert the Great to Duns Scotus (D135a, D135b) – Pt. I, $1.95; Pt. II, $1.75

A HISTORY OF PHILOSOPHY: VOLUME 3 – LATE MEDIAEVAL AND RENAISSANCE PHILOSOPHY (2 Parts) – Frederick Copleston, S.J. Part I – Ockham to the Speculative Mystics. Part II – The Revival of Platonism to Suárez (D136a, D136b) – Pt. I, $1.75; Pt. II, $1.45

A HISTORY OF PHILOSOPHY: VOLUME 4 – MODERN PHILOSOPHY: Descartes to Leibniz – Frederick Copleston, S.J. (D137) – $1.75

A HISTORY OF PHILOSOPHY: VOLUME 5 – MODERN PHILOSOPHY: The British Philosophers, Hobbes to Hume (2 Parts) – Frederick Copleston, S.J. Part I – Hobbes to Paley (D138a) – $1.45. Part II – Berkeley to Hume (D138b) – $1.75

A HISTORY OF PHILOSOPHY: VOLUME 6 – MODERN PHILOSOPHY (2 Parts) – Frederick Copleston, S.J. Part I – The French Enlightenment to Kant (D139a, D139b) – $1.45 ea.

A HISTORY OF PHILOSOPHY: VOLUME 7 – MODERN PHILOSOPHY (2 Parts) – Frederick Copleston, S.J. Part I – Fichte to Hegel. Part II – Schopenhauer to Nietzsche (D140a, D140b) – $1.75 ea.

These prices subject to change without notice

A 75–2